A Dictionary of Postmodernism

A Dictionary of Postmodernism

Niall Lucy

Edited by
John Hartley

With contributions by
Robert Briggs
Claire Colebrook
John Hartley
Tony Thwaites
Darren Tofts
McKenzie Wark

WILEY Blackwell

This edition first published 2016

Registered Office
John Wiley & Sons, Ltd, The Atrium, Southern Gate, Chichester, West Sussex, PO19 8SQ, UK

Editorial Offices
350 Main Street, Malden, MA 02148-5020, USA
9600 Garsington Road, Oxford, OX4 2DQ, UK
The Atrium, Southern Gate, Chichester, West Sussex, PO19 8SQ, UK

For details of our global editorial offices, for customer services, and for information about how to apply for permission to reuse the copyright material in this book please see our website at www.wiley.com/wiley-blackwell.

Library of Congress Cataloging-in-Publication data applied for

Hardback 9781405150774
Paperback 9781405150781

A catalogue record for this book is available from the British Library.

Set in 10.5/13pt Minion by SPi Global, Pondicherry, India
Printed and bound in Malaysia by Vivar Printing Sdn Bhd

1 2016

In memory of Niall Lucy, 1956–2014

"I am very impressed with your 'Dictionary' project. It seems to me that it is both a sharp and an exhaustive project and, of course, I want to say how grateful I am … Thank you for … keeping me informed about these beautiful projects in which I am proud and grateful to have a place."

Jacques Derrida
(Letters to Niall Lucy)

Contents

Acknowledgments

One of Niall's final wishes was that this book be completed, and I cannot thank John Hartley enough for accepting Niall's deserved trust in him to make it so, and for his dedicated and caring stewardship throughout. Niall would be honored that his longstanding friends Rob Briggs, Claire Colebrook, Tony Thwaites, Darren Tofts and Ken Wark also willingly and generously contributed their talents on his behalf. Thanks also to the team at Wiley-Blackwell for your professionalism across this and previous collaborations with Niall, especially Emma Bennett and Ben Thatcher for putting up with him for so long.

Niall was blessed to have many friends and colleagues who always supported his endeavors: thanks to Kerry Banting, Jill Birt, Peta Bowden, Paddy Buckley, Martyn P. Casey, Len Collard, Chris Coughran, Tim Dolin, Joseph Fernandez, Sean Gorman, Angela Glazbrook, Gillian Greensmith, Glynn Greensmith, Lisa Gye, Jane Hemery, Adrian Hoffman, John Kinsella, Monique Laves, Judith Lucy, Johnny R. Lucy-Stevenson, Alsy MacDonald, Jesse McGrath, Steve Mickler, Jane Mummery, Marnie Nolton, Dick Ounsworth, Pieta O'Shaughnessy, Cheryl Passmore, Elizabeth Pippet, Susan Pippet, Georgia Richter, Kim Scott, Mark Smith, Mark Snarski and Robert Snarski.

And finally, with thanks, love and pride to Niall's greatest legacy, our children: Dylan, Hannah and Jakeb.

Sam Lucy-Stevenson, January 2015

John Hartley thanks the co-contributors for their generous gifts of thought and talent, and thanks Sam Lucy-Stevenson for invaluable editorial assistance. The "Introduction" and "Culture" are reproduced from Niall Lucy's "The Acropolis of the Dragon," first published in *VLAK 4* (October 2013), by Litteraria Pragensia, Prague: our thanks go to editor-publisher Louis Armand.

Preface

This book is something of a postmodern hybrid. It's Niall Lucy's book, imagined, planned and executed by him, but it's also a collage, involving other writers. Niall wasn't able to complete it, but he was keen to see it finished. At his request, the contributors – friends and colleagues of his – have undertaken that task on his behalf. We have sought to keep Niall's project and his unique style in mind, but his mixture of erudition, wit, defiance and firm views on certain topics was all his own. An inevitable consequence of this is that our entries will sometimes reflect the contributor's interests and opinions rather than Niall's directly. Also, there are occasions when Niall has quoted work published by one of us. Thus, we have "signed" each entry, so that readers can avoid mistaking those passages for self-citation, or mistaking the parts he did not write for Niall's own work. The book is laid out as an encyclopedia, with entries in alphabetical order. Each entry is a short essay. In most cases each one has been completed by a single hand (rather than by collective authorship), in order to preserve Niall's characteristic mode of argument by example. The largest number of entries is by him, with the six contributors taking between four and six each.

The project has been a labour of love for all of us. This book is offered as *Niall Lucy's* Dictionary of Postmodernism, but it's also a Festschrift to him by a group of individuals whose lives and work have intersected with his, and in several cases with each other's too. We've all enjoyed his company, benefited from knowing and arguing with him, and feel confident that you, dear reader, will do too. For this is a working book, designed for readers to use and enjoy, and to dispute where necessary. In order to do justice to what Niall was attempting, we have tried to do justice to the topic.

There are varying views on postmodernism. In his *Postmodern Literary Theory* (1997) Niall Lucy wrote that it could be seen as the outworking of a literary–philosophical tradition that goes back to the Romantic movement in Germany and elsewhere. Postmodernism was what happened when that tradition, including its critics, eventually abandoned the idea that there was something central and intrinsically valuable about *literary* texts, and began to apply its considerable analytical, emotional and political resources to the consideration of *any* text, in a universe of knowledge where, to the perceiving subject, *everything* presents as a text, including context (as Derrida famously remarked, *il n'y a pas de hors-texte* – roughly translatable as 'context is everything'). Thus, postmodernism may be another way of discussing the historical experience, philosophy and practice of general textuality:

> What was once the romantic space of the literary becomes, for postmodernism, a general plane of human existence, on which concepts of identity, origin and truth are seen as multiple and structureless assemblages rather than as grounds for understanding human "being" and culture ... I think "postmodernism" refers to the generalization or flattening out of the romantic theory of literature, which marks it as a "radical" theory of the nonfoundational, structureless "structure" of truth. I do not think postmodernism is all that radical, in other words. (Lucy, 1997: ix–x)

Postmodernism, therefore, poses historical, political, theoretical and even "romantic" problems. Here, we set out to explain some of them. But as Niall wrote in the Preface to his *Derrida Dictionary*, "this will not have been a dictionary." Instead, as he put it: "My aim here has been to provide a series of outlines and interpretations of some ... key ideas and arguments, rather than fixed definitions. I discuss these ... within the widest context of Continental thought" (Lucy, 2004: xii).

Some of us may have strayed a little beyond the Continent in question. Niall had views about this. When he asked me to "see this through to publication," he warned me that compromise was needed:

> John, you'll need to tighten up a little. This can't be an opportunity to crack twee jokes, or to show that Lyotard and Barthes, say, know nothing about the world, which is best explained by a hard-nosed, street-smart approach. You have to pay at least some respect to theory and theorists, or this just won't work. (email, 8 May 2014)

Having spent some instructive and informative time working on the book with all those concerned – Niall himself, co-contributors Robert Briggs, Claire Colebrook, Tony Thwaites, Darren Tofts and McKenzie Wark, as well as Sam Lucy-Stevenson, Niall's wife and our colleague at Curtin University's Centre for Culture and Technology – I can say that it has worked. We have paid every respect to theory and its all-too world-knowing theorists, perhaps with one or two hard-nosed street smarts thrown in. Watch out for the jokes though.

John Hartley, January 2015

Notes on contributors

Author

Niall Lucy was Professor of Critical Theory at Curtin University where he co-founded the Centre for Culture and Technology. His books include: *Debating Derrida* (1995); *Postmodern Literary Theory: An Introduction* (1997); *Postmodern Literary Theory: An Anthology* (ed., 2000); *Beyond Semiotics: Text, Culture and Technology* (2001); *A Derrida Dictionary* (2004); *The War on Democracy: Conservative Opinion in the Australian Press* (with Steve Mickler, 2006); *Beautiful Waste: Poems by David McComb (The Triffids)* (co-ed., 2009); *Vagabond Holes: David McComb and the Triffids* (co-ed., 2009); *Pomo Oz: Fear and Loathing Downunder* (2010); *The Ballad of Moondyne Joe* (with John Kinsella, 2012).

Contributors

Robert Briggs, Senior Lecturer in the School of Media, Culture and Creative Arts, Curtin University, Western Australia

Claire Colebrook, Edwin Erle Sparks Professor of English, Pennsylvania State University, USA

John Hartley, John Curtin Distinguished Professor and Professor of Cultural Science, Curtin University, Western Australia; and Professor of Journalism, Media and Cultural Studies, Cardiff University, Wales

Tony Thwaites, Senior Lecturer in Literature and Cultural Studies, University of Queensland, Australia

Darren Tofts, Professor of Media and Communications, Swinburne University of Technology, Australia

McKenzie Wark, Professor, Culture and Media and Professor, Liberal Studies, The New School, New York, USA

Description

It is more or less canonical now to say that postmodernism resists definition, but this does not mean its key terms, concepts, figures and issues cannot be explained. Hence the aim of this book is to provide reliable (without claiming to be definitive) discussions of those terms, etc., in the form of essays rather than "definitions," the model here being my *Derrida Dictionary* (Lucy, 2004). In this way *A Dictionary of Postmodernism* is intended as an enduring reference, in contrast to throwaway introductions.

Limits have to be imposed on the number of entries, but the intention is for the book to be a comprehensive guide to the field. Here is a list of possible entries I was thinking about as I prepared this book:

> film, literature, sociology, art, music, architecture, [**new**] **media**, communications, fashion, technology, narrative, radical democracy, science, aesthetics, black, **modernism**, difference, assemblage, collage, genre, discontinuity, **differend**, fragment, construct, production, **culture,** subjectivity, film noir, decentring, capitalism, music videos, **modernity**, enlightenment, romanticism, humanism, **Jameson, Lyotard**, **Barthes**, Saussure, **Foucault**, Deleuze, **Deleuze and Guattari**, Freud, **Lacan**, gender, Chantal Mouffe, grand narratives [as **metanarrative**], **truth**, **Baudrillard**, signification, surface/depth, origin/copy, reality, **hyperreality**, **simulation**, knowledge, Wittgenstein, language game, consumption, commodity, crime fiction, **Derrida**, realism, reference, **representation**, self-reflexivity, relativism, interpretation, chance, silence, performance, Beck, absence, metonymy, desire, schizoanalysis, indeterminacy, **Hassan**, dada, rhizome, **Žižek**, **discourse**, existentialism, individual, reason, rationality, power, logocentrism, **Sokal affair**, Kuhn, philosophy, theology, film studies, television, theatre, cinema, critical theory, **cultural studies**, feminism, **Habermas**, post-colonialism, **poststructuralism**, Hegel, Heidegger, Nietzsche, nihilism, Kierkegaard, body, queer

theory, sexuality, **globalization**, **Charles Jencks**, Quentin Tarantino, play, language, authority, readerly/writerly, parody, irony, jouissance, Warhol, Duchamp, Rauschenberg, Robert Venturi, Borges, Paul Auster, Pynchon, Delillo, Barth, McLuhan, Harold Bloom, Adorno, Althusser, Bakhtin, Blanchot, Bruno Latour, Anthony Giddens, Merleau-Ponty, Tim Burton's *Batman*, Colin McCabe, Said, orientalism, Eagleton, **semiotics**, structuralism, Frankfurt School, Gramsci, hegemony, Haraway, Kristeva, Judith Butler, Charles Taylor, ethics, Husserl, cyborg, Marx, Sartre, Virilio, Kathy Acker, practice, nature, experience, meaning, Kant, Mondrian, Burroughs, Ridley Scott's *Bladerunner*, William Gibson, virtuality, Theodor Nelson, the Krokers, history, cyberspace, ethnicity, tradition, identity, Benjamin, style, context, gangsta rap, David Lynch, sampling, digital, panopticon, flesh, metropolis, hybridity, chaos

Some of these (in bold) appear in the book under their own name, others feature in discussion, a few are absent altogether, and some new entries have been added. So much for lists. Note also that not all items are intended to be seen as "belonging" to postmodernism: some (dada, existentialism, etc.) are there as quasi-antecedents, others (philosophy, architecture, etc.) are to be considered in terms of their relations to postmodernism without suggesting that there "is" such a thing as postmodern philosophy, say, or postmodern architecture.

Niall Lucy

Introduction

***Kaya*:** That means *hello* in one of the languages of the Noongar people, the traditional owners of the southwest region of Western Australia. But *kaya* doesn't mean *hello* in the way that 1 + 1 = 2. The exchange rate when it comes to translating a word from one language into another isn't calculable in advance, according to a universal formula, if only because language (if there is such a thing as language in this general sense, so that we might refer to language as we do to mathematics) … if only because language is always to some extent an inference or a projection, since in principle and in practice a language is never complete.

The English word (which is really the American word) *hello*, for example, was adopted as a popular greeting only in the late nineteenth century, in response to the new technology of the telephone. When the first telephone exchange was established in 1873, in New Haven, Connecticut, callers were greeted with "Ahoy! Ahoy!", a practice continued anachronistically by *The Simpsons'* Mr Burns to show how culturally out of touch he is. By 1889, though, central telephone exchange operators were known as "hello-girls," attesting to the newfound status of *hello* as a popular telephone greeting, which later spread to greetings in general. Previously, *hello* (or, in British English, *hallo*) was used not as a greeting, but as a shout for attention; via the introduction of the telephone, then, the word's exclamatory or declarative usage was exchanged for the performance of a social function. *Hello* doesn't really "do" anything except to signal an opening for the possibility of exchange with another, but in this way it is also always, perhaps, a kind of affirmation, always an answer to a call … even and especially when you

A Dictionary of Postmodernism, First Edition. Niall Lucy.

don't know who's calling. Strictly, when you pick up the phone and say *hello*, whether or not you recognize the number, you can't know for sure who'll be on the other end; you cannot know for certain whose call you're responding to. Often, indeed, we knowingly say *hello* to strangers, on the phone or in other social contexts, instead of demanding they identify themselves and state their business! (That would be an obsolete, by now ungrammatical, usage of *hello*.) So we use *hello* not em-phatically, but phatically, to open a line of communication, which is in a sense to say we do use the word emphatically—as an affirmation of our willingness to enter into an exchange with others. When we say *hello* to someone, especially to a stranger, we are also saying *yes!*

I prefer to think it's other than coincidental that *kaya*, the Noongar word for the English word, which is really the American word, *hello*, can also mean *yes*, as we know from Kim Scott's *That Deadman Dance*: "*Kaya*," the novel begins (Scott, 2010: 1), followed immediately by a full stop (as I began by repeating here). Far from opening a line of communication, however, the beginning of *That Deadman Dance*, at least for whitefella readers, is less a greeting than a declaration, and what it might be said to declare is something like the question of itself. But whatever the mark of its identity or the identity of this mark (since *kaya* is not immediately recognizable as anything so seemingly unitary as a word), it cannot simply be exchanged, cashed in, for an equivalence, which could be what the novel is all about. The very name of the main character, after all, Bobby Wabalanginy, stretches the limits of English pronunciation (English speakers can no more get their tongues around "Wabalanginy" than a trombonist can play the didgeridoo) and so the novel's colonial characters refer to him nearly always as "the boy" or "Bobby," a name not equivalent to his other name, but which instead takes the place of it.

So that's one form of cultural exchange, all too familiar to Australians: the exchange of one culture *for* another, the assimilation of one culture *into* another—the word *kaya*, for example, for the word *hello*. But is there no alternative to this hegemony; can there not be exchange without loss?

Before pondering the question of what a culture might risk losing, though, we should consider the question that precedes it: what do we mean by "**culture**" (q.v.)?

Niall Lucy

Barthes, Roland: *French structuralist and poststructuralist thinker, critic, linguist and semiotician, 1915–80*

Barthes's career is an exemplary one for this book. In close to three decades, he moves through many of the main intellectual currents of his time and place, and does it in an often thoroughly idiosyncratic way. Though he does not often name his contemporaries, the debts and homages are obvious; his work is alive with theirs, echoing, taking up and playing with their ideas with the stylistic virtuosity that is Barthes's signature.

One of his later books, *Roland Barthes*, gives his own view of his career to that point (1977b: 145). He began, like so many of his generation, as a broadly Sartrean Marxist, but by the time of the book that first brought him to general notice, *Mythologies* (1972 [Fr. 1957]), his project had become a much more Brechtian one of ideological demystification of the familiar. *Mythologies* brought together a series of short pieces he had been writing regularly for *Les Lettres nouvelles* on aspects of popular **culture** (ads for soap powders and margarine, Charlie Chaplin, food photography, Einstein's brain, wrestling …), and rounded them off with a new, long essay, "Myth Today." This essay is in turn something rather different: his first major foray into structuralist thought, and an attempt to imagine a general **semiotics** that might underlie the often impressionistic analyses of the pieces that precede it. Over the next decade, he would follow this up with some of the classic texts of structuralism: *Elements of Semiology* (1967 [Fr. 1964]), a book of first principles; "Introduction to the Structural Analysis of

A Dictionary of Postmodernism, First Edition. Niall Lucy.

Narratives" (in Barthes 1977a [Fr. 1966]); and *The Fashion System* (Barthes, 1985 [Fr. 1967]). Their method, as he begins by saying in the essay on narrative, is top down: because it's simply impossible to study all narratives and work upwards to an inductive synthesis, we start with

> a deductive procedure, obliged first to devise a hypothetical model of description (what American linguists call a "theory") and then gradually to work down from this model towards the different narrative species which at once conform to and depart from the model. (Barthes, 1977a: 81)

The danger of such an approach is that it can be pre-emptive. The essay on narrative is still suggestive, with its loose synthesis of all sorts of recent work into a framework for elaboration. But *The Fashion System* now looks particularly like a dead end: every possible move seems already there in the "minor scientific delirium" of its combinatories, as he will later describe it (Barthes, 1977b: 145), and so we have that odd and paradoxical thing, an exhaustive and exhausting book on fashion that can say nothing at all about the new.

At the same time that he is producing these high-structuralist analyses, however, Barthes is also working on a series of writings that take quite different directions. In particular, there are the well-known polemic "The Death of the Author" (1968, in Barthes, 1977a), the brief and rich "From Work to Text" (1971, in Barthes, 1977a), and the extraordinary *S/Z* (1970). In them, we see Barthes move from structural*ism* to what will become a multiplicity of poststructural*ist* investigations (**poststructuralism**).

S/Z is a book-length slow-motion reading of a Balzac short story, "Sarrasine." At first sight, it looks like a rather idiosyncratic form of structuralism. Barthes starts by saying that he will break the text up into a "series of brief, contiguous fragments," which he calls *lexias* (1970: 13). But these lexias are not syntagms, like sentences, products of the application of rules of syntax to a vocabulary. They're not structural, in other words, and this is no longer quite semiotics. There's something quite arbitrary about them: "sometimes a few words, sometimes several sentences" (1970: 13), whatever works best. As the name suggests, these bite-sized pieces are more like the grouping one does in the act of *reading* than they are like units of structure. Playing across each of these lexias will be several *codes*. Where it's a matter of raising a question in the narrative, articulating it with other features, delaying or giving an answer, Barthes proposes the term *hermeneutic* code (see **Eco**); where they refer out to common bodies of knowledge, we have a *cultural* or *knowledge* code; and so on. And again, neither are these codes structural: they're not units that are put together in the text, or rules for putting units together, they just name groups of effects that the words of the text have, directions they point in. And the five of them Barthes names here will, he says, be enough for this one. Presumably if we were describing a different sort of text altogether—a scientific paper, say, or a piece of legislation—we'd find it useful to bring in others, and mightn't need all of the original five.

What this mobile and flexible apparatus allows Barthes to do is trace through the unexpected vicissitudes of the story, taken a couple of lexias at a time with short interspersing commentaries. Rather than focus, as he does in the earlier structuralist piece, on the ways in which this story might be seen as the product of a formal system that can generate stories in all their variety, *S/Z* pays attention to the sheer singularity of this one story in particular, in its gradual unfolding across the time of its reading. He makes a distinction between what he calls the *readerly* work and the *writerly* text: in the former, the reader is addressed as a consumer, in the latter as an active co-producer of the text. It's tempting to see the readerly as the familiar routines of the realist novel, with the writerly being the more stringent demands of the avant-garde text. It's more accurate, however, to say that this is not so much a way of classifying literary objects (readerly works on one shelf, comfortably in reach; writerly texts on a shelf that's somewhat more difficult to get at), but as a sort of optic for viewing any literary object: look at it one way, and it might be familiar readerly realism, but look at it another way and you've got something quite different and unfamiliar.

And indeed, that's what we get here. Balzac is, after all, the epitome of a familiar mode of literary realism, a canonic author taught in schools – though it's unlikely that any curriculum would choose *this* particular story. Once we've read *S/Z*, though, "Sarrasine" looks as unfamiliar as anything from the avant-garde. What *S/Z* does is *queer* "Sarrasine," in all sorts of ways. If an important part of the comfort offered by the readerly is its reassuring management of sexual difference (and the so-called "marriage plot" is after all one of the genres at the heart of the classical novel), then *S/Z* shows a "Sarrasine" in which those anxieties implode. We see it in the title, where we have the "feminine" *S* that is nevertheless the initial of a man, the naïve Sarrasine who comes to Rome to learn to be a sculptor; and the "masculine" *Z* that marks the name of La Zambinella, the beautiful soprano with whom he falls in love on his first night at the opera. And between them, at the heart of the story, we have the slash of castration, for in his innocence Sarrasine has not realized that at this time all female parts on the Italian stage are still sung by castrati, as the church does not allow women on the stage. It's also the slash of death, his own death, for when he finds out the truth, Sarrasine will try to kill first Zambinella, then himself, only to be killed by a slash of the sword from the Cardinal who is Zambinella's lover and protector. And to multiply things out into **metanarrative**, the entire story is framed by the first-person narration of a failed heterosexual seduction at a lavish party: everything falls apart when the narrator tells the Sarrasine story to his companion, after her eye is caught by the entrance of a remarkable figure—none other than the now very old and no longer beautiful Zambinella. What "Sarrasine" traces out under Barthes's patient and spectacular reading is the death of narrative itself, at whose heart there is not the resolution of a marriage of opposites or complements, but the impossibility, as **Lacan** will say repeatedly, of the sexual relation. "The narratives of the world are numberless," as the first line of "Introduction to the Structural Analysis of Narratives" has it (Barthes, 1977a: 79). If the structuralist analysis of narrative suggests the plenitude of a system that is capable of generating infinite variety, then, with *S/Z*, narrative proliferates because of the slash of irreducible difference at the heart of it.

In one way or another, all of Barthes's later work turns from the global systematizing and grand narratives of structure to the more localized and less calculable effects of such singularities at the heart of all **discourse**. The "intertexts" that he names for these later writings in his summary in *Roland Barthes* are now no longer Sartre, Marx, Brecht and Saussure, but his contemporaries Philippe Sollers, Kristeva, **Derrida**, Lacan, and with them their great precursor, Nietzsche. *The Pleasure of the Text* (Barthes, 1975) deals with the paradoxical ways in which the *jouissance* of reading cuts across regimes of meaning, as a "sanctioned Babel" (1975: 3), a seduction that is also a wounding (1975: 38) to the extent that it lays bare the instabilities of the reading subject. *Camera Lucida* (1981) similarly speaks of the power of photography as lying not so much in its informational semiotics of meaning (which he calls its *studium*) as in the singular point or *punctum*, the small sometimes throwaway detail that barely belongs to that web of meaning but which stabs one to the heart. *A Lover's Discourse* (1978) hinges on the paradox of the singularity and intensity of the lover's experience and the necessary banality of the lover's vocabulary: what, after all, could be more banal yet more necessary than "I love you"? And *Roland Barthes* (1977b) itself is not so much a memoir as a meditation on memoir, testimony and writing a life; on what it means to say "I" in a text, and on signature and its effects—and thus the obvious antidote to the rather silly and hasty reading of

"The Death of the Author" as an embargo on discussion of authorship. The very form of the later books, like Nietzsche's, becomes aphoristic, fragmentary, sometimes even abandoned to the vicissitudes of an alphabetical ordering.

Tony Thwaites

Baudrillard, Jean: *French cultural theorist, 1929–2007*

Like David Bowie, to whom he has been compared (Poole, 2000), Baudrillard's work is notable for its many ch-ch-ch-ch-changes. From around the mid-1980s onward he became both a poster boy for postmodern theory and one of its most scandalous figures, the seeming "poetics" of his later work exemplifying the version of postmodernism parodied in the **Sokal affair**. Not even the editor of Baudrillard's *Selected Writings*, Mark Poster, however, himself a figure of some renown in postmodern and **new media** studies, could defend what he saw as Baudrillard's worst excesses, describing his early writing style as "hyperbolic and declarative" and accusing him of "refusing to qualify or delimit his claims" (Poster, 'Introduction', in Baudrillard, 1988a: 7). In scientific circles, meanwhile, Baudrillard's name stood for the perception that humanities scholarship had been corroded by vacuous jargon masking a lack of reasoned, evidence-based argument; indeed, what "Baudrillard" fostered was the retreat from reason altogether. US mathematician Alan Sokal and Belgian physicist Jean Bricmont thus find in Baudrillard's writing "a profusion of scientific terms"'serving only "to give an appearance of profundity to trite observations" (Sokal and Bricmont, 1998: 153), an assessment countersigned by evolutionary biologist Richard Dawkins in his review of Sokal and Bricmont's book for *Nature* (Dawkins, 1988). Nor is criticism of his work restricted to the natural sciences: British **Derrida** scholar Christopher Norris, for example, dismisses Baudrillard's later work as typical of the "bad philosophy" that postmodernism commits in "its uncritical adherence to a theory of language and **representation** whose extreme antirealist or sceptical bias in the end gives rise to an outlook of thoroughgoing nihilism" (Norris, 1992: 191).

Norris's complaints are directed at the third and last of Baudrillard's articles on the first Gulf War, an event that he famously claimed didn't happen. Written originally for European newspapers in 1991, expanded versions of the articles were later published as a book whose English translation,

The Gulf War Did Not Take Place, appeared in 1995. While the title may indicate a species of Holocaust denial, in fact Baudrillard's argument is that events in the Persian Gulf at the time didn't constitute a "war," but rather an atrocity dressed up to look like one. How could what took place qualify as a war when the resources of the US-led Coalition forces so vastly outweighed those of Iraq that, from the American perspective, "everything unfolded according to programmatic order" (Baudrillard, 1995: 73)? How could there have been a war when there could have been "[n]o accidents" (1995: 73)? Thus what took place was actually a media event staged as a real-time conflict for propaganda purposes, a "war" produced for American TV audiences. "We prefer the exile of the virtual, of which television is the universal mirror," Baudrillard writes, "to the catastrophe of the real" (1995: 28).

"We" postmoderns, then, prefer the condition of being in exile, a condition made possible by technologies of the virtual, to an experience of the catastrophic effects of reality. A catastrophe, however, denotes not only a calamitous event or a failure, but also the scene of resolution in classical tragedy; in ancient Greek, the catastrophic marked the point of narrative closure. But there is no equivalent of this when it comes to television, a medium that is irreducible to the screening of texts or objects in the form of individual programs and which is therefore permanently ongoing and perpetually in the now. Television is always "there," always "on," even when we aren't watching it, and what's on is always changing—a feature that today is greatly expanded or intensified by the Internet. Technologies of the virtual thus effect our exile from "the real" understood as closure, teleological certainty or the **transcendental signified**; and because reality is not simply a philosophical abstraction but also a social domain, such technologies offer escapist protection from "the brutalizing effects of rationality, normative socialization, and universal conditioning" associated with the real (Baudrillard, 1993b: 67).

Gaming is a good example. When I'm inside the open world of *Assassin's Creed II*, trying to bring the Desmond-Ezio plot to resolution, I am in a sense voluntarily in exile from the real, a realm governed by a political–economic imperative, if not also a moral imperative, to be productive. Gaming is not productive in anything resembling the "real" sense of this notion: all that is "produced" when I play *Assassin's Creed II* or any other game is my exile from the real, a mode of virtual production at best and which is also a product of my desire or will (remember that, for Baudrillard, we *prefer* the openness of the virtual). From mode to code, as it were. Thus gaming shows what Baudrillard calls the *reversibility* of a concept such as productivity, this being a logic or a strategy of disruption against the normalizing forces of the real. "Inject the smallest dose of reversibility," as he puts it, "into our economic, political, sexual, or institutional mechanisms and everything collapses" (Baudrillard, 1990: 47). If real time is spent productively, game time is spent in the pursuit of all but nothing: the gamer's purpose is to master a game that, once finished, is effectively obsolete, having been or about to be replaced by the latest version in a series (*Assassin's Creed III* was released in the US on October 30, 2012) or by the latest must-have game for sale. Like television, the game is always "on."

Democracy, Baudrillard notes, is based on equality before the law, "but that is never as radical as equality before the rule" (Baudrillard, 2001: 66). Everyone is equal before the algorithm. But such equality comes at the cost of a radical freedom, since the freedom to choose in game space is limited in advance by the rules of the game. Freedom, then, along with exile, is a **simulation** of the game: the gamer is never absolutely free, and never absolutely in exile from the real. Hence the reversibility that games enable is at best only an ambivalent force, especially if we were to think of games as commodities for staving off boredom. As McKenzie Wark argues:

> The interests of the military entertainment complex dominate policy, and policy's goal is to alleviate the threat of boredom. What is good for the military entertainment complex is good for America. And what is pronounced good is the war on boredom, which, like the war on drugs or the war on crime or the war on terror, can never be won—was never meant to be won—and is merely displaced, as the boredom index rises and falls. (Wark, 2007: 175).

The point here is that there's nothing that could count as the political or some other **essence** of gaming. Games are still commodities, and gamers are still subjects under capitalism. While it *can* be argued that games open a space for exile from the real, it can also be argued that that space has been coopted by capitalism as a relatively new means of turning a profit.

But the twist is that games may be seen as more real than the real itself. If reality requires our belief in it, gaming doesn't: I am not required to *believe in* the open world of *Assassin's Creed II*, but simply to move around in it within limits set by the rules of the game. My "freedom" to do so is both compromised and illusory. But isn't this how I move around in the world "outside" the game, within limits set by the laws of society? Should I transgress those laws I would be held accountable for my antisocial behavior regardless of whether I *believed* in "society" as such; my belief, in other words, is neither here nor there. So what the **hyperreal** or prosthetic environment of the game may reveal about technologies of the virtual is not that they are taking us away from "ourselves," but that they're taking us on an adventure:

> Perhaps we may see this [the technologization of the real] as a kind of adventure, a heroic test: to take the artificialization of living beings as far as possible in order to see, finally, what part of human nature survives the greatest ordeal. If we discover that not everything can be cloned, simulated, programmed, genetically and neurologically managed, then whatever survives could be truly called "human": some inalienable and indestructible human quality could finally be identified. Of course, there is always the risk, in this experimental adventure, that nothing will pass the test—that the human will be permanently eradicated. (Baudrillard, 2000: 15–16)

For Baudrillard, the scene of this adventure goes back further than the digital age. In his *For a Critique of the Political Economy of the Sign* (1981 [Fr. 1971]) he argues that the process of "artificialization" is a feature of modern industrial society, making hyperreality more or less coextensive with **modernity**. While conceding that the Marxist critique of commodity fetishism is an attempt to "get" this process, Baudrillard maintains that what prevents it from doing so is the inadequacy of the Marxist distinction between use-value (the utility of an object) and exchange-value (the commodification of an object expressed as a market price). The inadequacy proceeds from a failure to acknowledge the **semiotic** nature of objects under capitalism: "in the 'fetishist' theory of consumption … objects are given and received everywhere as force dispensers (happiness, health, security, prestige, etc.)," Baudrillard writes, but this forgets that "what we are dealing with first is signs: a generalized code of signs, a totally arbitrary code of differences" (1981: 91). Fetishism, in short, presupposes a real that is prior and a subject whose consciousness is non-alienated, but for Baudrillard there is no outside the generalized code of signs through which reality and subjectivity are always mediated:

> If fetishism exists it is thus not a fetishism of the signified, a fetishism of substances and values (called ideological), which the fetish object would incarnate for the alienated subject. Behind this reinterpretation (which is truly ideological) it is a *fetishism of the signifier*. That is to say that the subject is trapped in the factitious, differential, encoded, systematized aspect of the object. It is not the passion (whether of objects or subjects) for substances that speaks in fetishism, it is the *passion for the code* […]. (Baudrillard, 1981: 92)

It's in this context that the Gulf War may be said to have happened only in the televisualization (the artificialization) of an event that was therefore of the order of a non-event, an "event" that could be said to constitute a war only in its *signification* or at the level of the signifier. The "war" was produced in its conformity to the *appearances* of war (explosions, air strikes, combat uniforms, etc.), which of course is not to deny that tens of thousands of people died.

In postmodernity, reality is thus superseded by its appearances. This is perhaps the key to Baudrillard's writing and its scandalous reception, given the offence to common sense caused by such a statement. But if the task of serious criticism is to look *behind* appearances for the real, then what hope for "serious" criticism today if reality is now indistinguishable from its forms of manifestation? "Interpretation overlooks and obliterates this aspect of appearances in its search for hidden meaning," according to Baudrillard 1988a: 149), but "getting beyond appearances is an impossible task" (1988a: 150). Because the pursuit of hidden meaning blinds traditional criticism or theory to the **truth** about postmodernism (which is that "truth" is to be found on and not below the surface of things), theory must abandon its commitment to a scientific or realist mode of inquiry in favor of experimenting with new modes of relation to a world in which historical events, outstripping the capacity of **metanarratives** to explain them, increasingly resemble those of science fiction. Only by acknowledging the "impossibility of reconciling theory with the real" (Baudrillard, 1988b: 99) can we begin to respond to such a world. Hence the move towards what Baudrillard calls "theory-fiction" (or sometimes "anticipatory theory" or "simulation theory") in his later writing, where the scandalous drive to speculate overrides the critical imperative to be systematic; a move akin to **Lyotard**'s call to do philosophy differently for the sake of doing justice to the **differend**.

Niall Lucy

Cultural studies: Cultural studies is – note the singular: we're describing an intellectual enterprise here, not an archive of individual studies – cultural studies is a postmodern discipline. That's because its object of study is not only **culture** but also the study of culture. It's the discipline that investigates or irritates the politics of disciplinarity (Lee, 2003). As Stuart Hall (2007: 44) put it, when discussing the early days of the Centre for Contemporary Cultural Studies at Birmingham, studying culture seemed to necessitate a "break" with established epistemology, "by way of sustained conceptual interrogation and methodological self-reflection – as it were, 'working on the work.'"

"Working on the work" has characterized cultural studies throughout its short career, not only in the reform and modernization of concepts like culture, but also in an abiding interest in *cultural studies* as a topic for debate, such that there is an extensive literature on the question of what cultural studies *is*, a question typically resolved in favor of the political affiliations of the questioner. Thus cultural studies represents a turn from objectivity to *reflexivity* in knowledge: cultural studies is *about itself*.

One way to get to its relevance to *post*modernism is to approach it through **modernity**, specifically via the problem of disciplinarity. The growth of knowledge in formal, disciplinary systems grew like topsy in the nineteenth century. Modern disciplines, in process of formation since the Renaissance, received a massive boost from the secularization of education, the Industrial Revolution, consolidation of the nation-state, and the consequent explosion

A Dictionary of Postmodernism, First Edition. Niall Lucy.

of economic growth (McCloskey, 2006). However it was still thought possible to imagine a comprehensive "world system" (Wallerstein, 2011) of universal knowledge, to which all observation-based inquiry would contribute. To see what the resulting "tree of knowledge" might look like, you could do worse than check the Wikipedia entry: "Outline of academic disciplines."

This unprecedented and accelerating growth of formal knowledge was inevitably co-created with exploitation, imperialism and colonization (Lee, 2010). Specialist knowledge systems sought to be "objective" in the observational sense, but by the mid-twentieth century it was also clear that such objectivity was not neutral or disinterested. It had unintended but systematic human, ecological and political consequences. Its bastard brainchildren went viral across the world. In the end they threatened to overwhelm it: physics begat nuclear weapons; chemistry begat gas chambers; sociology begat apartheid; the humanities begat *difference.*

In the newly emergent "humanities" disciplines, difference meant discrimination, literally. In the hands of modern cultural critics from John Ruskin and Matthew Arnold onward, "discrimination" was a moral exercise based on *discernment* of cultural value. It was the duty of cultural and especially literary education to teach it. The idea was to "discriminate" good from bad art.

But in the wider world, cultural discrimination was turning from positive to negative, being seen as a prejudicial exclusionary tactic. Discrimination outside the humanities became *anti*-human, infringing newly identified "human rights" (again, check Wikipedia for a folksonomy of types of "discrimination" – the literary–cultural type is not listed among them). That reversal in the meaning of discrimination is also the history of cultural studies.

Originally, "the humanities" were based on Classics and designated human as opposed to divine knowledge (i.e. the subject of "divinity"), rather than being opposed to the sciences as is now routine. But by the late nineteenth century it became possible to study culture in English too, not just in the Classical languages. Interestingly this innovation was not a product of England, but of Scotland and the Scottish Enlightenment (Rhodes, 1998: 28). The world's first chair in English literature was established at Edinburgh in 1762; Glasgow followed in 1861. By contrast, Oxford didn't start an English department until 1894, or Cambridge till 1919, following the endowment of a "King Edward VII Professorship of English Literature" in 1911.

This chair was not initiated by the university itself, but donated by one of the original press barons, Harold Harmsworth, in the year following the award of his baronetcy. The Harmsworth brothers, better known to posterity as Viscounts Northcliffe and Rothermere, founded the *Daily Mail* and *Daily Mirror*. Younger brother Harold, who as Lord Rothermere inherited the whole empire in 1922, was a notorious fascist sympathizer and long-term admirer of Hitler, who used his newspapers to promote right-wing English nationalism of the kind still espoused by the *Daily Mail*, which in turn is still in the family, controlled by his great-grandson, Jonathan Harmsworth. Harold's jingoistic parvenu nationalism – not "culture" – was the material force driving the creation of English Literature at Cambridge: imperialism and "discrimination" of the negative kind were inbuilt, albeit at arm's length.

The most prominent of the King Edward VII Professors was the Cornish writer and critic Sir Arthur Quiller-Couch, known as "Q," the famous editor of *The Oxford Book of English Verse* (1900), who held the chair from 1912 until his death in 1944. His inaugural lectures were published during World War I. In a much-quoted passage, he spelled out how the study of English literature was a noble national service for the gentlemen who sat in front of him at Cambridge:

> But since of high breeding is begotten (as most of us believe) a disposition to high thoughts, high deeds; since to have it and be modestly conscious of it is to carry within us a faithful monitor persuading us to whatsoever in conduct is gentle, honourable, of good repute, and so silently dissuading us from base thoughts, low ends, ignoble gains; seeing, moreover, that a man will often do more to match his father's virtue than he would to improve himself; I shall endeavour … to scour that spur of ancestry [i.e. the "lineage" of English Literature] and present it to you as so bright and sharp an incentive that you … shall not pass out from [Cambridge] insensible of the dignity of your studies, or without pride or remorse according as you have interpreted in practice the motto, *Noblesse oblige*. (Quiller-Couch, 1916, Lecture VIII: 145–6)

Eng. Lit. was thought good for training governors, administrators, and civil/imperial servants in the "learning" (i.e. knowledge) associated with the acquisition of "cultured" taste, judgment (i.e. discrimination), and understanding (Rhodes, 1998: 27–8). It trained them to make "humane" decisions over the lives of the Empire's many and diverse "others." The *object* of study was the formation and government of the imaginative human *subject*, starting with the self.

Quiller-Couch's type of literary criticism was displaced at Cambridge in the 1930s by F. R. Leavis, who went on to become the most influential force in shaping English Literature as a discipline up until Leavisism in turn was displaced by cultural studies, but only then in line of filiation, because one of its founders, Richard Hoggart, was well known as a "left Leavisite." Leavis had been Q's protégé as a student at Cambridge (BBC, 1992), playing Robespierre to Q's Desmoulins, out-discriminating his mentor, who nevertheless took "discrimination" to the grave. Q's memorial plaque in Cornwall's Truro Cathedral proclaimed his epigraph in stone: he "KINDLED in OTHERS a LIVELY and•DISCRIMINATING•LOVE of•ENGLISH•LITERATURE" (Quiller-Couch Memorial, 2011).

Thus "discrimination" (modern, objective) and "noblesse oblige" (imperial, class-based) remained entangled until after World War II. By then British decolonization was under way and a popular socialist government installed at home. Returned working-class servicemen Richard Hoggart and Raymond Williams, unlike most of their peers, went to university (Leeds and Cambridge). Later Stuart Hall from Jamaica did too, with a Rhodes scholarship (Oxford). Despite the social changes consequent upon the war, universities were not democratized. Higher education was poised between the defunct "noblesse oblige" tradition and mass higher education, which only began to gather pace in the 1960s. Hoggart, Williams and Hall experienced at first hand the disconnect between the universalist claims of *cultural discrimination* on the one hand and, on the other, the *discriminatory* exclusion of pretty well everyone from a "non-U" background (Mitford, 1956). Small wonder that they felt *self-conscious*. Reflexivity was built in.

Not surprisingly, their critique of the disciplinary study of culture began with the problem of class. There was something wrong with the university set-up, sure, but more fundamentally, there was something wrong with knowledge. Literary discrimination, using methods like I. A. Richards's "practical criticism" or the New Criticism from Chicago, sought to reveal the objective qualities of texts (rather than focusing on their authors' literary biographies). To demonstrate that this mode of knowledge was systematically discriminatory required more than merely pointing to the demographics of student intake. What was needed was a rethink of culture itself, and this required new attention to knowledge – not only what was known, but how, and in which interests. Difference, distinction, discrimination all turned out to be social, political and competitive, not natural, cultural and universal (see **essence**). Studying culture as "discrimination" therefore did not admit such topics as popular media or class politics – the world of the user, if you like – into its remit. Cultural studies could not do otherwise than to start with culture as a *problem of knowledge*. Before too long, pioneering class analysis – critical-autobiographical (Hoggart), historical-political (Williams) and theoretical (Hall) – opened the way for studies of other social identities where distinction, discrimination and difference meant exclusion not discernment: gender, ethnicity, nation, age, sexual orientation, disability and more. Instead of being about value, culture was now about power (Gibson, 2007), especially its role in determining subjectivity in everyday life.

But at the same time, cultural studies was always about itself. Studying "the popular" *as culture,* without pathologizing it (as in psychology and criminology), was a major intellectual challenge. Luckily, and not for the first time, the French were on hand to take the blame for the result. Already, back in the eighteenth century, as Neil Rhodes has shown, the arts of rhetoric – masculine, sublime, pathetic, stentorian, gesticulatory and natively English, even Shakespearean – had been domesticated, as public speech was interiorized both literally (quitting the pulpit and public square for the salon and drawing room) and imaginatively (via the novel). It was transformed into reading and conversation, and feminized in the process. As Rhodes puts it, "The art of speaking well dwindled to the art of being well spoken," and rhetoric, already shorn of logic, was left only with the "feminine ornaments" of elocution. This change supplied the "cultural conditions" for the emergence of English as an academic subject (Rhodes, 1998: 32). For all of this, according to contemporary observers like the playwright Sheridan, the French were to blame, because they valued ornament and artifice over nature and "plain" language; the arts of duplicity over those of **truth** (see **Barthes**, **Eco**).

It was just the same in the 1960s and 1970s, when English (the subject) was again invaded by Frenchified theory. That's what came to be called postmodernism. What was French about it? First, it was based on *Continental* Philosophy (not "Anglo-Saxon" analytic philosophy or empirical science). Second, it was *unserious*: more interested in play, deceit, duplicity and media than in truth or reality. Third, it was actively engaged in undermining Anglo-Saxon (including American) knowledge bastions, introducing both Marxism, which in the Cambridge of the times was synonymous with treachery (BBC, 2003), and an "anything-goes" element into scientific inquiry (see **Sokal affair**). In short, the French were guilty, as ever (so the prejudicial discourse went) of overturning truth in favor of language. In cultural studies, they were guilty of Theory (as such), which dethroned not only cultural value, critical discrimination and the search for "truth in beauty," but also the very reading of literature itself, which was relegated thenceforth to the back seat in favor of up-front critical readings of ... *cultural studies* itself (see **paraliterature**).

Cultural studies was duly lampooned for its interest in popular media, famously by novelist Don DeLillo (see **hyperreality**):

> Murray [Siskind] was ... a stoop-shouldered man with little round glasses and an Amish beard. He ... seemed embarrassed by what he'd gleaned so far from his colleagues in popular culture. "I understand the music, I understand the movies, I even see how comic books can tell us things. But there are full professors in this place who read nothing but cereal boxes." (DeLillo, 1985: 10)

Early cultural studies was not all cereal boxes, but there was still something suspect about it. No one had objected to entire disciplines being devoted to art-forms that their aficionados *liked* (literature, cinema, music, painting), but *liking* pop culture and the practices of ordinary, everyday life was seen as inconsequential, trivial, even demeaning; not a sufficient basis for academic attention. So when Roland Barthes proclaimed "the pleasure of the text" and Jacques **Lacan** "the play of the signifier," it was taken as a provocation – and a French one at that – which struck at the foundations of value-based discrimination, foundations upon which imperial self-knowledge (now handed over to the Americans) had been secured.

Perhaps overcompensating somewhat, cultural studies found pleasure itself to be *political* (i.e. consequential), a site or sign of semiotic resistance to "dominant ideology." For example, it became possible, in Australia especially, to study the beach. The *Australian Journal of Cultural Studies* (1983–7), which later became the American-edited, London-published journal *Cultural Studies*, nominated the beach as a "cultural motif" (along with the barbecue) in its opening description of its aims and scope. The beach fascinated John Fiske, who marked his own arrival in Australia with an analysis of Perth's Cottelsoe beach, in "Surfalism and sandiotics" (Fiske, 1983). The odd title, a parody of Terence Hawkes's influential *Structuralism and Semiotics* (1977), was meant to demonstrate that sand and surf, indeed anything, could be "read like a text," this maneuver being the innovation that distinguished cultural studies in its "critical reading" phase. In *Myths of Oz* (1987) Fiske and his Australian co-authors explained what was both cultural and political about the beach: namely, *opposition* and exclusion, a new form of "discrimination":

> The beach's centrality to the culture is won by its appropriation of those attitudes most closely related to an Australian mythology while placing itself in opposition to those that are excluded. (Fiske, Hodge and Turner, 1987: 54)

"The beach" most often imagined in Australia is urban – Bondi in Sydney, Cottesloe in Perth – prompting Fiske *et al.* to pursue a city/ocean, culture/nature opposition as a myth-generating mechanism that addresses the increasingly urbanized reality of contemporary Australia. Meaghan Morris, however, pointed out that "the" beach in Australian culture and cultural studies is not representative of national identity so much as of national*ism* (Morris, 1992; 1998). It is mobilized as a founding myth of an unreflexive Anglo (i.e. white) version of Australian "ordinariness." The 2000 conference of the Cultural Studies Association of Australia took up the challenge of this theme. "On the Beach" called for studies of this "quintessential Australian icon," inviting readings of Australian texts (*Puberty Blues*, surf magazines), pastimes (surfing or tanning), the body and Australian cultural studies. Not surprisingly, the beach was found to be a "privileged site" for the exploration of national identity (Bonner, McKay and McKee, 2001: 270). Traditionally Australian identity had been located in the "red centre" and the bush, sites that enjoyed the status of being "authentic, timeless, pristine and past." By contrast, the beach is "more ordinary, everyday, tacky, familiar, mixed" (Bonner *et al.*, 2001: 273). Mark Gibson remarks on the Anglo-whiteness of Australian beaches. Whiteness is often central to the "semiotic cluster" that represents Australian beaches as the postcolonial antithesis of *English* ordinariness (Gibson, 2001: 275). Cultural studies has never given up on the beach as a nature/culture interzone. Christine Schmidt (2012) went so far as to claim the swimsuit as Australia's distinctive contribution to world fashion, linking sport, fashion and nation with gender, desire and creative industries.

Such topics were well suited to the "politics of pleasure" phase of cultural studies, where "politics" was personal and cultural, i.e. postmodern. The beach's signs of a partial and ethnocentric mythic imaginary were not understood as part of the modern public sphere. Not until the "Cronulla riots" of 2005, that is, when redneck, flag-draped Aussies did battle with what they saw as interlopers on their beach, i.e. multicultural (Middle Eastern) Australians. The resulting ugliness sent shockwaves around the world, which Hartley and Green (2006) saw as evidence of the beach *as* the public sphere, albeit for a short, incandescent burst. At last, cultural studies could read this inconsequential site of ordinary pleasures as a text of *discrimination*. The modern was reincorporated into its opposite (q.v.).

John Hartley

Culture: Culture (if there is such a thing) is an anthropological concept, referring only to forms of human life or organization and not to those of animals or machines. It might be granted, say, that all the various generations of Apple Macintosh computers share a roughly common operating system or "language," a kind of machinic DNA, but from this it would not seem credible to conclude that the machines themselves behave in ways that constitute a culture, even if (after the fashion by which we now refer to "business culture" or to the "culture" of a football club) we were to concede that Mac *users* comprise something like a "culture." Similarly, while animals may congregate in a pod, a pack, a school, a nest, a herd, a swarm and so on, these all denote forms of social organization that are not historical, but coded, as if they were hardwired into the members of a species at birth. Machines and animals are programmed to respond to their environments reflexively, and so they don't so much respond to those environments as react to them.

Culture, then, is proper only to humans and not to the animal-machine. The problem with this distinction, or with this system of oppositions, a system that may turn out to belong as much to the culture of philosophy as to the philosophy of culture, is that it's riven with tenacious contradictions. Some animals (and let's not forget there are only ever *animals* as such, since "the" animal, the hypostatic animal in general, is to be found nowhere outside a **discourse**) – some animals are capable of acquiring knowledge and passing it on to others in their group, who learn it by instruction or imitation. Among many examples, it has been discovered recently that a troupe of capuchin monkeys in the forests of northeastern Brazil has developed a sophisticated technique for extracting termites from their treetop nests (see Welsh, 2011). They begin by slapping the side of the nest, provoking soldiers to swarm to the area under threat, before twisting a small branch through the outer wall, and this rotating or drilling motion serves both to enlarge the hole made by the insertion (thus reducing the risk of breaking the branch on withdrawing it) and to maximize the number of termites attracted to the "aggressive" object. Since the capuchins' technique is more successful than any devised by human cultures that eat termites (Viegas, 2011), it would surely seem that culture is less anthropological than "zooanthropological," to use the term preferred by **Derrida** in the first volume of *The Beast and the Sovereign* (2009).

So we begin (no doubt all too hastily and familiarly) with the problem of the threshold: the threshold separating humans from animals, especially any animal with a discernible head and a face, is far from indivisible, and what is a threshold that is always divided and less than absolute from the start? This is a general problem, which I will come to in a moment. But for now let me quickly respond to an imagined, ludicrous objection: that the example of the Brazilian capuchins commits me to saying that the culture of Jack Russell Terriers in Brisbane differs from the culture of Jack Russells in Perth or anywhere else. To see the threshold separating humans from animals as problematic is not, in other words, to see the nonhuman as indistinguishable from the human; to suggest that culture is not quite proper to man, that it does not belong to humans exclusively or sovereignly, does not deprive the concept of culture of any force, but rather clouds its purity, a purity that presupposes that the concept must be indivisible.

This doesn't mean our starting point (one of several by now), our first tentative proposition, as it were, should be that culture is *not* anthropological, but simply that it's not indivisibly anthropological. Indeed, the Greek root *anthropos*, so often glossed as "man" or "human being," also means "man-faced," "having the face of man," and so must be allowed at least to countenance, if not to include, those animals I referred to previously, animals with a discernible head and a face – in a word, most but not all mammals. In this way the science or the discipline of anthropology would be distinct from that of zoology only by convention, through the imposition of an artificial or arbitrary limit disguised as an indivisible threshold, because in a sense anthropology ought to refer not simply to the study of man, but of the man-faced, to creatures resembling or which in some way may be thought to share an equivalence, an equivocal or nonabsolute equivalence, with humans. It would be debatable as to whether this would lead to a new taxonomy of living beings or simply account for a longstanding but informal, unscientific or inexact, but not ineffectual, distinction between the faced, the less than faced and the faceless. While we may see something of ourselves, in other words, in monkeys, bears, dogs, cats or wolves, we see rather less of ourselves in chickens or reptiles, and nothing or almost nothing at all in jellyfish. The animals to which we are attracted the most and with whom we form the strongest attachments, whose welfare summons our strongest considerations and about whom we are the most keenly ambivalent when it comes to eating them, are those with a head and a face. The animal with a face is not human, but it is not therefore, automatically, unquestionably, *non*human.

My distinction, I repeat, is not a scientific one. What we might call faciality is not recognized by the sciences of anthropology or zoology as a discriminator in the classification of living beings. Indeed, my distinction (which I get from Derrida in *The Beast and the Sovereign*, vol. I, and so which is not quite "my" distinction, not indivisibly mine) is not really a distinction since it doesn't clarify but rather blurs whatever might be held to separate the human from the nonhuman, the human from the animal-machine. But again this blurring, which is not an erasure, does not justify (and is not intended to justify) thinking that humans and animals are the same; yet neither can the question of how they might differ from one another be settled on the basis of choosing between an idea of the indivisibly human and of the indivisibly nonhuman.

Here we come back to (but of course we've never been far from) the general problem of the threshold. For science, or for a certain way of thinking we might call scientific or scientistic, every threshold is indivisible, a principle exemplified by the periodic table of the elements. The threshold at which water boils or at which this compound, when mixed with that compound, turns into another compound, is calculable and unvarying. Or, to take another example, it must be supposed that between the numbers 1 and 2 there exists a discrete series of indivisible calibrations even though the series may go on indefinitely: 1.01, 1.001, 1.0001, etc. But when you cut a 75 cm length of pipe to repair the plumbing in your kitchen, you don't ponder the endless divisibility by which the pipe could be too long or too short. For all practical purposes, let alone for the purpose of sending probes to Mars, scientific thresholds are indivisible, which is fine because "scientific" differences are nondiscriminatory: sodium and the number 7 aren't victims of historical or political oppression at the hands of nitrogen and the number 5.

What holds, though, for scientific or natural differences (as they might also be called) doesn't hold for cultural differences. As we know from Saussure (see **semiotics**), language is a system of differences without positive terms; hence the word-sign *sodium* (to précis the lesson of Saussure 101) means or functions by virtue of its difference from *odium* or *podium*, for example, although at some point, outside this system, the referent of sodium is understood to be fundamentally different, different in essential ways, from the referent of nitrogen. From this it could seem that language is a system simply for naming things that exist in the world already, prior to being named.

Enter, the dragon. If language is a system for naming pre-existent things, how come we all know what a dragon is? The problem here would be that we acquire knowledge of dragons in ways that don't differ, in a pure and unconditional sense, from those in which we acquire knowledge of people from other cultures. We know dragons as we know others, but of course we also know that others, unlike dragons, exist prior to our knowing them and in ways that are independent of their **representations** or of the fact we can know them only *through* their representations. But this latter argument – that there is no outside the text, as it were, since we cannot interface with what we call reality except in ways that are always mediated and contextualized – doesn't mean we can't develop a sophisticated knowledge of others, especially of others who are like ourselves. Cultural understandings, then, as we might refer to them, as distinct from scientific understandings, may be informal, but they are not therefore imprecise or unreliable for appearing to be based on a nudge and a wink, a point that is well illustrated by the shared community knowledge of the characters in *Desperate Housewives*, for example, and that TV series' nineteenth-century precursor, the Elizabeth Gaskell novel, *Cranford* (1851–3), itself appearing originally in serial form. Among the women of the fictional provincial town that lends its name to Gaskell's novel it would seem impossible to keep a secret, so intimately are they acquainted with the goings on in one another's lives:

> The Cranfordians had that kindly *esprit de corps* which made them overlook all deficiencies in success when some among them tried to conceal their poverty. When Mrs Forrester, for instance, gave a party in her baby-house of a dwelling, and the little maiden disturbed the ladies on the sofa by a request that she might get the tea-tray out from underneath, everyone took this novel proceeding as the most natural thing in the world, and talked on about household forms and ceremonies as if we all believed that our hostess had a regular servants' hall, second table, with housekeeper and steward, instead of the one little charity-school maiden, whose short ruddy arms could never have been strong enough to carry the tray upstairs, if she had not been assisted in private by her mistress, who now sat in state, pretending not to know what cakes were sent up, though she knew, and we knew, and she knew that we knew, and we knew that she knew that we knew, she had been busy all the morning making tea-bread and sponge-cakes. (Gaskell, 1987: 2)

This little deception that is shared by the women of Cranford exemplifies a commonly held distinction between humans and animals: namely, that animals are incapable of lying. But surely the threshold separating human from animal deception, where the latter is owed to anthropomorphic decree, is rendered less than indivisible when we consider the fox who leaves a false trail to mislead her would-be captor, or the family dog who feigns to look away from the ball he drops at his owner's feet, only to snatch it back again as soon as the owner goes to reach for it. We may join in wondering with Derrida, then, by what right are certain characteristics considered to be human denied to animals? Again, this does not lead to supposing that humans and animals are the same:

> It is less a matter of wondering whether one has the right to refuse the animal such and such a power (speech, reason, experience of death, mourning, culture, institution, politics, technique, clothing, lying, feigned feint, effacement of the trace … etc. – the list is necessarily indefinite, and the most powerful philosophical tradition in which we live has refused *all of that* to the "animal"). It is more a matter of wondering whether what one calls man has the right, for his own part, to attribute in all rigor to man, to attribute to himself, then, what he refuses to the animal, and whether he ever has a concept of it that is *pure, rigorous, indivisible, as such*. (Derrida, 2009: 130)

Keeping in mind the non-indivisibility of this distinction by which culture would not be essentially proper to man alone, for which "distinction" is not quite the right word since in this case it gestures to an order of difference that doesn't correspond to the structure, or the governing logic, of the periodic table of the elements, we might wonder what to make of cultural differences per se. When I said earlier it would be ridiculous to argue that Brisbane Jack Russells are *culturally* different from Perth Jack Russells, no doubt the absurdity I was invoking should be ascribed to the notion of *canine* culture. Yet the example of the Brazilian capuchins shows that animals are capable of developing practices that, among humans, we do not hesitate to call cultural practices, so that (we may extrapolate) it's far from incontestable to say that animals are incapable of deceit or effacement. But note that I'm not the author of the *absurdity* of the Jack Russell proposition, nor of its *immediacy*: if the notion of canine culture is instantly outlandish, it must offend something we regard as fundamental to reason. It's absurd because it doesn't make sense. The assumption here, though, would be that sense, or good sense, conforms to principles unaffected by the force of culture, history, context or mediation; principles we associate with *scientific* thinking, or reason. Reason, then, or sense, refers to a way of thinking (understood as thought in general) that in its broadest usage is ineluctably scientific, or scientistic; and so the notion of canine culture, like the term "square triangle," could make sense only as art or poetry, but otherwise would be dismissed as stupid or insane. Again, the problem we're encountering pushes at the limits of the threshold.

To posit, on the one hand, a cultural difference between Jack Russell Terriers in Brisbane and Perth would seem a nonsense, while on the other it would be uncontroversial to suppose that between the people of Brisbane and Perth there *are* cultural differences. Why the reluctance or the refusal to acknowledge the authority of this "are"? Let's consider at least two possible responses to this question.

1. **Deconstruction** (if there is a such a thing) refuses the authority of every "is" (see Lucy, 2004: 11–14). In this way deconstruction (if there is such a thing as deconstruction so that we might refer to it as we do to "language" or the "animal") would be the continuation of the Enlightenment by other means, as John D. Caputo is fond of saying (1997: 59–60); to attempt to deconstruct something, then, would not be to oppose it outright, and especially not in order to deprive it of all possible force. So it's not a question of the absolute denial of something *like* cultural differences having an explanatory role to play in distinguishing Perth from Brisbane, and vice versa, but rather of refusing the purity and the rigor of those differences, which must be supposed to go all the way down to each city's "own" cultural identity or **essence**. To what level of atomic specificity, however, should we descend in order to reach the foundations of that identity?

   The idea of the city as an expression of its citizens goes back at least to Plato's *Republic* (380 BCE), where the city of Athens both reflects an ideal human temperament and models such a temperament. Just as democratic city life is nurtured by orderly prohibitions, so, too, in the soul of man, must wanton desires be governed by reason and passion, lest "the concupiscent soul, no longer confined to her own sphere, should attempt to enslave and rule those who are not her natural-born subjects, and overturn the whole life of man" (380 BCE: Book IV, 442b–c). What Plato calls "the acropolis of the soul" (380 BCE: Book IV, 460b), then, mirrors the soul of the acropolis: city and citizen, or nation and citizen in today's terms, produce and *re*produce one another. There would seem to be no way out of this circle by which culture is both the achievement of a people *and* the expression of a people's nature: culture is artificial (historical, and therefore deconstructible), on the one hand, and, on the other, *at the same time*, it is indivisibly natural.

   But if *The Republic* provides a warrant for associating culture with city life, and city life with culture, it doesn't seem to bring us any closer to knowing what should count as forms of cultural specificity. For example: I once attended a conference at the University of the Aegean, in Rhodes city, the capital of the small Greek island of Rhodes, where smoking was banned on campus for the two or three days of the conference proceedings. So far as I could tell, this was the only place on Rhodes you weren't allowed to smoke, since everyone, it seemed, at least just about everyone over the age of 12, appeared to be a smoker, and no one looked inhibited whenever, or wherever, they felt like lighting up. Waiters took orders and served food while smoking; shop assistants smoked as they handed you change; people smoked out on the streets, in parks, and inside cars, bars, delis and cafes. The only enclosed space in which I *didn't* see people smoking was inside elevators, and no doubt that wasn't because they suddenly became health conscious when they stepped into a lift; they just didn't want to risk dying in a fire trap!

It seems to me the only reason not to regard smoking as a cultural practice of Rhodes would be if some cultural practices were considered more cultural than others. This couldn't be a distinction that was pure and unconditional, though, or surely the Australian federal government wouldn't have intervened on behalf of the victims of child sexual abuse only in remote Indigenous communities in the Northern Territory; surely it would have intervened by now also on behalf of the victims of child sexual abuse by Catholic clergy, and, as a symbol of the state's refusal to condone the anti-modern culture of the church, sent in the military to take over St Mary's Cathedral in Sydney and surround it with troops. The point, then, is that there's almost nothing that couldn't count as a cultural practice, on the basis of which we couldn't point to a cultural difference … which is one reason for hesitating to accept that cultural differences just "are."

2. Another reason: unless we challenge the authority of *indivisible* culture, we'll never see how often culture is used to disguise or excuse differences that have political and economic causes. To call smoking on Rhodes a cultural practice is to forget that the people of Rhodes are less prosperous than the people of Sydney, where, even in this comparatively affluent demographic, affluent by world standards, smoking rates are higher, as they are everywhere, the lower down you go on the socio-economic scale. To call smoking a cultural practice, then, is to forget or to ignore that, broadly speaking, smoking is class based: the less "cultural" power you have, within your "own" culture or in the world at large, the more likely you are to be a smoker.

   Forgive me for succumbing to temptation at this point by not being able to resist drawing a corollary: if you're a Catholic priest, you're more likely to be a pedophile than if you're not. The systemic sexual abuse of

> children by the church should not be downgraded to an institutional "pathology," the result of a few bad eggs unable to cope with the pressures of celibacy, but seen as an effect or an outcome of the *culture* of that institution, if, as we are sometimes only too quick to conclude, the serial mistreatment of women by one or more players at a football club is to be understood as a product of that club's "culture."

Briefly: the problem with culture would seem to be that either it's too general and too easily generalizable, and is therefore always outside the text, or too specific, too overdetermined, and therefore prone to an essentialism that is always outside the text. Either culture is supplementary (historical and therefore perfectible), or else there's a primary sense of culture as something that comes before history but is always outside of history, an originary culture that would be more primordial, more historical, than history as such. From what we've been calling a scientific point of view, these doubled and divided usages would be equivalent to supposing that sodium can sometimes mean nitrogen, and sometimes potassium: a structure of exchange or of interchangeability, then, that would in fact be the opposite of a structure; an asystematic system that would always be in a state of breaking bad. But this is not to say that culture's many meanings are the result of sloppy, nonscientific thinking, as though it must always come down to choosing between the indivisibly scientific or the indivisibly nonscientific: sense or nonsense. The human, or the animal-machine.

I don't propose to know how to think beyond this impasse, outside the limits of this logocentrism, which, to the extent that its roots are "European," is therefore cultural through and through. We might ask, then, whether the philosophy of culture, which is what we might be said to have been doing here, could ever be separable from the culture of philosophy, for which there has always been something like an elemental difference between the human and the animal, and thus, if only informally, something like a periodic table of living things. But if periodicity turned out to be no less cultural than philosophical, surely we would have to start again.

Niall Lucy

D

Deconstruction: Deconstruction – despite its association with **Derrida** who insisted upon its *not* being a method – is nevertheless fairly easily defined against what it is not (Derrida, 1985; see **semiotics**). Methods proceed by way of orderly construction, grounded upon principles that allow us to proceed from premises or axioms or evidence towards conclusion. Modern philosophy was founded upon method: begin with what can be established indubitably before proceeding (Descartes, 1999). If there were some ultimate presence, whether that be nature, life, humanity, matter, God, reality, culture, language or meaning, then forms of reading, speaking and writing would be constructive. One would begin speaking or thinking or reasoning from what is given, and then proceed in an orderly fashion.

When Derrida wrote about Western thought being a history defined by the "metaphysics of presence" he seemed to be making a grandiose claim about philosophy of a certain type: classic instances of a metaphysics of presence would begin with the notion that there is some ultimate Being that governs and orders all other beings (Derrida, 1976: 73). Such a Being might be the creative principle from which all other beings are generated, and we could then think of this tradition as onto-theology, where a concept of foundational being is defined through some ultimate cause or God. Philosophers from Plato, who placed the world of sensations and fictions as secondary to an always-present truth, to Heidegger (who argued that we need to think of being *not* as some special entity but as the unfolding of

A Dictionary of Postmodernism, First Edition. Niall Lucy.

time) can be seen as clear instances of what Derrida targets as the metaphysics of presence.

However, the real force of deconstruction lies well beyond claims regarding the history of philosophy and Derrida's reading of foundational texts. In the 1970s and 1980s deconstruction took hold of literary studies, in part following the translation of Derrida's work into English, but also due to the work of a series of other thinkers, including (but not limited to) Paul de Man, J. Hillis Miller and Barbara Johnson (all three of whom were part of a Yale school that included others less inclined to the mode of writing deconstructively). Rather than thinking about deconstruction as a claim regarding metaphysics and claims about ultimate being, literary deconstruction abandons the ethos of construction: that there is some given *from which* criticism, reading and even experience begin. If one thinks of literature as the way in which a writer expresses an intent, or a political mindset is given form, or a world is disclosed, then the literary text can be placed as the sign or **representation** of something other than itself. If this were so, then criticism would re-trace a path of literary construction: how the text emerges from its context, reality, meaning or intention. Reading would be constructive, building meaning and reference from the text. Literature would also be a highly specific domain and practice: other disciplines – such as history or geography – would begin from realities that were material, but literature would deal with texts (where texts may have a material form in books, paper, celluloid or canvas but where the object of literary reading would be some ideal sense that tied the material signs to the material world).

Against this method of the supposed secondariness of the text that needs to be traced back from the presence or ground from which it emerges, literary deconstruction argues for a more general understanding of the trace. There is no given presence that is then differentiated or re-presented; in the beginning is difference. Deconstruction refuses the orders and constructive paths that define a certain conception of reading; texts are not material objects that need to be translated back into the reality that accounts for their sense. What we tend to think of as matter – as that from which complexity and relations emerge and as that which is represented by texts – is itself a text. Matter is not some presence that provides an order or givenness that allows us to read the world. Rather, what looks like the secondary matter of a text in the narrow sense – a literary text that does not have an attached reality but that requires some work of construction in order to generate meaning and reference – characterizes matter in general (de Man, 1996).

What looks like a specifically literary mode of formalism – to consider a text as not having any natural referent, and to demand a form of reading that composes or builds relations that are always contingent and capable of being undone – is, for deconstruction, the way of the world (Miller, 1987).

This is not to say that, for deconstruction, there is no reality and that all we have is language without any hope of **truth**. Rather, truth and reality are necessary outcomes of the unavoidable predicament of reading. To experience oneself or one's world is to experience a presence, but that experienced and natural presence occurs by way of positing – beyond all the dispersed traces and marks that we experience – something that is simply there and that is seen (after the event of reading) as having been the cause of experience.

In addition to the literary modes of deconstruction (and that demand that all disciplines become mindful and responsible of the ways in which there is no foundation that can be set outside the time and space of dispersed difference), there have been specific forms of deconstruction focused on race, sex, class and gender. Rather than think about a single and universal humanity that is then (inappropriately) differentiated into races and that should (ideally) be considered as one global family of "man," writers such as Gayatri Spivak have argued that inclusion of "others" within a global humanity erases forms of difference that cannot simply be included within what is taken to be the self-present norm of "humanity"; "difference" is textual, not because we understand others only through the construction of language, but because experience as such is differential: always involved in multiple systems of relation that can never be grounded or reduced (Spivak, 1990).

Deconstruction needs to attend to the ways in which forms of racial otherness are structural to establishing the supposedly universal presence or **essence** of the human. The very production of the man of liberal reason has a complex history involving forces of differentiation that are economic, geographical, military, textual (in the narrow sense) and temporally dispersed (see **Foucault**). Rather than see cultural systems of gender, for example, as being ways of representing a simple and underlying sex, one needs to see the supposed presence and origin of sex as the imagined underlying unity that emerges from an ongoing structure of differences (Butler, 1990).

What makes deconstruction as a general movement *postmodern* is its anti-foundationalism: there can be no appeal to a foundation outside the general predicament of text. To say that there is nothing outside the text, is *not* to say that there is no reality; it *is* to say that reality is composed from relations, differences, distances and delays. Any appeal to a foundation takes place in space, time, language, experience and difference and cannot exempt or except itself from the web or mesh of relations.

Where deconstruction differs from postmodernism as the embrace of difference is in the impossibility of arriving at some post-foundational liberation from modern desires for critique. Modern forms of critique begin from some term, such as the subject who can reason and doubt, and then place what is given under scrutiny. Deconstruction acknowledges that critique must begin from some assumed premise, and that a liberation from presence never arrives but must proceed tirelessly. In this respect, deconstruction accepts postmodernism's criticism of foundations, but does not arrive at a postmodern relativism. If modern thought posits a reason that would negotiate competing claims, postmodernism sees reason as one voice among others; against the attempted relativism of postmodernism, deconstruction recognizes that any relativizing voice is one more form of accounting for all voices as relative *to* some unavoidable center. Seemingly relativizing gestures – such as placing all truths within history, **culture** or social construction – are ultimately metaphysical insofar as they use one term to explain and subordinate all others.

Deconstruction is *not* a form of social constructivism, nor does it reduce everything to being an effect of language. On the contrary, rather than see any structure (such as writing, nature, history or culture) as the cause of everything else, it argues that all the features we tend to think of as effects of structure pervade everything: rather than argue that language is a dispersed, differentiated and ungrounded system that allows for the communication of a stable reality, reality "itself" is already constantly differing from itself, always becoming other than itself, never fully self present. Everything that we think of as pre-textual and as providing a ground for reality (whether that be mind or matter) is like a text or trace.

Claire Colebrook

Deleuze, Gilles: *French philosopher, 1925–95*

Guattari, Felix: *French psychotherapist and activist, 1930–92*

On the one hand Deleuze and Guattari can be included within a post-1968 generation of French theorists who defined themselves against traditionally moral forms of politics and critique (those that opposed capitalism by appealing to some purer outside such as the individual or the worker). The student protests of 1968 throughout Europe (which were not supported by the Communist Party of France) challenged the notion that resistance and revolution needed to be generated from those whose economic position as workers granted them a privileged insight into the fundamentally economic forms of capitalist repression. Instead, after 1968 the profound political problem was not one of economic repression but of desire: why is it that individuals willingly have "interests" such as those of a good job, stable family life, being an upright citizen or decent taxpayer? For Deleuze and Guattari any reference to some natural or proper humanity – such as the working man who would think freely if only he became aware of his true interests – covers over a history of desire. This history does not begin with the human individual; for what we know as the individual – especially the "worker" – has been produced from social relations or "assemblages" that enable the broader system of capitalism, individualism and humanism. In this respect Deleuze and Guattari, like their contemporaries, begin with structures of difference (such as the economy, language, gender relations, race, ethnicity and so on) and explain the individual as an effect of social codes. In the beginning are differentiating structures *from which* stable entities, such as "man," "family," and "law" are effected.

On the other hand, Deleuze and Guattari differ significantly from other **poststructuralists** (or those who see reality as effected by way of structures and relations of power or text), by way of their insistence on desire. Although Gilles Deleuze had a career as an individual philosopher (in which he wrote on major figures in the history of philosophy), and although Felix Guattari had a career as a radical therapist who was critical of the focus of psychoanalysis on the individual psyche (see also **Lacan**, **Žižek**), it was their co-authored project of *Anti-Oedipus* (1983) and *A Thousand Plateaus* (1987) that coupled a universal history with a criticism of contemporary capitalism. Capitalism is not a modern aberration; rather, life begins with the "warding off" of the free flows of desire that would eventually be fully decoded in capitalism (but then captured by markets.)

The first volume, *Anti-Oedipus* (1983 [Fr. *L'anti-Oedipe* 1972]), argues that the subject of psychoanalysis – the individual who must submit to the structures of law and recognition or risk falling into the chaos of psychosis – is the outcome of a broader history of social formations. Following both Marx and Kant they argue for three historical stages, and three forms of synthesis. The first "primitive" stage assembles bodies into territories, and at this stage investments (or the channeling of desire into a specific mode) is collective: when a body is scarred, tattooed, burned or marked it is felt and lived by the entire tribe. A territory is formed when bodies assemble to establish a relatively stable whole; the identity of each body is given through collective sensations: in the witnessing of a tribal bird dance "we" become a single body formed through a common rhythm. Rather than bodies who have a psyche and who use language to communicate, there are collective sensations that establish a tribal body. The second "despotic stage" is one of de-territorialization: if a tribal leader manifestly enjoys success – delighting in the pain inflicted on another's body – then one body is set outside the social whole. The assemblage or territory becomes subordinate to a body elevated above relations: if a despot enjoys the pain inflicted then the acts of violence can be seen as punishment; bodies are coded and read. With despotism we are on the way to privatization, which occurs in the final historical stage of capitalism and re-territorialization. Vision and sensations are no longer collective – as in despotism, where torture allows us all to feel the force of law – but become private: everything becomes a sign of who I am and what I must desire. Rather than an external despot, who operates by inflicting pain and displaying the excesses of his own enjoyment, we submit to "morality," or what makes us "human." We are guilty, or indebted: something in us – our humanity – already subjects us to an ongoing journey of submission. Everything is internalized and rendered as an effect of our supposedly universal and timeless nature: I am a subject who speaks, and I must therefore accept the law of language or fall back into chaos. I imagine that there must have been some undifferentiated desire prior to language, but acceding to that desire would be psychosis. Deleuze and Guattari see the Oedipus complex in its narrow form – the self who must submit to authority rather than enjoy the plenitude of pre-social desire – as the coding of a long history of oppression that has channeled desire into stable assemblages.

The modern subject is an effect of capitalism (and capitalism emerges from a long history of desire): all social assemblages stabilize difference, but capitalism no longer does so by external codes (the tribe or the despot), but by de-coding. Anything is possible and acceptable as long as it is my choice and as long as it takes part in the general exchange of markets. "We" accept that there is no law or presence other than that of the differentiating structures of language and exchange. What Deleuze and Guattari argue for, against this acceptance of the structures of language and capital, is *schizo-analysis.* How did the psyche – the subject who submits to the laws of language and the market – become the basic social unit whose *interests* are now those of being a good worker and citizen? In *Anti-Oedipus* the history is fairly straightforward and proceeds from the tribe as collective assemblage to the family and the Oedipal individual who assumes that *either* one accedes to the law *or* one falls into psychosis. This is what they refer to as the disjunctive synthesis: one is *either* a man *or* woman, a moral citizen *or* psychotic, a rational individual capable of communication and consensus *or* a dysfunctional "schizo" in need of therapy and integration. Against this, Deleuze and Guattari argue that we see the unified psyche as an effect of the repression of desire, where desire is directly revolutionary. This theory of desire is made clear in their second volume, *A Thousand Plateaus* (1987 [Fr. 1980]).

Why do we think of language and social units such as the family, as privileged codes for thinking about life? Why do we, for example, trace the individual's desires back to her family history, and not trace the family back to its emergence from broader social assemblages? And why do we not think of the human social assemblage, in turn, as having its historical condition of emergence in geological and microbial life? Language and the economy are legitimate systems of difference, but they form only one stratum among many, and both language and money have their origin in earlier human and inhuman relations. Deleuze and Guattari therefore argue for *desire*, which is not human: in the beginning is some force that enters into relation with another force. From the "pre-biotic" soup or "intense germinal influx" relations among forces allow for the emergence of single-celled organisms, which allow a history of light, oxygen and carbon to produce a history of bodies. The task for thinking is not to move from organized bodies to some single "Body Without Organs," for there are always multiple and divergent strata that produce systems of relative stability. Rather one moves from organization to a disorganization which is also a higher level of difference, ever more complex and ever more intensive. For Deleuze and Guattari, continuing the project of schizoanalysis from *Anti-Oedipus* (1983), "higher deterritorialization," requires taking any seeming stability – such as "man" or the subject (see **Foucault**) – and then opening up the organized whole to the fluxes of desire from which it emerged. From the differentiated to the more and more differentiated, Deleuze and Guattari use the concept of desire to open the notions of language, structure and economy to radically inhuman and inorganic forces.

In *A Thousand Plateaus* (1987) Deleuze and Guattari undertake multiple analyses of life, all of which begin from a different stratum or register. We could, for example, begin with metallurgy, and argue that what we now know as human social life emerged from a history of forging talismans, weapons, armor and body adornments; or we could begin from sound and argue that life proceeds by way of pulsations of rhythm and chromaticism; or we could begin from space and argue that life needs to be understood as a smooth space that is striated by movements and tracings that generate stability and places. Or we could begin by thinking of rhizomes – root structures that do not have a center – and then think of trees as being secondary formations that appear centered but that overlay a far more complex and multiple structure of growth and proliferating inter-connection. The concept of desire is therefore, for Deleuze and Guattari, not a thing within life or the world; it is a way of thinking relations, and a way of producing a theory that *is* movement. Take any force – from art and literature to war and viruses – and that force can be understood as being *what it is* by virtue of its encounters. Humans become speaking individuals because of the ways they have encountered other humans, the earth, time and light. There is no single thing or force in the world that explains all other forces, but each force relates to all other forces in its own way. We can refer to this "plane of immanence" (or mesh of relations that has no foundation, ground or outside) as *desire* because it tends toward something other than itself, and produces and transforms itself in relation. Politics is therefore not an art of looking at bodies and what they want and what they do, but looking at the desiring forces that compose bodies. Politics is not a question of ideology (what we believe) or power (a force that structures from above). Politics does not begin from the modern assumption of liberal anti-foundationalism (where the absence of any ultimate law requires us to give a law to ourselves). Politics is *postmodern* because there are always too many foundations (or there is always one element of completion missing); there are a thousand plateaus by means of which the totality of relations can always be understood by beginning from any relation that can never contain the open whole.

Claire Colebrook

Derrida, Jacques: *French philosopher, 1930–2004*

Before you even start reading, the sheer volume of it is striking. Benoît Peeters's biography lists Derrida as the author of 58 books in French, and collaborator on a dozen or so more (Peeters, 2013). There are more to come, as the vast archive of his papers at the University of California at Irvine is gradually edited and published.

This extraordinary output is all, of necessity, a continuing work in progress. It comes back on itself, rethinking where it has been and reconsidering alignments. For example, it's often been a commonplace among commentators to see Derrida's work as characterized by a shift toward the ethical somewhere around the 1990s. *Given Time* (1992) looks at the problematic of the gift; a series of essays from 1997 focuses on questions of cosmopolitanism (2003), hospitality (2000) and mourning (1999; 2001); *The Gift of Death* (1995) has a long meditation on the story of Abraham and its centrality to Western thought on ethics; and three of the important books so far published after his death – (*The Animal that Therefore I Am* (2008) and the two volumes of *The Beast and the Sovereign* (2009; 2011) – are to do with the question of the animal. Or again, it's often suggested that despite his own personal engagement with the Left in his early career, his work itself remains somewhat apolitical until *Specters of Marx* (1994), after which we see an increased engagement with overtly political topics, and work on the new Europe, cosmopolitanism, "rogue states" and 9/11. We can trace a number of smaller about-faces and reconsiderations; if Derrida's first published piece on Freud, "Freud and the Scene of Writing" from *Writing and Difference* 1978 [Fr. 1967]), is critical of what it sees as Freud's inability to see the implications of the machineries of writing in his own theories, then by 1980 and *The Post Card* (Derrida, 1987a [Fr. 1980]) he will be reading Freud in a much more thoroughly sympathetic fashion.

These are the type of changes we might expect from a work in progress spanning over 40 years. It's the very logic of a work in progress to do that. With Derrida, though, it's not only a description of his own work, but also in many ways what that work investigates. How is it that a particular argument, a particular piece of writing, is capable of doing unexpected things when one returns to it? How can it come to show aspects of itself that were not apparent the first time through, but which now stand out so strongly that they cannot be ignored? For Derrida, it's a false question to attribute this to the magical agency of an always-inventive human subject. The more interesting question is how this can be a property of the argument, the writing itself.

This is one reason Derrida's writing is, and has to be, so often leisurely and willing to take its time. It's writing that so often begins with another text, and that sees its first duty as the careful reconstruction of what that text says or argues: not in order simply to disagree with it, but in order to do something more complex and more interesting – to see how that text necessarily, as a condition of what it's doing, disagrees with itself. So, for example, just over half of the early *Of Grammatology* (1976 [Fr. 1967]) is taken up with an examination of Rousseau, focusing famously on the unexpected peculiarities of that term "supplement." A supplement is both something that is unnecessary to the basic functioning of what it supplements (a weekend newspaper would still be a newspaper without the color supplement, if a less desirable one), and at the same time something that is necessary, without which what it supplements just wouldn't work properly (as with a vitamin supplement). The supplement is, in short, impossible: it's at one and the same time gratuitous and essential. Derrida traces the trajectory of the idea of the supplement across Rousseau's work, cropping up as it goes in almost every genre that he works in: memoir, political philosophy, educational theory, writing on music, theory of language.

The aim of this is not to show that Rousseau is wrong, or to correct him, or to suggest that supplements don't exist, or that the supplement is a bad idea on which to base an argument and that the whole project is thus based on a false premise. It's here that Derrida's work of **deconstruction** refuses to be a sophisticated tool of Marxian *Ideologiekritik*, a way of pointing out and correcting the ideological errors that others make. The supplement, with all of its instability and inconsistency, is not an error. Not only is it not in need of correction, it cannot be corrected in this way; any attempt to do that can only result in the very same thing cropping up again elsewhere. The supplement is persistent. More, it's constitutive.

Let's stop for a moment at that point. One of the frequent complaints by critics of Derrida (who reveal in making the complaint that they simply haven't read him with any of the care that Derrida gives to the texts he reads) is that this is a sort of nihilism or relativism (both of which always stand as terms of condemnation that are always ready to hand). The conclusion one has to draw from Derrida's argument, they say, is that rigorous argument is simply impossible. Logic itself, Derrida says (they say) is full of holes, and we are adrift in pathos on a sea of words without purchase on the real world, or any possible commitment to it. We find this complaint in Fredric **Jameson**'s early work, for example and above all, in that title, *The Prison-House of Language* (1972). It is inherited by figures such as Terry Eagleton and his polemic against falling into the endless sea of semiosis (see **semiotics**) in his best-selling *Literary Theory: An Introduction* 1983. This is to see the Derridean move as one that tries to point out and correct errors, to which one's own move should be, in turn, to point out Derrida's errors. In this case, the "naïve" error that Derrida is supposed to be correcting is that language can and does have referents in the real world; and the reaction to it is to argue that that very move itself would be an error, and a naïve and politically disabling one, because it makes all arguments fall apart before they're even uttered and leaves powerless those who would use argument as a weapon against power.

Perhaps the argument to be made against this is to go one step further: the supplement is not an erroneous idea, not because it's a correct idea, but because it's not even really an idea in the first place – and this is its point. Derrida famously says of another of his coinages, *differance* (with an *a*), that it is neither a concept nor a word, though it does of course look like both. Why is the supplement not a concept? Even to suggest it surely sounds like precious self-parody, the sort of thing that so easily gets cited to demonstrate how much Derrida (or postmodernism, or **poststructuralism**, name your poison) has left all common sense behind. And yet, it is not at all difficult to see supplementarity not as a particular logical operation or conceptual relation, but as a way of trying to give a name to what makes concepts and their logics possible in the first place. Before there is the apparent consistency and coherence of the concept, or the strength of systematicity in which concepts exist, there is just *differance*, a differing-from, a supplementation. Difference itself has no consistency, no unity, no boundaries. Woven out of pure differences, signs and concepts thus have at their heart the potential to differ even from themselves: put them into connection with another set of differences, and they may turn themselves inside-out, revealing something that had been profoundly unexpected – which is, among other things, the *Aha!* reaction of the moment of illumination.

Without such formal instability, which is that of differentiation itself, there could be no concept. The cost of it, though, is that the concept cannot govern this movement of supplementarity. Supplementarity is one of many names for what comes before the concept – not in the sense of something primal or originary, but just for that ever-shifting differentiability. The difficulty is that the supplement tries to think something that is before the concept, to name something that is necessarily prior to **discourse**. Without it, we'd have neither a system of concepts nor the ways of saying them, but because of that priority the supplement will never fit comfortably into those systems, which it inhabits as a series of dislocations, unpredictable effects, the possibility of novelty at the heart of the familiar.

Over and over, as Derrida shows, Rousseau's work keeps returning to that point of supplementarity. Derrida is not interested in describing it as an error Rousseau makes repeatedly, but in *reading* the moves he is making at these points. (To declare something an error is, after all, always a useful way of declaring that something does not *need* to be read, or even that it shouldn't be read, as we know in advance all that we'd ever conceivably need to know about it, which is that it's wrong. It's to absolve one in advance for not reading.) To do this, he tries to carefully and meticulously reconstruct Rousseau's argument at each stage, to show just what work the supplement is doing wherever Rousseau invokes it.

Two things emerge from this. One is that Rousseau himself begins to appear not just as a thinker who across a large number of disciplinarily different investigations (into justice, the development and education of children, democracy, autobiography ...) finds himself obliged to supplement his argument in ways that never quite cohere in the ways he might wish, but *as a thinker of supplementarity itself*. Across all of these investigations, Rousseau is clearly and cogently thinking the implications of supplementarity, wherever it appears. The paradox is that Derrida, in thinking how supplementarity works in Rousseau, cannot help but show that Rousseau was there before him. Before Derrida, Rousseau was already thinking Derrida-thinking-supplementarity – but of course, we didn't think that before reading Derrida on Rousseau. Derrida's reading changes our idea of what Rousseau has been about all along. And this is, after all, neither more nor less than the claim we make for a major thinker: that they change our ideas of what thinking *has been*, of what whatever came before them had been all along. Under Derrida's reading, Rousseau is Derrida before the event.

And from that (second point), what Derrida's reading of Rousseau has attempted to do in its careful tracing-out of Rousseau's argument is show that not only is there another and very different sort of argument there than the familiar philosophy of liberty and equality and the essential and improvable goodness of human nature, but that this new and different argument occupies the very same texts, even at times the very same *sentences*; that it is demonstrably and rigorously Rousseau's argument, because the terms and the ways of dealing with those terms are his; and that one finds this argument not by an act of traducing Rousseau or imposing another system upon him from outside, but oddly by being rigorously and meticulously faithful to him in this reading. What Derrida shows is that Rousseau's philosophy has within it the possibility of what we can call *novation*: it can be read in ways that are rigorously and carefully faithful to its own procedures, and that yet produce something that is quite unforeseeable, incalculable from those procedures. The gap that opens up in Rousseau's text is thus that of history itself, if we are to think of history as the vicissitudes of the real and their escape from law (see **Foucault**). Far from closing down the possibilities of thinking the political and the historical, what Derrida's reading does is install that at the heart of any text, as its very possibility. Far from closing things off into the solipsism of thought that would buffer itself from the world with a defensive undecidability, it turns thought into an endless spilling-over.

Tony Thwaites

Dialogue: **Dialogue**'s roots as a word go back to Ancient Greek (*dia* = "through" + *legein* = "to speak"), where it occurs in contrast to other such terms – prologue, monologue, epilogue and so on. It appears in relevant specialist domains, such as drama studies, literature and linguistics, and in Socratic-Platonic philosophy, where dialogue is a method. Thence, it has become familiar in ordinary language, where dialogue is recorded conversation between two or more speakers.

The conventions of recording multivocal speech may seem an unlikely place to look for a new theory of language in general, but this is indeed the situation that the concept of dialogue has inspired. It has emerged as a new answer to an old question: "where does meaning come from?" Ferdinand de Saussure's (1974 [Fr. 1916]) model of language (see **semiotics**) was that of an abstract system of rules, which produced signs whose chief property was that they *differed* from others in the system. For Saussure, meanings bore an *arbitrary* relation both to the speaker (whose utterance or "*parole*" did not control the system or "*langue*" but was spoken by it, as it were), and to the "concept" that was signified (signs were "unmotivated" by their object). In one blow, Saussure removed both *subjectivity* (speakers, and their intentionality) and *realism* (where signs were thought to bear a trace of the real referent) from the workings of language, and thus from the determination of meaning.

Saussure's abstract model of language downplayed the social element of interactive speech (parole), and had no theory of change, especially of how social life might determine change and transformation of the abstract system of language (see **poststructuralism**). Tony Bennett (2003: 57–8) lists four objections to Saussure's model: (1) reductionism; (2) formalism; (3) idealism; (4) anthropologism. One might add individualism, for despite its abstraction and systems-based model, it remained individualist or monologic in the sense that discourse was seen as a product of individual choice ("paradigm") and combination ("syntagm") of elements from the system.

But, almost from the beginning, an alternative – dialogic – model of meaning's origins had been available. "Dialogism" emerged from the revolutionary ferment of Russia in the early part of the twentieth century, where Russian Formalism, Marxism, Futurism and other intellectual movements that explored the links among artistic, imaginative and political life were cross-fertilizing and arguing with each other (Bennett, 2003; Brandist, n.d.). Translations of their main texts were slow to cross the ideological Iron Curtain into English or French, and Cold War hostilities slowed further the reception of writers from the Eastern bloc. Thus the influence of many of their most innovative ideas was not felt in the West until decades later – after Saussurean semiotics had gained a foundational place in the emerging fields of communication, media studies and literary theory.

The best-known proponents of dialogism were Mikhail Bakhtin (1981), Valentin Vološinov (1973 [Russian 1929–30]), and later Yuri Lotman (1990; 2009). The idea of dialogue as the foundational act of meaning-making emerged from a reaction among the "Bakhtin Circle" to the arrival of Saussurean theory in Russia (Brandist n.d.), where it was taken up by the Formalists (Bennett, 2003; Hawkes, 1977), who substituted literature for language, such that "texts" are the units in a "literary system," and intertextuality the play of difference that produces literariness. Instead of such a closed-system approach, the Bakhtinians wanted to open language to social determination, newness, change and struggle, including the dialectics of difference between official and popular socio-cultural forces: authority and carnival; literature and popular culture; the discourse of the intelligentsia and that of the denizens of the "carnival square." In his writing on Dostoyevsky, Bakhtin (1984) contrasted what Craig Brandist has dubbed "the forces of cultural centralization and stabilization: the 'official strata', unitary language, the literary canon and so on," with, on the other side, "the decentralizing influence of popular culture: popular festivity and collective ridicule, literary parody, and the anti-canonic novel" (Brandist, n.d.).

This is dialogism at the macro- or *system* level, where large-scale meaning systems ("literature" vs. "popular culture") clash and interact, producing new meanings out of their difference, which is historical, social and political as well as formal and structural.

Bakhtin and Vološinov were also convinced that dialogism occurred at the micro-level of the sign. In *The Dialogic Imagination*, Bakhtin writes:

> The word is born in a dialogue as a living rejoinder within it; the word is shaped in dialogic interaction with an alien word that is already in the object. A word forms a concept of its own object in a dialogic way. (Bakhtin, 1981: 279)

There's no such thing as a signifier without an interlocutor-role already working within it, causing it to be "born" with its "rejoinder" already present. Vološinov used that idea to propose the "multi-accentuality" of signs, where the same sign can be accented (used) to mean different things to different speech communities. Signs are therefore "polysemic," allowing not only for difference among signs but also for differences among users; and for change to occur as a result of social process, including class struggle (Volšinov, 1973: 68–9). Thus, "understanding" – knowledge – is only possible through dialogic process, in which the sign is mutable, contested and always incomplete:

> Any true understanding is dialogic in nature. Understanding is to utterance as one line of a dialogue is to the next … meaning belongs to a word in its position between speakers: that is, meaning is realized only in the process of active, responsive understanding. (Vološinov 1973: 102)

Both Bakhtin and Vološinov were interested in the speech of the street as well as that of the state or salon, seeing a vibrancy in it that was dialogic both in the local situation of utterance (requiring the presence of imagined or real interlocutor and social context to make sense) and as a whole, especially in its interactions with authoritative (class or state) discourses. Here the Bakhtin circle shared an interest in what the novelist Anthony Burgess would later call "low-life language," which, like George Orwell (1946), he saw not in negative terms but as "the home-made language of the ruled, not the rulers, the acted upon, the used, the used up. It is demotic poetry emerging in flashes of ironic insight" (Burgess 1992, cited in Carr, n.d.). Burgess cites an example of dialogism that requires an understanding of context, use, and multi-accentuality, where the same sign is made to perform the role of no fewer than five different parts of speech across the span of a mere seven words:

> I once heard an army motor mechanic complain of his recalcitrant engine by crying "Fuck it, the fucking fucker's fucking fucked." (Burgess, 1992, cited in Carr, n.d.)

Burgess's interest in the state/street clash of languages was put to powerful fictional effect in his own best-known novel, *A Clockwork Orange* (1962). It peppers the underclass/subcultural argot of disaffected urban youth with Russianisms, supposedly imbibed from Soviet propaganda, but repurposed dialogically to suit the life and style of the book's "Nadsat" (teen) antiheroes.

Vološinov and Bakhtin too were interested in the energy and irony of demotic speech, especially when it achieves literary status in Rabelaisian satire and bawdy, which reflexively comment on the "speech genres" they send up or undermine. Bakhtin saw the unification-in-dialogue of literary forms with "low-life language" as a Renaissance achievement, inaugurating the modern era: Marlowe, Shakespeare and Cervantes may be mentioned alongside Rabelais, although Bakhtin wrote almost nothing about Cervantes. However, the critic Walter Reed (1987) cleverly explains this absence as a kind of dialogic homage:

> It seems to me that Cervantes himself mounts powerful arguments against our tendency to assume that, in the dialogue of theory and practice, literary theory can and must have the last word. Both Cervantes and Bakhtin demonstrate, from opposite sides of the critical fence, that the privilege and authority of all theory are on loan from the creative imagination but also that the escapism and delight of the literary imagination are vehicles for serious philosophical investigation. (Reed, 1987: 37)

This type of dialogism – between high and low culture, theory and practice, philosophy and literature, insider and outsider, presence and absence – is the direct source of change, dynamism and social determination in language: the origin of liveliness if not life itself, the source of the "everyday English" that George Orwell saw as the "first step towards political regeneration":

> If you simplify your English, you are freed from the worst follies of orthodoxy … Political language … is designed to make lies sound truthful and murder respectable, and to give an appearance of solidity to pure wind. One cannot change this all in a moment, but one can at least change one's own habits, and from time to time one can even, if one jeers loudly enough, send some worn-out and useless phrase – some *jackboot, Achilles' heel, hotbed, melting pot, acid test, veritable inferno* or other lump of verbal refuse – into the dustbin where it belongs. (Orwell, 1946)

Such sentiments require that *all* utterance is dialogic and at the same time political, because the use of one register – say, educated, Latinate "orthodoxy" (i.e. weasel words) – implies the neglect or suppression of another possible choice ("everyday" simplicity). Like many others, Orwell thought that renewal from below was the best defense against totalitarianism. What might happen without it inspired his novel *Nineteen Eighty-Four* (1993 [1949]), where the state's monstrous crimes were hidden in the corruptions of *Newspeak*. Many have claimed that Newspeak has now become a social as well as fictional reality – a **hyperreality** – for instance as a "speech genre" that has been adopted by Fox News (*Huffington Post*, 2011).

Thus dialogism is at one and the same time a macro-level systems phenomenon, a feature of meso-level institutional or inter-communal relationships, and a micro-level property of individual signs. It explains in linguistic terms the social (group-based) determination and clash of contested meanings.

This approach was taken a stage further by Yuri (also Juri) Lotman (1990; 2009), whose work has provoked perhaps the most radical extension of dialogism. Lotman's concept of the semiosphere extends dialogism to planetary proportions, on the model of the biosphere. Like the biosphere (all life, its interconnections and conditions of existence), the semiosphere is infinitely varied and dynamic, evolutionary and interdependent. In the biosphere, each species and each specimen of life require all the others as part of their space/time conditions of existence (including evolved characteristics and relations of predation, competition, cooperation, and reproduction). Each living cell requires a previous cell and other cells. Eukaryotic organisms (nucleus-bearing cells enclosed in membranes) include all animals, plants, fungi, and single-cell protists. These separated out from the other two forms of life, Bacteria and Archaea, about two billion years ago. Each one needs (1) to be aware of itself (the boundary between its own system and the environment, including hierarchies of organization that distinguish complex multicellular organisms from *their* environment), (2) to perceive the environment (filter incoming information) and (3) to process its perceptions about threats and opportunities related to self-maintenance (fuel, security, reproduction) such that it can act (expend energy) in its environment. All of these activities are *communication* (Luhmann, 1991; 2012; 2013), not just information-transmission but semiosis.

Each organism – from protista to Stephen Hawking – lives in an *Umwelt*: "the phenomenal worlds of organisms, the worlds around animals as they themselves perceive them" (Hoffmeyer, 2010: 369). All *Umwelts* are semiotic. Each human *Umwelt* interacts with others; each interaction occurs within – and so constitutes – the semiosphere. It is impossible to communicate except through the semiosphere: "Any two *Umwelts*, when communicating, are a part of the same semiosphere" (Kull, 1998).

It follows that the elementary and initiating act of semiosis is *translation* – the strongest form of dialogue, if you like. This fundamental dialogism is the basis of *biosemiotics* (Hoffmeyer, 1996). Kalevi Kull (1998) summarizes its claims:

- semiosis arose together with life, which means with the first cells;
- semiosis, symbiosis, and life process are almost identical (or, isomorphic);
- life is mainly a semiotic phenomenon, the real elements of life are signs.

Life, in short, is a precipitate of dialogue.

John Hartley

Differend: Part of what the Enlightenment gave us to believe is that disputes can be resolved rationally. Through the application of reason it can be decided which case or argument in a dispute represents the **truth**, where "truth" is understood as transcendental. In this way truth is always prior to and independent of the means that might be used to express it, or any claim to speak on its behalf. This kind of scientific or positivist ideal of truth is a good example of what **Lyotard** means by a **metanarrative**, which, after Auschwitz, no longer holds universal sway. It was the Third Reich's metanarrative of Aryan supremacy, after all, that justified the persecution, torture and killing of millions of Jews, Bolsheviks, gypsies, gays, the mentally ill and others who were denied a chance to speak under the oppressive reign of a single, "unifying" **discourse**. So what might have been intended to unify the members of the Third Reich did so not only at the expense of different versions of the truth, but also out of a necessity to exclude, silence and ultimately to obliterate such differences. The work of unification (at least on the evidence of the Nazi case) necessitates the exclusion of others, demanding an attitude of intolerance toward difference. To unite, then, is also to exclude. The desire for sameness (unity, unification) confronts difference (multiplicity, hybridity, heterogeneity and so on) as a problem, to which the final solution is genocide. If others are different, if they don't or won't conform to an ideal prescribed by a given system of thought and being – kill them! "Problem" solved.

Put like that the Holocaust seems rational, a sensibly practical solution to the problem of difference. But notice how this explanation presupposes that difference is always already a problem to be overcome, while assigning a positive value to unity and instrumental reason. If this were the only available or allowable explanation of the Holocaust, then, how could you contest it? How would you be able to account for being different – as a Jew, a gay or a communist – in terms other than those which construct "difference" as a problem to be overcome? In all such cases the truth is determined by a single discourse that accords it the status of being absolute and independent, and so the possibility of "competing" or "alternative" truths is ruled out in advance. (Consider the warring claims for ownership of Gaza and the West Bank: in the context of US-backed Israeli claims, Palestinian territorialism is defined only as terrorism.) The Third Reich didn't see Jewishness as a legitimately different form of ethnic identity or regard communism as a legitimate alternative to Nazism; it saw them as degenerate perversions of "true" ethnicity and government. So in any dispute between the Third Reich and others, whom it defined as deviant or simply different, there would always be what Lyotard calls a *differend*, which occurs whenever one side in a dispute is rendered effectively speechless through the impossibility of putting its case in a way that makes sense within the terms of the other side's controlling discourse.

Now in many situations it is vital, of course, to insist on there being hard-and-fast truths, even if these are only functional rather than transcendental. You wouldn't want to live in an apartment building designed by an architect who thought there was an alternative truth to the law of gravity or that the principles of geometry were open to free association. While knowing that the "absolute" truths of science change from time to time, all the same at any given time it is sensible to regard them as unquestionable. One day, perhaps, the law of gravity (as we understand it now) may turn out to be less than absolutely true, but in the meantime it functions as a perfectly good rule of thumb to keep in mind when designing buildings.

For Lyotard, however, it isn't differends that might be said to occur in nature which interest him, but differends in **culture**. No doubt a daffodil can't explain itself to a gum tree, and so there may be many incommensurable differences within the botanical world. But since plant-life isn't ethical in the usual sense, plants can't be accused of being oppressive, violent or invasive; this accusation can be leveled only at ethical, decision-making beings, among which differends arise whenever one side fails to make itself heard according to the other side's controlling terms of reference. This didn't happen only in Nazi Germany; it's happening all the time. What causes it to happen is that in contrast to the plant world, where something like universal forces and conditions might be said to apply, in the world of culture there is no such thing as universal meaning, a universal language … or universal anything. Human cultures are made up of any number of differences. These have to be overlooked in order to define a culture or a community in terms of sameness (as a nation, for example) on the basis of an **essence**, a supposedly homogeneous set of common features or shared values. What gets lost in this formation is the absolute singularity of individuals, whose differences cannot be expressed under a regime of overarching sameness, uniformity or consensus. Condemned to silence, the individual is victimized. But here victimhood (which is a condition of the individual's absolute singularity or radical otherness) needs to be distinguished from a wrong, which Lyotard associates with litigation. Concerning litigation, wrongs are compensable; concerning differends, they are unpresentable.

What, for example, could be more radically other than the nonhuman, and how could it present a wrong to us in a language we might understand? "That is why," Lyotard writes, "the animal is a paradigm of the victim" (1988b: 28). This doesn't mean that animals are more deserving of justice than people (though some people argue that they are), but simply that animals are victimized by their inability to communicate with us in ways we recognize as a language. Unable to "speak" for themselves, their lot is only ever to be spoken for. Because they are "deprived of the possibility of bearing witness according to the human rules for establishing damages" (Lyotard, 1988b: 28), animals are constituted as victims and the wrongs inflicted on them are unable to be presented as wrongs.

But what could possibly count as evidence of a wrong that couldn't be presented? How would you even know such a wrong had occurred? For Lyotard, however, such questions miss the point, because they take "evidence" to mean only what is determinable or objective from a positivist point of view:

> Either the differend has an established reality for its object and it is not a differend but a litigation, or, if the object has no established reality, the differend has no object, and there is simply no differend. – So speaks positivism. It confuses reality and referent. (Lyotard, 1988b: 28)

Lyotard is alluding here to what can be called the problem of **representation**, where a representation is understood to reproduce something that is prior to and independent of its reproduction in the form of a painting, a photograph, a novel, a newspaper article and so on. This assumes that every representation is always a re-presentation of something preceding it, which has the status of being real. It's on the basis of this succession (from a thing's reality or essence to its representation) that successful litigation is possible, where wrongs are understood as prior and determinate; ultimately, then, one side's representation of a wrong is taken to be true at the other's expense. By contrast, damages pertaining to differends are of the order of the unpresentable and so their only "representation" is silence:

> In effect, the differend is not a matter for litigation; economic and social law can regulate the litigation between economic and social partners but not the differend between labor-power and capital. By what well-formed **phrase** and by means of what establishment procedure can the worker affirm before the labor arbitrator that what one yields to one's boss for so many hours per week in exchange for a salary is *not* a commodity? (Lyotard, 1988b: 10)

From this might be drawn the crypto-Marxist conclusion that antagonistic social forces are incommensurable, such that conflicts between the fundamentally different interests of labor and capital could never hope to be resolved in a fanciful "middle" ground of compromised consensus. It is possible for a worker to appear before an arbitration court as a complainant, in other words, but not as a victim. "The one who lodges a complaint is heard, but the one who is a victim, and who is perhaps the same one, is reduced to silence" (Lyotard, 1988b: 10). Even if he or she is a plaintiff, the victim remains unrecognizable to legal discourse (since victimhood is unpresentable) and suffers not only a damage but also, and crucially, "the loss of the means to prove the damage" (1988b: 5).

Lurking in the shadows of Kant's sublime – where something experienced as "an outrage on the imagination" cannot be re-presented, "and yet it is judged all the more sublime on that account" (Kant, 1790: §23) – differends call for a non-prescriptive, case-sensitive rule of judgment that isn't really a rule at all. Certainly it isn't a rule in the sense of being universally applicable, since Lyotard insists there is no such thing as "a universal rule of judgment between heterogeneous genres" (Lyotard, 1988b: xi). This is not to say there isn't something like a universal response to Auschwitz, for example, or to injustices generally, but simply that we don't respond to these according to pre-given rules (atrocities on the scale of Auschwitz are not instances of a general type, mere cases subsumed under a universal). Nor is our response motivated by an *object*, as though an event like "Auschwitz" could be represented as the sum of so many calculable facts and figures whose totality could be litigated. Such an event – like a work of art – leaves us with the feeling that when all is said and done, there is more to say and do. Art, calling for what Kant terms reflective (in contrast to determining) judgment (see Lucy, 1997: 172–9), is exemplary in this regard, for what a work of art "is" remains inexhaustible because art is irreducible to an object understood as something prior to and independent of discourse. Art, Kant says in the Third *Critique*, is what gives us the feeling that what it "is" can't be determined objectively or cognitively, having to do with "the assent of all to a judgement regarded as exemplifying a universal rule *incapable of formulation*" (Kant, 1790: §18, emphasis added). No commentary on a work of art could be mistaken for the work it comments on or be thought to provide the final solution to the mystery that the work evokes and which "is" the work. Art, in short, beckons us to something like the limits of thought or understanding, posing itself as the *question* of "itself."

Reflective or aesthetic judgment, then, differs from practical and rational judgments. First, we don't judge art according to what it is "for" (Kant insists that art is non-purposive, or at least that its purpose is unknowable), and secondly the question of what art "is" remains open-ended. These, too, are features of the differend, defined as "the unstable state and instant of language wherein something which must be able to be put into phrases [base units of meaning or sense, not restricted to language] cannot yet be" (Lyotard, 1988b: 13), so that differends have no utility from the point of view, say, of a legal system, which thinks to mete out justice by evaluating competing sets of determinable statements and measurable facts in search of the truth. Like a work of art, however, the differend is what is unpresentable to such a system, and therefore can't be represented from within it. But unlike the sublime, which Kant associates with the colossal (a skyscraper or a cyclone, for example), the unpresentability of differends occurs at the mundane level of the everyday, multiplying victimhood into the bargain.

So while the sublime is a rare occurrence, differends are common as muck. Here, moving forward almost two centuries, the work of the later Wittgenstein (which might be taken to show that there is no such thing as "language") is an important influence on Lyotard's thinking. For Wittgenstein, what we think of as language – a universal system – is in fact a heterogeneous mix of multiple rule-governed, game-like micro-systems having "countless different kinds" of use (2001: §53). Language games, he calls them. Just as the rules of baseball make it possible to score a home run, which would not be possible otherwise, language games, rather than reflecting pre-existing truths or reality, simply allow us to "do" certain things. Baseball doesn't re-present home runs; it produces them. The rules of a game are tools for getting things done: striking out a batter in baseball, bowling a maiden over in cricket, checking an opponent in chess. None of these makes any sense outside of the games that make them possible, and whatever sense they make within particular games is not transferable to other games. It would be gibberish to say that a batsman in cricket was struck out or a baseball pitcher bowled a maiden over. Similarly, knowing how to bowl a yorker in cricket won't help you to pitch a changeup in baseball and vice versa.

On this model, the meaning of a word isn't representational but rather an effect of its usage as determined by the rules of a particular language game. Just as, for Kant, art is not to be found "in" objects, so for Wittgenstein meaning is not a property "of" language as such but rather of the multifarious ways in which language is used in ever-changing social contexts, and to the extent that each of these positions is anti-teleological it is also anti-Enlightenment: the careful accumulation of knowledge concerning art and language won't lead to their ultimate definitions. This is why Lyotard refers to the later works of Kant and Wittgenstein as "epilogues to **modernity** and prologues to an honorable postmodernity" (Lyotard, 1988b: xiii). Although separated by more than 150 years, the later works of these philosophers open modernity to an "incredulity toward metanarratives" that characterizes what Lyotard calls "the postmodern condition" (1984: xxiv), their later works bearing witness to "the decline of universalist doctrines," as Lyotard puts it (1988b: xiii), and which he associates with a philosophical mode or attitude rather than an epoch. Postmodernism belongs, as it were, not to history, but to philosophy.

It's not as if differends suddenly started happening for the first time, one day back in the 1960s or thereabouts. While they occur "in" history, differends aren't quite historical through and through to the extent that they are also necessary or in-principle effects of differences between language games or phrase regimens. Since the proliferation of such differences may be said to begin as a consequence of the Enlightenment's refusal of church authority and aristocratic privilege, however, differends are modern phenomena: the refusal of the authority of metanarratives of social rank and human destiny opens truth to questioning, leading to the claims and counter-claims of competing micro-narratives. Hence, dating from the Enlightenment, there has been increasing acknowledgment of the rights of social minorities, for example, which is to say that "minority" differences have won increasing legal recognition and protection. Legally, then, justice has been done, and wrongs have been turned into rights. But since a legal system makes decisions on the basis only of what is presented to it, how is justice to be done in the case of what remains *unpresentable*?

The problem here has to do with the structural positioning of the victim as a plaintiff, to whom falls the burden of proof. "Reality," Lyotard writes, "is always the plaintiff's responsibility" (1988b: 8). The onus to verify the wrong done to him or her rests with the victim as plaintiff, who must verify it to the court's satisfaction "by means of well-formed phrases and of procedures for establishing the existence of their referent" (Lyotard, 1988b: 8). Such means are not universal. Not everyone has the capacity to produce phrases judged to be felicitous according not only to the rules of cognitive or quasi-scientific discourse, but also, as Lyotard puts it in *The Differend*, to the centuries-old prejudice "that there is 'man', that there is 'language', that the former makes use of the latter for his own ends, and that if he does not succeed in attaining these ends, it is for want of good control over language 'by means' of a 'better' language" (1988b: xiii). In order to bear witness to differends, then, it is necessary to acknowledge that "man" is not a universal subject, nor "language" a universal system. This in turn is to acknowledge the necessity, both ethical and political, that others need not be like "us" (who approximate an ideal of "man") and may speak a "language" that is irreducible to words (a shrug of the shoulders, a knock on the door, a facial expression or even silence can be a phrase). What calls for a response, to cite one of the many dialogic entries in *The Differend*, can take many possible forms:

> French *Aïe*, Italian *Eh*, American *Whoops* are phrases. A wink, a shrugging of the shoulder, a taping [sic] of the foot, a fleeting blush, or an attack of tachycardia can be phrases. –And the wagging of a dog's tail, the perked ears of a cat? –And a tiny speck to the West rising upon the horizon of the sea? –A silence …? (Lyotard, 1988b: 70)

If, therefore, the means available to the plaintiff (a certain form of language-use coupled with procedures for attesting to and verifying a certain form of truth) are inadequate to the needs of the victim, then in order to bear witness to differends we must find *other* means. This "must" is akin to Kant's "categorical imperative," from which he derives the following maxims: (1) act only in such ways that your actions would become universal laws; (2) treat everyone, including yourself, as an end rather than a means; and (3) always act as if you were a legislator in the "kingdom of ends" (a hypothetical realm of rational beings whose conduct accords to universal laws) (see Kant, 1785). Again, though, differends are unpresentable and can't be determined rationally – and yet Kant insists on seeing the categorical imperative as a command bearing on the exercise of pure pragmatic reason, a faculty "we" all possess. But for Lyotard this faculty is a product of consensus, belonging not to members of a noumenal "kingdom" but to "the manufacture of a subject that is authorized to say 'we'" (Lyotard and Thébaud, 1985: 81). Such a subject is of course no less authorized to say "they," since to include is also to exclude; indeed, inclusion *begins* with exclusion. So for Lyotard the (postmodern) categorical imperative is this: act not in (fanciful) imitation of a universal model of sovereign subjectivity, but, "in matters of justice, act in such a way as to regulate all your actions to be in conformity with the [no doubt the intention was to say *an*] idea of multiplicity" (Lyotard and Thébaud, 1985: 94–5). On this account, reason alone is not enough to pre-empt or redress instances of injustice. It may be reasonable to regard the dead children of Gaza as "collateral damage" in the "war on terror," but to be offended by this rationalization is to undergo what Lyotard, rephrasing Levinas (1969; 1998), calls an "event of feeling" that takes one "out" of oneself. Others – the dead children of Gaza, the stolen generations of Aboriginal people in Australia (see Lucy and Mickler, 2006: 95–105) – "befall the ego," writes Lyotard, "like a revelation" (Lyotard, 1988b: 110). What is revealed is the ego's difference from itself, in submission to a force of obligation that does not proceed from the ego as autonomous source or agent.

For Kant, individual will is "a law unto itself" (1785) such that moral obligation is not external to human reason. The Kantian individual, then, is the self-conscious site and source of his or her own decisions, including the decision – made freely and rationally – to be morally obligated. By virtue of reason in general, the individual wills actions that would become universal laws. Lyotard's problem with this, however, is not so much the unconditionality of obligation, but the unvarying, systematic nature of decisions that, in their generality, scarcely count as decisions at all. In this way others and ourselves alike conform to a singular, cognitive ideal of "man" that violates the non-identical singularities of others and ourselves. But for Lyotard (strongly influenced by Levinas) obligation is unpresentable, before and beyond a normative sense of mutually binding duty. Lyotard's obligation is asymmetrical; it is owed to victims without recompense, without any expectation of being owed *by* victims in return.

This is not simply a "personal" obligation, and neither is it exclusively ethical or political in nature. For it is also philosophical. "The time has come," Lyotard writes at the outset of *The Differend*, "to philosophize" (1988b: xiii). The time has come to "do" philosophy over, differently, for the sake of those who cannot speak, or speak "philosophically," according to the language game of universal cognition. Postmodern (post-Enlightenment) philosophy is obliged to take the risk of becoming – *as* philosophy – something other than "itself." Or, to cite a **remix** of Lyotard by Avital **Ronell**:

> Philosophy has to stop testifying for the institutionally self-satisfied defense team, stop kissing up to state-sanctioned power plays, and instead get into the untested regions of new idioms, new addresses, new referents; it has to abandon its conciliatory habits. Rather than continue its traditional pursuit of conciliation, philosophy, more or less according to Lyotard, needs to be invaded by new inconsistencies and to saturate itself with the *feeling* of the damaged. The differend must be put into phrases with the understanding that such an act cannot yet be accomplished. In sum, philosophical thought must come up with a link to the feeling-tone of the unaccounted for, and offer privileged protection to the unaccountable refugees of cognitive regimens. (Ronell, 2004b: 494–5)

But this doesn't mean philosophy must renounce all links to the past. Far from it. *The Differend*, for instance, is written as a series of numbered fragments, in imitation of Kant's *Critique of Judgement* and Wittgenstein's *Philosophical Investigations*. The very "look" of Lyotard's writing recalls two of the great, if controversial, works of the canon, suggesting that in order "to philosophize" today, to do philosophy differently, it isn't necessary to abandon everything associated with philosophy since the Enlightenment.

All the same, philosophy needs to get out more if it wants to find ways of responding, as it must, to new idioms that belong not to the universal time of academic discourse, but to our times today. This sets philosophy a new task: no longer to ascertain the truth, but – far more difficult – to "bear witness to the differend" (Lyotard, 1988b: xiii).

Niall Lucy

Discourse: As with a handful of other terms in this book, "discourse" is a word that you can find not just herein but also in dictionaries of "ordinary" language, where it is likely to be defined either as "communication of thought by words," "talk," "conversation" or as "a formal discussion of a subject in speech or writing, as a dissertation, treatise, sermon" (see, for example, dictionary.com). Of course, the fact that the term is included in this book as well signals that for postmodernism discourse has another, more specialized meaning.

Yet in many ways it's this idea that the *significance* of words – or speech or communication more generally – lies in their definitions or signified meanings (see **semiotics**) that postmodern analysis of discourse seeks to challenge. In this regard, what's specialized about postmodernism's discourse is its *approach* to speech, communication, and so on: its *way of analyzing* signification. Thus when **Foucault** – the figure who is most regularly credited with developing a new concept of discourse – reflected on the principles underpinning his early work, he saw in that work a task of analysis "that consists of not – of no longer – treating discourses as groups of signs (signifying elements referring to contents or **representations**) but as practices that systematically form the objects of which they speak" (Foucault, 1972: 49).

The first thing to note in this formulation is that it reverses the conventional order of things: instead of looking for a meaning or point of reference that exists prior to the enunciative act (or what Foucault calls a "statement") and which is then given expression in that act, the focus is on meaning or reference as an *effect* of communication processes. Discourse doesn't convey ideas or speak about objects, in other words, so much as *ascribe* meaning to the things it appears to be about. Accordingly, the task is to analyze not what a given statement means, but how it operates and what it does. The second thing to note is the absence of any reference to who's speaking. Foucault approaches discourse and communication as radically depopulated regions, in the sense that the identity of the individual speaking subject is far less important than the fact of statement itself. To the extent that the speaking subject is significant in this analysis, it's only as an effect of discourse and of the "rules" governing the assignment of speaking positions, along with other discursive positions or roles. Hence discourse as an object of analysis starts to include far more than simply the words spoken or written, let alone merely their signified contents, and extends to include an entire enunciative field, consisting of such "facts of discourse" as "principles of classification, normative rules, institutionalized types" and more (Foucault, 1972: 22).

On this model, literary discourse, for example, does not designate simply a collection of great works of literature, nor the kind of writing or language use exemplified by literature, nor even the totality of everything that gets said about literature. Rather, it is a particular *way* of thinking and speaking about literature, which constructs the literary object in very specific terms: as an aesthetic achievement, which is created by an author and expressive of some insight (construed as the work's theme) into human nature or the contemporary conditions of existence, and which is to be evaluated according to defined criteria (originality, narrative coherence, social and psychological realism, complexity of characterization, and so forth). Compare that to the terms which commercial discourse, for instance, would use to make sense of the same object – as a commodity, which is produced in a quasi-industrial process by a production team (author, editor, marketer) and intended to meet consumer demand, and which is thereby to be assessed in terms of popularity, gross sales figures, profit margins, buzz generation, and so on. In this competing discourse, questions of meaning and practices of interpretation are marginal, if not altogether missing, in contrast to their seeming centrality to the operation of literary discourse.

Further, it's not just the literary object that is given its meaning and its status in or by discourse. Through "a complex operation," Foucault argues in a famous discussion, literary discourses serve also to construct "a certain rational being that we call 'author'" (1984: 110). Thus constituted, the author, as the text's creator, hence master of its meaning, is accorded the sole privilege of speaking the work's **truth** – which is undoubtedly why Writers Festivals are a dime a dozen but Readers Festivals are few and far between. To the extent that the latter are imaginable, moreover, it's only as a celebration of the joy of reading, where reading is understood as an undifferentiated, unproductive capacity or enthusiasm that resides, potentially at least, in all of us. Within the terms of modern literary discourse, that is, readers have no authority over the text (whose limits are to be identified with those of the book) and no creativity to speak of. Their role is to uncover "what the author was trying to say" from textual clues, and if they find in it some other personal relevance, this significance remains subordinate and inessential to the meaning of the text. What's more, this isn't anything that anyone simply says, but is more what gets taken for granted; to the extent that we speak these ideas, it's perhaps largely in the form of habituated practice.

But if all this sounds thoroughly deterministic – a "prison-house of language," as **Jameson** (1972) argued (see also **Derrida**) – it should be recalled that Foucault's historiographies always demonstrate the relative fragility of the "discursive formations" he analyzes. Discourse is not an eternal and immutable system but something more like a social and historical fact (as it were); and if the various projects associated with **poststructuralism** have anything in common, it's a demonstration of the contingency, multiplicity and errancy that *persist* within or in the face of seemingly totalizing structures of language (or laws of history, systems of production, and so on). The "author-function" that we inherit from **modernity**, then, not only operates in an uneven and discontinuous fashion – being central to the identification of literary texts, yet superfluous to the authority of scientific texts, a difference which amounts to a "reversal" of the order of things in the Middle Ages and Renaissance era (Foucault, 1984: 109) – but also draws much of its authority from the emergence of a system of ownership – "strict rules concerning author's rights, author–publisher relations, rights of reproduction" (1984: 108) – that today appears to be "threatened" by **remix** culture and the use of **new media** technologies for "unauthorized" reproduction of copyrighted materials.

And so it might be that, notwithstanding the regulatory power of discourse, we are today witnessing a mutation in the author-function, such that the **phrase** "each individual reader has his or her own personal interpretation of literary and media texts" has come to make perfect sense. That statement is often (wrongly) ascribed to postmodern theory (and sometimes to **cultural studies**), though its sayability is perhaps owed more to the prolific expansion of popular media production across the late twentieth century and the corresponding intensification of niche media consumption, which play their part in "fragmenting" a sense of a universally (or even nationally) shared cultural text. Even so, there's no doubt that postmodernism – through its rethinking of ideas of authorship, **culture** and textual **essence**, among others – has made its own interventions within literary discourse, with the result of multiplying the possible aims, practices and pleasures of reading (see **deconstruction**). Hence this unauthorized version of Foucault's concept of discourse, provided here – for you, dear reader – in order to further multiply and disseminate such *ways* of engaging with the discursive practices of reading, writing and thinking.

Robert Briggs

Eco, Umberto: *Italian semiotician, essayist, newspaper columnist, philosopher, literary critic and novelist, born 1932*

A theorist of stories, Eco discovered late in life that his very name is a story, or at least an acronym: E.C.O. stands for "*Ex Caelis Oblatus*" (Latin: "a gift from the heavens"). His grandfather, a foundling, was apparently given this surname by a city official (Dingee, 2011). Reflecting on his first and best-known novel, *The Name of the Rose* (2014 [It. 1980]), which was published when he was approaching 50 years of age, Eco wrote: "I rediscovered what writers have always known (and have told us again and again): books always speak of other books, and every story tells a story that has already been told" (Eco, 2014: 549). With that, Eco brought his "creative writing" self together with his "critical theorist" self, for he was already the illustrious author of one of the foundational texts of **semiotics** (Eco, 1976). What motivated him to turn from theory to practice? He told an interviewer in 2011:

> I don't know why exactly I started. Probably I just had some wish to. But there were scholars who spent their whole lives wishing that they were novelists. Take the great Roland **Barthes**. A genius. He died with this sort of bitterness, not to have written what stupid people call "creative writing," as if Plato and Aristotle were not writing creatively. In fact, Barthes was writing creatively his whole life. And in a way all of my essays have a sort of narrative structure. So, I always say that I've had a narrative impulse.

A Dictionary of Postmodernism, First Edition. Niall Lucy.

> I satisfied it in part by telling stories to my kids, but unfortunately they grew up. (Dingee, 2011)

The "narrative impulse" of the novelist and the genius of the theorist (from Plato to Barthes) are one and the same: both build creativity on the ground of **truth**; truth on the wings of creativity. If there's a difference between theory and practice, for Eco it is simply one of scale: fiction offers the chance to reach "more of an audience"; those readers, like children, who may not have access to other narrative channels such as scholarship.

However, once embarked on the path of narrative, Eco "rediscovered what writers have always known," that the country traversed is not natural but semiotic. Every story is telling another, and every story has already been told. This is certainly a postmodern gesture, because it does not proceed from a desire to limit the domain of story any more than it seeks to legislate a particular truth. Indeed, one of Eco's founding insights in *A Theory of Semiotics* is that truth and lies are co-extensive:

> Semiotics is concerned with everything that can be *taken* as a sign. A sign is something which can be taken as significantly substituting for something else. This something else does not necessarily have to exist or to actually be somewhere at the moment at which a sign stands in for it. Thus *semiotics is in principle the discipline studying everything which can be used in order to lie.* If something cannot be used to tell a lie, conversely it cannot be used to tell the truth: it cannot in fact be used "to tell" at all. (Eco, 1976: 7)

With a characteristic twinkle in his eye, he remarks: "I think that the definition of a 'theory of the lie' should be taken as a pretty comprehensive program for a general semiotics" (1976: 7). Well, it's a joke, but one that should be *taken* seriously, because Eco chooses his words carefully: *Italicizing* the word ("everything that can be *taken* as a sign"), the wily *Italian* reminds us that the act of signification is not constrained by any real referent, which need not even exist; instead, communication is an act of appropriation, or, in simpler language, theft. This is the "theory of the lie": the profound realization that there is no ground in language on which the Trickster or liar is not already present. Truth and deceit are, semiotically speaking, the same process. There's no telling anything without both being co-present.

There's an anthropological and historical dimension to this insight, one that was brought to life by Lewis Hyde in his book on *The Trickster* figure in global mythology (1998). Citing Eco, he situates the very first move of human signification – one that precedes the word – in the lie (see **dialogue**), and with it the conditions of possibility for human sustenance and thus survival:

> A worm with no hook in it … has … no significance, but the worm that says "I'm harmless" when in fact it hides a hook tells a lie and by that lie worms begin to signify … Only when there's a possible Lying Worm can we begin to speak of a True Worm, and only then does Worm become a sign. (Hyde, 1998: 60)

It should come as no surprise to find that in ancient myth, Hermes (Mercury) – patron deity of thieves and communication alike – was credited with the invention of language, not least by Plato (Hyde, 1998: 75–6), and thence of oratory, in the form of Hermes *Logios*. Hermes' own act of larceny – stealing Apollo's cattle on the very day he (Hermes) was born – was marked not by the functionalism of catching food but a humanizing act of semiosis. Hyde (1998: 58–61) argues that it is only when animal appetites are deferred (Hermes does not eat Apollo's cattle, but hides them) that mere meat (nature) becomes a sign (culture), thereby allowing something much more important to arise – consciousness, and with that, knowledge. But note that it arises from what has been stolen and hidden: from the lie. Hermes is the Trickster.

Hereabouts is where Umberto Eco came in, for although he is a semiotician and novelist, he started out as a medievalist. He approaches the abstract problem of signification from the library (he's reputed to own 50,000 books: see Farndale, 2005), with long-honed erudition about how language, life, signification, communication and knowledge have been entangled since ancient times. In Classical mythologies and medieval learning, the god of theft and communication was also credited with founding magic and thence science (knowledge). Well versed in the arcane secrets of the "hermetic tradition" (*hermetic* = "of Hermes"), Eco has brought this depth of interpretative or hermeneutic scholarship (*hermeneutic* = "of Hermes") – his own and history's – to bear on his theory of semiotics.

Like many others (see **dialogue**; **semiotics**), Eco (1976: 14–17) starts from Saussure (also C. S. Pierce), but his approach is at once more literary and more social than Saussure's. In fact he never abandons the role of the reader in his quest for understanding what he calls the "paramount subject matter" of semiotics, namely "*semiosis*" (1976: 316). It's not just the *system* of "signification" that adds up to semiosis, it's also the *act* of "communication." Further, any text (a phenomenon belonging to signification) can itself "act" in two ways, which Eco calls "*open*" and "*closed*" (Eco, 1984). An open text is polysemic (the concept originated in an early study of James Joyce). It is open to interpretation, which involves a creative co-production of meanings: author and reader are actively *forming* meaning. A closed text is ideological, leading the reader to what **cultural studies**' Stuart Hall and others would later call a "preferred reading" (Hall, 1973). This distinction echoes the one Roland Barthes makes between writerly ("scriptible") and readerly ("lisible") texts.

But Eco, credited as a pioneer of "reader response" theory, is also an opponent of unlimited readings. Texts and works may be "open," just as signs refer only to other signs, thereby initiating an "infinite regression" of "unlimited semiosis" (Eco, 1976: 69, citing C. S. Pierce). But, if pursued too far, that way madness lies. Eco explains the limits to "overinterpretation" in terms of the hermetic tradition. Dennis Dutton, commenting on Eco's book *Interpretation and Overinterpretation* (1992), summarizes how he gets from Hermes to here:

> Eco begins by identifying what he calls the hermetic tradition in interpretation … second-century hermeticism … searches for a truth it does not know. Since the books in which it hopes to find the truth contradict each other, truth will be seen mysteriously to reveal itself in allusion and allegory. "Secret knowledge," he says, "is deep knowledge" for the hermeticist: truth must be probed for beneath the surface of the text. The result of the hermetic outlook is that "interpretation is indefinite," and that we must accept "a never-ending drift or sliding of meaning." On the one hand all phenomena become linguistic, while on the other language itself loses its communicative ability. Every revelation yields to yet another secret, ad infinitum. (Dutton, 1992)

Although this insight might be read as a spoiler for *The Name of the Rose*, and even more so for *Foucault's Pendulum* (1989), that's OK because, as the novelist and critic Anthony Burgess (1989) pointed out in a review of *Foucault's Pendulum*, the joke's on us: distinctions between fiction and information, entertainment and enlightenment, observation and interpretation are more apparent than real:

> For while it is not a novel in the strict sense of the word, it is a truly formidable gathering of information delivered playfully by a master manipulating his own invention – in effect, a long, erudite joke. … To see what Mr. Eco is really getting at, the reader of his fiction or pseudofiction should consult his scholarly works, where observation and interpretation are not disguised as entertainment.

> I don't think "Foucault's Pendulum" is entertainment any more than was "The Name of the Rose" … To be informed, however, is holy. (Burgess, 1989)

What Eco is doing, as much in his fiction as his scholarly discourse, is showing that although he himself is capable of imagining almost infinite possibilities of interpretation, and sharing those with his readers, not least via the interminable lists of which he is a connoisseur, interpretation as communication is not infinite, and that constantly looking for secret meanings known only to other initiates is – in the real world, fictional narrative and the scholarly domain alike – dangerous. Eco knows from experience that "every story tells a story that has already been told," but that does not mean that anything goes, without consequences. The observer, critic, joker-trickster is always present, *taking* knowledge.

In Eco's hands, the hermetic tradition can "read" (hermeneutically) contemporary America *as* "neomedievalism" (Eco, 1986). Indeed, *Travels in Hyperreality* (published in the USA as *Faith in Fakes*), in which Umberto marvels his way across the mixture of fact, fiction, fabrication and faking that is the contemporary USA (see **hyperreality**), may be said to be one of the best "road movies" ever scripted, on a brilliant par with another European writer's all-too-knowing travels through America with his erudite eyes wide open, namely Vladimir Nabokov. When Nabokov's *Lolita* came out (1955), Eco was of course already watching. He noted the similarity between his own forename and that of Nabokov's antihero, Humbert Humbert, and before long published a short-story spoof of *Lolita* called "Granita," where "Umberto Umberto" pursues a geriatric granny with "whitely lascivious locks," an upside-down Lolita (Eco, 1993 [It. 1959]). His own hermeneutic (as opposed to hermetic) "road trip" across America resulted in remarkably compelling essays: "Travels in Hyperreality," "Dreaming of the Middle Ages," and "Living in the New Middle Ages" (Eco, 1986). Eco shows what you can do with a postmodern sensibility that trained itself on St Thomas Aquinas. Reality – in the form of medieval fantasy film, fiction and games – is still stumblingly catching up.

Thus, interpretation is the name of the game, but only because there's so much reality to read:

> If anything marks the personality and writing of Umberto Eco, it is an insatiable curiosity, love, and sense of wonder about the world. He's having a good time, to be sure, but good times aren't the point. It's rather that the world itself – in all its intractable, intricate, deliciously ambiguous, quotidian reality – is to Eco so astonishingly rich. (Dutton, 1992)

This is the secret, as it were, of Eco's unwillingness to allow the endless play of signifiers that always-deferred last word. He's too interested in *things.* We should have known. He remarks at the beginning of *A Theory of Semiotics* (1976: 5): "An atomic scientist knows very well that so-called 'things' are the results of a complex interplay of microphysical correlations, and nevertheless s/he can quite happily continue to speak about 'things' when it is convenient to do so." Eco thinks it "uselessly oversophisticated" to over-interpret, to segment and typologize endlessly when "things" are nevertheless what we're interested in, to produce only an "*n*-chotomy of various modes" (1976: 5), even though he will devote a chapter to doing just that.

Early in his career Eco worked at RAI (1954–9), the Italian state-owned broadcaster, equivalent in those pre-Berlusconi days to the BBC in Britain, that is, as a nation-building institution. In keeping with his later predilection for popular culture as well as learning, which had in fact been nurtured by childhood delight in American comics (Jaggi, 2002), Eco was positive about television, setting his own views apart from those of the then critically prevailing Frankfurt School critique of media. As he recalled in a 2002 interview:

> "It [working at RAI] was an important experience," he says. "I followed the story of television from the beginning, from inside." In the 1950s "the Frankfurt school of [Theodor] Adorno was attacking the media. I elaborated a view that this instrument could be used in different ways. TV played an immense role in the linguistic unification of Italy, which was still a country of dialects." (Jaggi, 2002)

Typically, he turned that "important experience" into scholarship. One of the earliest of his analytical works to be Englished, "Towards a Semiotic Inquiry into the Television Message" (1972 [It. 1966]), was published in Stuart Hall's Birmingham house journal, *Working Papers in Cultural Studies.* It introduced the concept of "aberrant decoding" as a feature of even the most ideological texts, and laid out a program for cultural studies that is still unfolding. This was an early manifestation of another fundamental aspect of Eco's theory of semiosis, i.e. that it doesn't apply to language only, but to anything that signifies, including mass media, popular culture, and "things," all of which "instruments" are thus the "subject" of semiotics. Obviously Eco wasn't the only theorist to make this leap out of language (although it is not prefigured in Saussure), but he was among the first to identify these "pansemiotic features" (Eco, 1976: 310), and to consider popular culture in analytic and elegant detail.

The question for a book such as this is whether and how any of all that may add up to postmodernism. Let Eco, still pursuing Granita perhaps, answer that question, in his "Postscript" to *The Name of the Rose* (first published in 1984 [It. 1983]):

> I think of the postmodern attitude as that of a man who loves a very cultivated woman and knows that he cannot say to her "I love you madly," because he knows that she knows (and that she knows he knows) that these words have already been written by Barbara Cartland. Still there is a solution. He can say, "As Barbara Cartland would put it, I love you madly." At this point, having avoided false innocence, having said clearly it is no longer possible to talk innocently, he will nevertheless say what he wanted to say to the woman: that he loves her in an age of lost innocence. (Eco, 2014: 539–77)

Reflexive, self-referential, funny, "cultivated," as much at home in "readerly" popular consumerism as in "writerly" intellectual knowledge, this postmodernism is clever enough to create innocence; knowledgeable enough to feel love; textual enough to communicate; and all the while modulating between (i.e. co-producing) what is real, true, and personal with story piled on story. As fellow novelist Anthony Burgess says: "No man should know so much. It is the work not of a literary man but of one who accepts the democracy of signs" (Burgess, 1989).

John Hartley

Essence: Around about the time that some of the biggest names in postmodernism were gaining notoriety in the English-speaking academic world, my mother was making cakes. Not professionally, I should hasten to add; nor even with a great regularity, but with an occasionality and purpose more or less consistent with the baking "duties" assigned (without being assigned) to housewives from Australian working-class families in the late 1970s and early 1980s: children's birthdays, weekend morning-teas with visiting friends or family, the odd special treat. Accordingly, our kitchen pantry was – like most of our neighbors' – always stocked with a kaleidoscope of small bottles of food colorings and flavorings, including the truly iconic – in my neck of the woods, at least – Queen (*Est. 1897*) Imitation Vanilla Essence.

If food additives were metaphysical entities, the otherwise perfectly ordinary scenario recounted here would represent all kinds of wrong. For a thing's essence, according to the logic and precepts of philosophy since Plato, is its very heart, its nature, its *what*ness: that aspect or quality or substance that makes the thing (or idea, or event) in question *what it is*, and not something else – least of all some poor imitation of that thing (idea, event, etc.). Further, the essence of a thing is what the thing *has* to be or *has* to have, if it is to be the thing that it is. It stands to reason, moreover, that an essence is what is fixed or unchanging, to the extent that an object or idea undergoing *essential change* becomes another thing entirely. An object's essence, then, is to be distinguished both from the qualities that the object just happens to possess, and from any of its attributes that might be transformed or replaced with something else. So, on this model, one determines the essence of something by stripping away all that is accidental or arbitrary or optional about it, no matter how frequently such qualities may be empirically associated with the object in question. If the success of the Prince song "Little Red Corvette," for example, means that type of sports car will forever be associated with one color only, nevertheless "redness" does not define the essence of Corvettes, because Corvettes can sometimes be black or white or blue or gold, and some might even be painted – heaven forbid! – in plaid.

So an essence defines what a thing absolutely and forever has to be – further, *only* what it has to be – in order to actually and authentically be the thing that it is. To that extent, an essence defines that thing as such, which raises the question: what would an "imitation essence" be? Metaphysical **truth** probably isn't answerable to 1970s baking ingredients, but interestingly it's through a question not too dissimilar to this one that postcolonial theorist Homi Bhabha (1994) has sought to analyze and interrogate the history and **discourse** of European colonialism, including its conceptual basis in Western philosophy. While many postcolonial theorists would perceive (fittingly, as we'll soon see) an ambivalent relation between postmodernism and postcolonialism, the two are bedfellows not only to the extent that influential postcolonial critics such as Bhabha, Gayatri Spivak (1990) and even Edward Said (1978) have made use to varying degrees of the works of **Derrida**, **Foucault**, **Lacan**, **Deleuze** and others, but also because the colonial moment largely coincides with the era of **modernity** and modern philosophy that postmodern thought routinely calls into question. For those forms of postcolonial critique that do make use of postmodern ideas, moreover, it is modern, colonial discourse's appeal to the constancy of *essence* – "the essential duplicity of the Asiatic or the bestial sexual licence of the African" (Bhabha, 1994: 66) – that warrants critique for its construction of markers of ethnic difference, predominantly in the form of stereotypes, that in turn serve to legitimize a system of colonial subjugation.

By the same token, as Bhabha sees it, this recourse to essence is the feature that most troubles the colonial strategy. For European powers have routinely sought to legitimize their rule over the colonies through their avowal of a "civilizing mission" whose objective is to help to lift the colonized Other out of its condition of political and cultural immaturity and towards its historical destination, alongside the West, in and as the form of modern "Man." The dependence of this narrative on an Enlightenment **metanarrative** of historical progress, hence on the notion of the *essence* of Man, is unmistakable. But it also hinges on an essential "separation" – "*between* races, **cultures**, histories, *within* histories" (Bhabha, 1994: 82) – that justifies ongoing colonial government. "By 'knowing' the native population" in terms of a racial, cultural or ethnic difference that is simultaneously historical (as "immaturity" or "underdevelopment") and essential (as "racial otherness"), Bhabha argues,

> discriminatory and authoritarian forms of political control are considered appropriate. The colonized population is then deemed to be both the cause and the effect of the system, imprisoned in the circle of interpretation. What is visible is the *necessity* of such rule which is justified by those moralistic and normative ideologies of amelioration recognized as the Civilizing Mission or the White Man's Burden. (Bhabha, 1994: 83)

At the same time, this "necessary" rule sets for the colonized the goal of attaining a self-mastery that is *modeled on* the sovereignty of the West, which is the very realization of the potential of "Man." The civilizing mission is thus construed on the basis of a desire for, quite literally, an *imitation essence* that is both demanded as an ideal and deployed as a governmental strategy. "Colonial mimicry," which names – simultaneously, hence undecidably – *both* the ironic desire of the colonized "to emerge as 'authentic' through mimicry" of the colonizer (Bhabha, 1994: 88), *and* the colonial authority's "complex strategy of reform, regulation and discipline, which 'appropriates' the Other as it visualizes power," is thus "constructed around *ambivalence*" (1994: 86).

Bhabha recalls this ambivalence by describing its logic of appearance: "almost the same, *but not quite*" (1994: 86), which in the colonial context ultimately reveals itself to mean "*almost the same but not white*" (1994: 89). But if that refrain appears to couch otherness in terms of imperfection or incompletion, it's perhaps the fundamental doubleness and splitting implied in the idea of ambivalence that most speaks to the postmodern rethinking of essence. As a form both of domination and disavowal, that is, colonial ambivalence ultimately reveals an object that is thereby produced as *hybrid*, "at once disciplinary and disseminatory" (1994: 112). Insofar as colonial authority presumes knowledge of (modern) Man as well as apprehension of the (primitive) Other, moreover, "hybridity" goes much further than simply naming a combination or mixing of two fundamentally separate races or cultures, whose differences occasionally take the form of a conflict that must then be resolved. Rather, hybridity here names the division and displacement of the very essence of culture:

> Colonial hybridity is not a *problem* of genealogy or identity between two *different* cultures which can then be resolved as an issue of cultural relativism. Hybridity is a problematic of colonial representation and individuation that reverses the effects of the colonial disavowal, so that other "denied" knowledges enter upon the dominant discourse and estrange the basis of its authority … What is irremediably estranging in the presence of the hybrid … is that the difference of cultures can no longer be identified or evaluated as objects of epistemological or moral contemplation: cultural differences are not simply *there* to be seen or appropriated. (Bhabha, 1994: 114)

For Bhabha, this situation not only describes the effect of colonial power but also allows "an important change in perspective" with regard to its analysis. As ambivalent texts, the symbols and strategies of European imperialism themselves enable "a form of subversion, founded on the undecidability that turns the discursive conditions of dominance into the grounds of intervention" (1994: 112) – a strategy of intervention which we might also suggest is akin to a certain version of **deconstruction**.

To the extent that hybridity "estranges" cultural differences generally, however, the condition or desire or "problematic" that Bhabha describes is not unique or confined to the context of (post)colonialism. This is perhaps why the theme of hybridity has been taken up not only by postcolonial theorists but also in many forms of analysis that broadly adopt or identify with a postmodern disposition. It is in this vein, for example, that Donna Haraway, in a highly regarded essay first published in 1985, introduced a seminal figure of hybridity – the cyborg – as the "basis" (as it were) for a political thought and praxis formulated "in the utopian tradition of imagining a world without gender" and appropriate both to "socialist-feminist culture" and to "theory in a postmodernist, nonnaturalist mode" (Haraway, 1990a:

191–2). By the same token, the fact that Haraway had to *affirm* the image of the cyborg as a way of "grounding" politics serves as a reminder that the postmodern critique of essence has often been received as politically "disabling" (see **globalization**). Certainly, she was mindful of the extent to which both critical theory and "lived experience" in the late twentieth century foregrounded the fragmentation of political identity, such that any attempt to re-establish such forms of identity could only be accompanied by further exclusion and disenfranchisement (Haraway, 1990a: 196–7). By way of the image of the cyborg, then, Haraway sought to "build an ironic political myth faithful to feminism, socialism and materialism" (1990a: 190), one which could account for both the reality and (in Bhabha's terms) the ambivalence of "lived social relations," perhaps giving expression to an "imitation essence" of another kind:

> By the late twentieth century, our time, a mythic time, we are all chimeras, theorized and fabricated hybrids of machine and organism; in short, we are cyborgs. The cyborg is our ontology; it gives us our politics. The cyborg is a condensed image of both imagination and material reality, the two joined centers structuring any possibility of historical transformation. (Haraway, 1990a: 191)

"[R]esolutely committed to partiality, irony, intimacy, and perversity," moreover, the cyborg "is oppositional, utopian, and completely without innocence" (Haraway, 1990a: 192) – which is as much as to say that, even when Haraway calls it "our ontology," what is named is less a metaphysical foundation than a critical attitude or ethos (see **Foucault**), an "argument for pleasure in the confusion of boundaries and for responsibility in their construction" (1990a: 191).

The debt that this theoretical trope owes to contemporary science fiction narratives is obvious. While Haraway appeals predominantly to critically acclaimed works of feminist speculative fiction to give shape to its features, an arguably more enduring image of the cyborg was first making its appearance around the time Haraway was writing – in the James Cameron-directed film *The Terminator* (1984). "Part-man, part-machine," "living human tissue" over "a hyper-alloy combat chassis," as the character Kyle Reese describes it, the Terminator T-800 (played to perfection by Arnold Schwarzenegger) is a military infiltration unit designed and manufactured by the artificial intelligence system SkyNet for the purpose of fulfilling its mission of exterminating the human race. In the projected timeline of the film, SkyNet is built in 1984's near future by defense technology firm Cyberdyne Systems for the purpose of controlling the US military's computer network, thereby eliminating the possibility of "human error." Faithful to a by-now classic sci-fi trope, the system becomes "self-aware" days after its activation and commences a campaign to remove any threat to its existence by destroying all who would try to deactivate it – in other words, every person on the planet – including the future leader of the human resistance John Connor, whom SkyNet plots to eliminate by sending a T-800 back in time to 1984 in order to kill John's mother Sarah before John is even born!

As both a key piece of weaponry in SkyNet's mission to end all traces of humanity and a product – albeit a fictional one – of the masculinist "military industrial complex" (see Eisenhower, 1961), the Terminator would, of course, make for an unlikely model of reason, good conscience or progressive politics. But for Haraway the cyborg is not a figure of moral purity, embodying simply a "good" (hybrid) subjectivity as against the uniformly "evil" forces of multinationalism and militarism. Utopian science fiction functions as only one "source" of our contemporary existence as cyborgs, with cybernetic organisms and human-industrial processes figuring in many facets of our time: the prosthetics and genetics of modern medicine; the assembly lines of modern manufacturing; and the "cyborg orgy" of modern war (Haraway, 1990a: 191). Even as an ideal, then, Haraway's cyborg is divided, ambivalent and hybrid, "the illegitimate offspring of militarism and patriarchal capitalism, not to mention state socialism." "But", she adds, "illegitimate offspring are exceedingly unfaithful to their origins. Their fathers, after all, are inessential" (1990a: 193).

And so, crucially, science and technology remain for Haraway laudable projects and important resources for progress and development. Accordingly, "taking responsibility for the social relations of science and technology means refusing an anti-science metaphysics, a demonology of technology" (1990a: 223). So much for the argument that postmodernism is resolutely "anti-science" (see **Sokal affair**)! It's thus a fitting coda to Haraway's story – an extratextual one, as it were – that Cameron's hybrid man-machine assassin returns (and not for the last time, either) in *Terminator 2: Judgment Day* (dir. James Cameron, 1991), albeit this time fighting on the side of human survival, having been captured and reprogrammed by the human resistance and then sent back to the world of 1991 with the mission of protecting John Connor from execution at the hands of a newer, model T-1000 Terminator. If this fictional subversion of techno-terror doesn't quite confirm the quasi-existentialist slogan carved by Sarah Connor into a table in *Terminator 2*

("No fate but what we make"), it may at least serve as something of a metaphor for the ambivalence that pervades a cultural heritage, even so-called "dominant discourses," and which continues to provide the means and occasion for structures of power to be reprogrammed, for meaning and authority to be **remixed**, even if always under the threat of "counter-strike" from the colonial-military-industrial complex.

Robert Briggs

F

Foucault, Michel: *French historian-philosopher, 1926–84*

As the prefix "post-" makes clear, the very thought of "the postmodern" raises the question of history. Yet, interestingly, few of the key figures associated with postmodernism have forged reputations as historians. Even in the case of those theorists who define contemporary culture in terms of a systemic break with the past, their histories tend to be broad brushed, taking the form of a succession of cultural totalities, epochs or stages in the development of some central component or foundation to existence – knowledge (**Lyotard**), the sign (**Baudrillard**), capital (**Jameson**) – rather than detailed studies of historical dates and dusty documents.

It's perhaps understandable, then, that the body of archival analysis that Foucault produced over the course of his lifetime is championed for its attention to the historical specificity of its objects of analysis – so much so that he has often been approved, particularly in **cultural studies**, as presenting a materialist alternative to the apparent "ahistoricism" of Saussurean **semiotics** and the **poststructuralism** that spawned in its wake (see, for instance, Weedon, Tolson and Mort, 1980). While the complaint that **Derrida** and **Lacan** (among others) fail to appreciate the force of history is easily belied (see **simulation**), there's no mistaking Foucault's commitment to historical inquiry. Under the rubrics of "archaeology" (Foucault, 1972) and "genealogy" (see "Nietzsche, Genealogy, History" in Foucault, 1984), Foucault's monographs present historiographies of such endeavors and

A Dictionary of Postmodernism, First Edition. Niall Lucy.

experiences as psychiatry (*Madness and Civilization*, 1967), medicine (*The Birth of the Clinic*, 1973), the human sciences (*The Order of Things*, 1970), punishment and training (*Discipline and Punish*, 1979), as well as sex and sexuality (across the three volumes making up *The History of Sexuality*, 1980; 1985; 1988). In these books – as well as in countless other works historicizing a diverse range of practices and institutions like authorship ("What is an Author?" in Foucault, 1984), architecture ("Space, Knowledge, and Power," in Foucault, 1984), health ("The Politics of Health in the Eighteenth Century," in Foucault 1984) and government (Foucault, 1991), to name a few – Foucault pursues his objective of producing what he has called "a history of the different modes by which, in our culture, human beings are made subjects" (Foucault, 1984: 7). By the same token, these works, and others reflecting explicitly on the question of "method," make it clear that "history" for Foucault entails an analysis very different from the exercise in rationalism and positivism promoted by a traditional conception of historical method, which, in Foucault's words, "aims at dissolving the singular event into an ideal continuity – as a teleological movement or a natural process" (Foucault, 1984: 88).

Indeed, it's as much through this rejection of a familiar concept of history as through his specific historical investigations that Foucault accomplishes his critical objectives, since that familiar concept is one which sees "the subject" not as made but as *given*, in the form of "Man" or "humanity": the human subject. In this conventional **metanarrative**, "Man" – as the subject of knowledge, as the one who knows himself and his world – is the ground of historical experience and consciousness insofar as he acts on the basis of the stock of knowledge he has built over time. Advancing his knowledge, improving his literary, scientific and political endeavors, "Man" thus lifts himself out of his ignorance, prejudice and subjugation in a progressive march toward his civilization. From the vantage of this final standpoint, we can look back and see that, if it is only now, today, that we take our proper, civilized form, this is so because the course of human history has been nothing but the slow realization of what was already immanent to us in and as our very **essence** or nature. The fundamental of human freedom and equality, in this view, has come to find its final, true expression in the form of liberal-democratic government; the full potential of human reason has at last been actualized with the institution of universal education and a social commitment to the disinterested pursuit of scientific knowledge.

In this way, the figure of "Man" or of human nature functions as the ultimate point of reference, a **transcendental signified**, anchoring all historical meaning and putting historical inquiry to the service of an anthropology in the form of a humanist philosophy. The human subject thus sits outside history, located both at the "origin" and at the "end" of history, but remaining a constant throughout it. In proposing to analyze the "modes of objectification which transform human beings into subjects" (Foucault, 1982: 208), then, Foucault reverses the accepted logic of "history" by situating humanity not as the producer of history but as its product: "man is an invention of recent date," Foucault famously writes in *The Order of Things*; "[a]nd perhaps one nearing its end" (1970: 387). More significantly, when the figure of the human subject is no longer assumed to organize and account for the entire social field, specific institutions and practices are able to be seen as relatively autonomous in their operation and effects, having their own variable and contestable rationales. Rather than education being the means of developing a uniform and well-defined literacy that gives expression to our innate and constant capacity to think, speak, learn and imagine, in other words, literacy becomes a product of specific pedagogical and disciplinary techniques – a variable aptitude subject not to the authority of fixed "laws" of reason and morality but to ongoing revision in response to changing ideas, values and practices, both inside and outside education (see, for instance, Lucy, 2010b: 33–53).

In contrast to the continuity and sameness foregrounded by the figure of "Man" and "his" "history," therefore, Foucault's archaeological and genealogical investigations introduce the possibility of difference and transformation into "human" institutions by way of showing up the discontinuity and dispersal, the accidents, ruptures and mutations, which constitute the very fabric of history. The "great problem" for historical analysis, Foucault writes, "is no longer one of tradition, of tracing a line, but one of division, of limits; it is no longer one of lasting foundations, but one of transformations that serve as new foundations, the rebuilding of foundations" (Foucault, 1972: 5). In short, who or what "we" are can change. And the proof lies in the fact that we've been changing all along, have never really been self-same for very long, or certainly not for eternity. "Real" history – non-anthropological and non-metaphysical history; what Foucault calls (after Nietzsche) "effective history" – shows that everything we take to define the human as such, everything we take as closest to ourselves – our freedom and our aptitudes; our capacity for reason, imagination, emotion and judgment; our bodies, sex, sexuality and taste – has a history in which that quality can be found to have changed in character or significance, to have split or merged with something else, to have waxed and then waned:

> We believe that feelings are immutable, but every sentiment, particularly the noblest and most disinterested, has a history. We believe in the dull constancy of instinctual life and imagine that it continues to exert its force indiscriminately in the present as it did in the past. But a knowledge of history easily disintegrates this unity, depicts its wavering course, locates its moments of strength and weakness, and defines its oscillating reign. It easily seizes the slow elaboration of instincts and those movements where, in turning upon themselves, they relentlessly set about their self-destruction. We believe, in any event, that the body obeys exclusively the laws of physiology and that it escapes the influence of history, but this too is false. The body is molded by the rhythms of work, rest, holidays; it is poisoned by food or by values, through eating habits or moral laws; it constructs resistances. "Effective" history differs from traditional history in being without constants. Nothing in man – not even his body – is sufficiently stable to serve as the basis for self-recognition or for understanding other men. (Foucault, 1984, 87–8)

It's easy to see in this description of effective history a ruinous anti-foundationalism that would undermine every attempt to attain certain and lasting knowledge of the conditions of human existence. It decenters the human subject, denies constants or foundations, emphasizes discontinuity and dispersal over continuity and sameness, and affirms history over essence. All of this appears exemplary of a postmodern and thus anti-Enlightenment approach to history, knowledge and freedom. However, Foucault himself did not appear to understand his work unambiguously in those terms. For example (and notwithstanding his early tendency to divide history into a series of epistemes, or eras of knowledge), a rich and inspiring essay Foucault wrote only a few months before his death proposes a very different way of relating to the "age" of Enlightenment and to postmodernity. In "What Is Enlightenment?" Foucault turns to the work of German philosopher Immanuel Kant in order to characterize what he calls "the attitude of **modernity**":

> I know that modernity is often spoken of as an epoch, or at least as a set of features characteristic of an epoch; situated on a calendar, it would be preceded by a more or less naïve or archaic premodernity, and followed by an enigmatic and troubling "postmodernity". And then we find ourselves asking whether modernity constitutes the sequel to the Enlightenment and its

> development, or whether we are to see it as a rupture or a deviation … Thinking back on Kant's text, I wonder whether we may not envisage modernity rather as an attitude than as a period of history. And by "attitude," I mean a mode of relating to contemporary reality; a voluntary choice made by certain people; in the end, a way of thinking and feeling; a way, too, of acting and behaving that at one and the same time marks a relation of belonging and presents itself as a task. A bit, no doubt, like what the Greeks called an *ethos*. (Foucault, 1984: 39)

The Kantian text referred to here is not any of the three great *Critiques* for which he is most famous, but rather a brief essay written in response to a German periodical's call for answers to the question, "*Was ist Aufklärung*?" (What is Enlightenment?) (Kant, 1784). What interests Foucault about this text, in which Kant describes the Enlightenment and the public use of reason as our "way out" of "immaturity," a kind of release from our acceptance of established authority over our own use of reason, is the way that it appears to link the Enlightenment's project of critique to a practice of historical inquiry: "the reflection on 'today' as difference in history and as motive for a particular philosophical task" (Foucault, 1984: 38). In this way, Foucault characterizes "the" Enlightenment not as a period in intellectual history, nor as a set of doctrines, nor even as the realization of an authoritative rationalism, but rather as the emergence of a certain way of doing philosophy, a "type of philosophical interrogation … that simultaneously problematizes man's relation to the present, man's historical mode of being, and the constitution of the self as an autonomous subject" (1984: 42).

"Enlightenment" thus names the roots of "a philosophical ethos that could be described as a permanent critique of our historical era" (1984: 42). In its "positive" dimension, moreover, this ethos would direct Kant's cherished public use of reason toward the practical challenging and transgression of the limits placed on freedom by arbitrary authority. "It seems to me," Foucault writes, "that the critical question today has to be turned back into a positive one: in what is given to us as universal, necessary, obligatory, what place is occupied by whatever is singular, contingent, and the product of arbitrary constraints?" (1984: 45). And again: "I shall thus characterize the philosophical ethos appropriate to the critical ontology of ourselves as a historico-practical test of the limits we may go beyond" (1984: 47). In whatever "law" or "fact" of existence we inherit as *given*, in other words, how far exactly does its authority go, and what further freedoms can we reclaim from it?

Far from rejecting Enlightenment thought, let alone undermining **truth** and the possibility of critique, therefore, Foucault's reading of Kant's text lends much support to the argument that postmodernism amounts to a continuation of the Enlightenment's project of critique by other means (see Lucy, 2010b: 54–86). But note in this suggestion a simultaneous insistence on both continuity and discontinuity, on "tracing a line" (continuation) *and* on registering a difference (by other means), which suggests (perhaps against some versions of Foucault) that an alternative name or model for "history" might be found in **deconstruction**'s notion of a "text" or textuality in general as a "site" in which the familiar and the new lie together as mutually oblivious bedfellows (see **Derrida**). Note, too, that the upshot of Foucault's reflection on the attitude of modernity is that "theory" or "critique" – *as* an attitude or a practice – "has a history," as Ian Hunter has recognized (2006), one which therefore demonstrates that the ideals embodied or produced by critique are far from timeless and universal, but are instead the outcome of a historically constituted, hence contingent, context of academic practice. By the same token, critical reflection's inevitable "failure" to arrive at some transcendental idea or experience, which could then be taken as having "grounded" and "legitimated" the reflection in the first place, if not also as laying the foundations for a better world, need not be understood to delimit or confine critique's import and effects purely to the scholarly and pedagogical spaces of university humanities departments, as Hunter implies (2006: 86). Undoubtedly, the institutions and disciplines of humanities instruction will constitute the primary mechanisms by which the attitude of modernity may be cultivated and distributed, but once released from that site who knows where or how that attitude will be activated, or to what specific effect?

Whatever the context, and whatever the specific outcome, the point is not so much to expand humanity's "stock of knowledge," but to expand our forms of freedom, such that critique takes the form of an engaged experiment with liberty rather than of a "detached" search for timeless values. Indeed, critique's lack of universality, its non-transcendence, is precisely what might give it meaning, a specific existence, a link to the world in which we live:

> If we are not to settle for the affirmation or the empty dream of freedom, it seems to me that this historico-critical attitude must also be an experimental one. I mean that this work done at the limits of ourselves must, on the one hand, open up a realm of historical inquiry and, on the other, put itself to

> the test of reality, of contemporary reality, both to grasp the points where change is possible and desirable, and to determine the precise form this change should take. (Foucault, 1984: 46)

Another inheritance from the Enlightenment, then, in the form of a renewed demand for freedom. In the wake of Foucault's experiment with the heritage of the Enlightenment, however – if not following postmodernism more generally – such freedom takes the form not simply of a freedom to question the authority of humanist doctrine or Kant's putative "moral law," but also the freedom to *value* the liberatory and transformative potential of the Enlightenment ethos. Rather than laying waste to the project of Enlightenment and modernity, in other words, Foucault's approach to history is able to *embrace* a sense of affinity with that project, hence to choose to feel and to respond to a transformable, non-authoritative sense of obligation with respect to that task of critique, if not the demand for justice (see Derrida, 1994; Lucy and Mickler, 2006), which that critical project bequeaths.

Robert Briggs

G

Globalization: By now, globalization is a just portmanteau term, of use to publishers, readily disaggregated into various fields of specialist study: globalization *of* (environment, crime, disease); globalization *and* (development, power, identity); globalization *for* (neoliberalism, progress, emancipation) … and so on. But there was a period – around the time of the fall of the Berlin Wall, collapse of the Soviet bloc and of international socialism – when the idea of globalization generated plenty of heat. In some hands it was used as a kind of rod with which to beat postmodernists (for example, **Lyotard**, 1984), who, ironically, had pointed to its emergent cultural forms in the first place. For a while, there was an intellectual politics of globalization (with postmodernism as the political football) when the term escaped from the world of facts to the world of values (where it was subsequently overtaken by another term designed to draw tribal-ideological boundaries – neoliberalism).

Of course, there were theories and examples of globalization before this flare-up. Karl Marx was a pioneer theorist, with his concept of the "world-historical" status of the modern mode of production:

> The more the original isolation of the separate nationalities is destroyed by the developed mode of production and intercourse and the division of labour between various nations naturally brought forth by these, the more history becomes world history. Thus, for instance, if in England a machine is invented, which deprives countless workers of bread in India and China, and

A Dictionary of Postmodernism, First Edition. Niall Lucy.

> overturns the whole form of existence of these empires, this invention becomes a world-historical fact. (Marx, 1845: Ch1.B)

Marx was remarkably quick off the mark here, for "world-historical facts" would have been a very novel discovery in 1845. They imply not only that global forces were at work in human affairs but also that these could be grasped in a single intellectual framework (Wallerstein, 2011). The history of globalization as a process is uneven and very long run, but knowledge of it is much more recent (Castells, 1996).

Globalization as an *anthropological* fact was achieved once *H. Sapiens* had colonized the whole world. The migration of this species out of Africa commenced about 75,000 years ago, but it was not completed globally until only about 750 years ago, when Polynesians colonized Aotearoa/New Zealand, the last sizable landmass to be settled by a premodern society (Irwin and Walrond, 2012). In other words, it took 99 percent of the time that has elapsed since human diffusion began before "globalization" of the species was completed.

Long before then, certain kinds of *knowledge* had been widely (but not universally) diffused, especially after the rise of ancient monarchies and medieval empires. Trade and warfare accelerated the spread of technologies (e.g. smelting, pottery, weapons), know-how (e.g. farming, brewing), social arrangements (e.g. states, cosmologies, slavery), and artifacts (e.g. silk, spices; later, Gutenberg's printing press, which reached China, Japan, and South America within a century of its invention in 1450). But in no case did a single culture grasp the full extent of the world within its own knowledge system, until **modernity**. In fact, it was only in the nineteenth century that an accurate understanding of the planet as a natural and geopolitical unit began to be achieved. Knowledge of it was rapidly consolidated, albeit as an accompaniment to European (and subsequent settler-society) expansionism, imperialism, colonialism and nation-state competition, but also, as the example of Marx attests, because of critique, opposition and active resistance to those developments. Global knowledge soon exceeded its instrumental provenance (McCloskey, 2006; 2010; forthcoming).

The accelerated expansion of scientific, commercial, political and cultural knowledge ensured that *technologies* were globalized very quickly thereafter, for instance in communications, using the Atlantic crossing as a proxy for the process:

- first transatlantic steamship 1838 (*Great Western*);
- first transatlantic telegraph cable 1858 (Cyrus Field);

- first transatlantic radio signal 1901 (Marconi);
- first transatlantic satellite TV signal 1962 (Telstar);
- first transatlantic shipping container 1966 (Malcom McLean) (Levinson, 2006).

It was only once these physical, technical and organizational arrangements were in general use that the kind of globalization with which we are now familiar could emerge. Thus, commercial globalization was first crystallized as a concept by Ted Levitt in 1983, in *Harvard Business Review*. Around the same time, certain postmodern philosophers, notably Lyotard (1984) and **Baudrillard** (2003), and also Paul Virilio (see Armitage, 2000), were elaborating an account of globalized technological culture. Globalization seized the sociological imagination in the 1990s, precipitating a spate of books and some heated argument.

David Harvey (1989) mounted a critique of postmodernism that was subsequently influential in the political economy approach to globalization. Harvey's title, *The Condition of Postmodernity*, pushed back against Lyotard's (1984) *The Postmodern Condition*. Harvey wanted to analyze globalization (which he called "time-space compression") through a Marxian lens, through which he espied postmodernism as a retreat from adversarial politics. He held writers like **Derrida**, **Foucault**, Lyotard and even Jonathan Raban (1974) personally responsible for what he saw as the "relativism," "defeatism" and "pragmatism" that result from postmodernism. Its celebration of the "mutability and fragmentation of language" was a symptom of "schizophrenia" and "paranoia." Postmodernists insist, he wrote, that "we cannot aspire to any unified representation of the world, or picture it as a totality" (Harvey, 1989: 52–3). That being so: "How can we possibly aspire to act coherently with respect to the world?" Harvey conceded that the postmodern interest in surfaces, media and cultural forms is connected with a discernible "time-space compression" of global dimensions, but he accounted for this as another ruse of capitalism. Harvey came close to saying that globalization is all TV's fault, for globally "promoting … the production of needs and wants, the mobilization of desire and fantasy, of the politics of distraction, as part and parcel of the push to keep … capitalist production profitable" (1989: 61). His Marxist-modernist framework of thought wanted to hang on to exactly that modernist **metanarrative** of "totalization" (comprehensive knowledge) that postmodernists critiqued. He wanted globalization to be understood as a product of capitalism, not culture, and he wanted to mount a "coherent" or *global* response to it.

He blamed postmodern theorists for the "loss" and "collapse" of modernist universals, and cast them as mere apologists for capitalism in its new, "flexible" phase. It becomes clear that the "condition" of postmodernity signaled in his title was, for Harvey, *psychological* (1989: 53–4) – or, more accurately, in his view, psychotic – something to be cured, not copied.

This strange book set the rather mean-spirited tone for a burgeoning sociology of globalization, which henceforth ditched postmodernism (even as an object of critique), and reduced globalization to economic and ideological terms: it was a ruse (or success story, take your pick) of capital. After that, during a period that saw the collapse of the Iron Curtain, the Berlin Wall and international socialism, discussion of globalization became preoccupied with the values of the analyst as much as the facts of the case. Those who saw globalization in a positive light, such as postmodernists, were cast as celebrants or dupes of capitalism, standard-bearers for neoliberalism, now even including Foucault (see Flew, 2014). The only "critical" option was to castigate globalization from a pessimistic viewpoint – a position that Derrida (2005) explicitly rejected.

Theorists of globalization saw postmodernists as fair game, suitable fall guys for knockabout argy bargy. Oddly enough, this has brought the social theorists and postmodernists back together again. For among the most pessimistic observers of global capital are writers like Baudrillard; and among the most rational of upholders of Enlightenment values is Derrida. Baudrillard, on the pessimistic side, makes a distinction between "globalization" and "universal" values, where "universal" refers to the democratic spirit that animates the Universal Declaration of Human Rights (United Nations General Assembly, 1948), for instance. He writes:

> What globalizes first is the market, the profusion of exchanges and of all products, the perpetual flow of money. Culturally, it is the promiscuity of all signs and all values. At the end of this process, there is no longer any difference between the global and the universal. The universal itself is globalized; democracy and human rights circulate just like any other global product – like oil and capital. (Baudrillard, 2003: 89–90)

Globalization means the commodification of everything – signs, values, democracy, rights. Hmmm, no metanarrative of progress there then. But Baudrillard's point is echoed by Nobel prizewinning economist Joseph Stiglitz (2002). He noted that globalization results in global economic *governance* without global *government*. Nonetheless, something can be done about it, as no less a figure than Derrida has argued. Derrida was not a fan of the term "globalization" – he prefers "*mondialisation*" (Derrida, 2005: 107, 117; see also Dalgliesh 2013). Doubting that globalization is even taking place, given the low proportion of those touched by its benefits among the global population, Derrida is however interested in a global *movement* among non-state agencies and society. This is *mondialisation*, which signifies holding the world in knowledge, not as a resource for exploitation, but as a social and historical world (*monde*), and acting in it accordingly:

> QUESTIONER: … "Globalization" creates serious social problems in the world … Looking particularly at the global situation, what might be the contribution of philosophy? …
>
> DERRIDA: I am thinking of a worldwide solidarity, often silent, but ever more effective … It is not recognized in states or international organizations dominated by particular state powers. It is closer to nongovernmental organizations, to some projects called "humanitarian"; but it also goes beyond them and calls for a profound change in international law and its implementation … Those who belong to this International are all the suffering, and all who are not without feeling for the scale of these emergencies – all those who, whatever civic or national groups they belong to, are determined to turn politics, law, and ethics in their direction. (Derrida, 2005: 125–6)

This is the duty of the intellectual, postmodern or otherwise: to participate in a determined globalized (*mondialised*) movement to "turn" politics and economy toward justice.

John Hartley

Habermas, Jürgen: *German sociologist and philosopher, born 1929*

Habermas's relation to postmodernism lies both in the importance of his theory of **modernity** for those who defined postmodernism against Habermas's claims for enlightenment, and in Habermas's ongoing critique of postmodernism and his claim for the completion of the modern project. When **Lyotard** defined postmodernity in his appendix to *The Postmodern Condition* he situated his own theory of micro-narratives or *petit recits* against what he saw as the "slackening" of Habermas's theory of communicative action (Lyotard, 1984: 71). Whereas, for Lyotard, postmodernism needed to embrace multiple and incommensurable registers, **phrases** and language games, Habermas insisted that philosophy should maintain a critically reflective approach: rather than offering some ultimate foundation that could be appealed to as already in existence or that could be deduced as a presupposed ground, Habermas insisted that despite all the distinct ways of speaking, reasoning, writing and composing the world, philosophy could think about the relation among these various worlds (Habermas, 1972).

Key to Habermas's claim for continuing, rather than abandoning, the tradition of enlightenment was a shift from reason as something that was a property of the subject or the individual self, toward reason as achieved through a theory of communicative action (Habermas, 1992). Reason is not something that one possesses as an ability or property, and that precedes and allows one to evaluate relations among humans. Rather, in order for any human to act – or to want to do something – there must already be a world

A Dictionary of Postmodernism, First Edition. Niall Lucy.

of presupposed purposes and meanings: we do not face reality as isolated individuals but are born into a world of language, tradition, other humans, **dialogue**, practices, habits and institutions. Habermas follows the tradition of phenomenology in referring to this presupposed milieu of meaning and other subjects (or intersubjectivity) as the lifeworld or *Lebenswelt.* If we accept that existing as a human being already presupposes a world of meanings and habits then it follows that everything we do is communicative: to act, desire, speak, disagree, argue or even to refuse reason and communication is always intersubjective, always oriented to a horizon of possibilities that includes others. Habermas therefore argues that postmodernism is a self-refuting project: to refuse reason and consensus – to make a claim for unreason and dissensus – is still a form of argument (Habermas, 1987). Communication or a relation to others (rather than some assumed human faculty of reason) is a transcendental horizon – not a transcendental foundation so much as what we must accept in the absence of any foundation.

Postmodernists who refuse reason and argue for discontinuity, incoherence and the multiplication of fictions and phrases have too narrow a conception of **truth** and reason. This is where Habermas argues that modernity needs to be completed rather than abandoned (Habermas, 1997). Modernity's completion occurs not with the arrival of a grand state of illumination, but with the recognition that in the absence of any foundation or any *metaphysical* ground – for there can be no appeal to anything outside all the ways in which we live our world – what we have is an ongoing practice of reflection. Reflection occurs not with an individual assessing the function or validity of claims (although those forms of reflection take place within specific practices). Social and reflective reason occurs when practices enter into relation. Habermas argues that modernity and reason have been far too narrowly construed as instrumental reason: the reasoning that works out the best way to achieve certain ends. But there are other communicative practices and modes of reason distinct from the sciences and technologies that are typified by instrumental reason. Art and literature are, for Habermas, "world disclosive." If we accept the phenomenological theory that the world we live is given through historically sedimented practices, habits, meanings and ways of speaking and desiring, then art-forms such as novels allow us to think about the forming of worlds; we see what we take to be immediate as mediated by specific ways of living. In addition to science's technical, instrumental or means–end rationality, and art's capacity to display our world *as a world*, Habermas insists on public and communicative forms of reason that would negotiate the relations among the assumed norms of distinct practices.

Crucial to achieving this mode of reason would be the ongoing project of establishing an enlightened public sphere: institutions, practices and forms of media that enabled the discussion, critique and refutation of facts, and the reflection on values or norms. Whereas modern or enlightenment thinkers appealed to reason as a faculty possessed by a subject or individual, Habermas sees reason as a social and historical process that needs to be achieved and constantly reflected upon.

Criticizing what he sees as the attempted nihilism of postmodern thought, or the embrace of a world without reasons that refuses any binding truths, Habermas argues for a viable relation between facts and norms (1996). All facts emerge from institutions and practices and therefore rely upon established forms of communication and validation; rather than abandon truth and reason once we acknowledge their necessarily political and institutional emergence, we should accept that facts emerge through realms of value and intention, and then establish ways of reflecting upon knowledge and human interests (Habermas, 1972). Facts are already values, but this does not mean we should abandon truth and accept that everything is fictive or constructed. It does not mean that philosophy is just another story or fiction. On the contrary, every scientific practice or assertion of facts is part of a broader communicative world where we can – and indeed must – be subject to ongoing processes of legitimation (Habermas, 1988). There is not an incommensurable divide between the brute facts of science, and the values that are the outcome of human decision. Nor is there only a world of invented values that has no basis or validity that could be subject to critique. Rather, we should maintain the modern project of critique – of questioning any supposed fact and refusing any supposed unquestionable foundation – but should not simply accept that all we have are fictions and assertions. Postmodernists have, for Habermas, too readily accepted a narrow conception of truth as brute fact and reason as universal human faculty (Habermas, 1987). Truth and reason are not substances or properties that lie outside or beyond human communication; they are procedural and emerge from unavoidable normativity. To speak with others, even when we disagree, is nevertheless to embark upon an ideal of consensus. We should embrace disagreement, multiple **discourses** and incongruent norms *not* because we accept incoherence and incommensurable and untranslatable divides, but because multiple narratives and norms necessarily generate a common space of discussion and understanding.

Habermas was writing from the German tradition of critical theory as it was articulated in the Frankfurt School (see **Jameson**). One of the hallmarks of the Frankfurt School was the ongoing analysis of the manifest failure of reason: if Western thought, or humanity, were rational and progressing toward enlightenment then how can we explain the monstrosities of the twentieth century, such as fascism, totalitarianism and acts of mass genocide? Whereas earlier philosophers, such as Theodor Adorno, argued that reason possessed a totalizing tendency that needed to be counteracted by thinking of an otherness that could not be captured by language or reason (Adorno, 2008), Habermas argues that reason is crucial – in its intersubjective, public and communicative mode – to counteract the abandonment of political striving that has been the hallmark of postmodernity.

Claire Colebrook

Hassan, Ihab: *Egyptian-American literary theorist, born 1925*

Like many other theorists attempting to define the postmodern, Hassan inevitably does so (initially) in opposition to its predecessor. Accordingly he sees **modernism** as formalist and hierarchical, postmodernism antiformalist and anarchic, "a vast, revisionary will in the Western world, unsettling/resettling codes, canons, procedures, beliefs." This "heteroclite" *thing* called postmodernism is at the same time cumbersome, untidy, an ill-fitting, loose and baggy character eclectically teasing our inherited history of ideas, as Hassan gently parodied this rough flâneur in *The Postmodern Turn* (1987: xvi). Drawing on writers as varied as de Sade, Lautréamont, Rimbaud, William Burroughs and Samuel Beckett, Hassan's most singularly figurative idea that he pursued in the name of the postmodern was the experimental, narcissistic and agonistic counter-tradition he called the "literature of silence" (Hassan, 1967). While Beckett was its totemic figure, silence was nothing so literal as atrophy, quiescence or the "revolution of the word" (as it was for the writers of the modernist avant-garde who courted Eugene Jolas's *Transition* magazine of the late 1920s). More arduously it was a metaphor for language pushed to extremes of "radical doubt" (Hassan, 1987: xiii).

Hassan didn't restrict his critical attention to writers who "give themselves to silence" (Hassan, 1982: xvii). His paracritical interjections into the tidy, typographic space of the page enact his strong polemical assertion that critics at the "frontiers of criticism" must "improvise on the possible" (Hassan, 1972: 3). Hassan's *criticism concrète* anticipates similar experiments with **discourse** as page space that reinscribes the language and practice of criticism, confronting and enacting the "implications of its own queries" (1972: xv). Theoretically and typographically self-conscious, paracriticism's affinities lie with the dynamic multimedia style of Marshall McLuhan and Quentin Fiore in *The Medium is the Massage* (1967), the "autocritique" of French poststructuralism such as **Derrida**'s typographic collage *Glas* (1990 [Fr. 1974]), **Barthes**'s meta-code work *S/Z* (1970) and in their turbulent wake the choragraphy and applied grammatology of American theorist of the *post*-age, Gregory L. Ulmer (see, for example, 1985). (This list is only indicative.)

Rather than assertive, analytical or declamatory paracriticism is self-reflexive and performative of Hassan's desire to break out of a dominant critical practice that is predicated on the certitude and transparency associated with the modern episteme. Timothy J. Reiss in *The Discourse of Modernism* describes this historical dominant as "analytico-referential discourse," a language of assertion and possession that is structured syntactically using "elements that *refer* adequately through concepts to the true, objective nature of the world" (Reiss, 1982: 31). Paracriticism contrariwise is "provisional disconfirmation, discontinuity, silence, space, and surprise … typographic variation and thematic repetition, serialism and its parody, allusion and analogy, query and collage, quotation and juxtaposition" (Hassan, 1972: xii). Punctuated by "frames," "slippages," "frames within frames" and perturbed interrogations of what he has written, Hassan's writing works polemically and aesthetically on the page as well as in the mind like speculative and self-inspecting creative writing (see Lucy, 1997: 90).

For instance. T. S. Eliot's influential "*Ulysses*, Order, and Myth" (1923) is suggestive of the epistemology of the modern critical discursive mode of analysis, reference and evaluation. Eliot was writing at a time when the "usylessly unreadable Blue Book of Eccles" was an epiphenomenon, *cause célèbre* and still barely reviewed (Joyce, 1975: 179). In attempting to express how Joyce's daring experiment was for, as well as of, its time, Eliot's brief but concise articulation of the "mythical method" in *Ulysses* announced a "step toward making the modern world possible for art," thereby "giving a shape and a significance to the immense panorama of futility and anarchy which is contemporary history" (Eliot, 1923). Hassan's 1970 "Fiction and Future: An Extravaganza for Voice and Tape" by contrast is a carnivalesque, postmodern ontology (see **dialogue**) in which the performative effects of critical practice become the object of attention, speaking them rather than speaking of them. "Criticism," he tidily asserts in *Paracriticisms* was "born to behold literature [and] must still do so." But crucially, it must also "look beyond itself" (1972: 14). If literature has changed, so too must criticism.

But criticism, he curiously and sagely observes, "is no country for old men" (1972: 14). At this point things become curiouser and curiouser.

A Eureka moment. Hassan's "no country for old men" anachronistically anticipates as well as echoes (at the time of *this* writing) the title of the Coen Brothers' 2007 film *No Country for Old Men*. A fortunate coincidence perhaps, but a convergence that the paracritical temperament can't let fall into the silence of its own impossibility. In the spirit of OULIPO (*ouvroir de littérature potentielle* or "workshop of potential literature": see **remix**) this uncanny enjambment implies, if not promises a potential literature that is self-conscious of its own making. And this potential is implicit in the accident, the capricious enjambment of the title of a 2007 film and Hassan's 1971 bibliography of postmodern criticism (see Hassan, 1972).

The Coen Brothers' film has been critically read as a sophisticated and canny allegory of good and evil and the blurring of the two into an unrepentant nihilism that prevails right until the last man standing. This is a take on the film that is derisorily expressed by one critic who reviewed it for the World Socialist Web Site. The taste of bad faith and disappointment in the mouth of this writer for such an unpleasant world view is summed up as the "film's complete unwillingness to represent and deal with a genuine human feeling" (Saccarelli, 2007). And suffice to say the last man standing without any right to be is the merciless and inhuman killer Anton Chigurh. In other words here is an inexcusable film in which everything goes wrong: the good guys die violently (with the exception of Tommy Lee Jones's Sheriff Bell) while the bad guy hobbles into the sunset with a broken arm to wreak havoc another day. For Emanuele Saccarelli (2007) it is not only the Coen Brothers who have stuffed up here but "film" itself. Or rather a humanist attitude toward what film should be. Drained of human qualities, "the nobility of suffering and of the hope for redemption … are clinically excised" (Saccarelli, 2007). However, imagined as an allegory of the modern tradition's agonistic hustle with the coming of the postmodern, the film can be read very differently. In one sense the film does thematically trace the weary passing of an old and familiar world of reassurance. In its place something resembling William Butler Yeats's "rough beast, its hour come round at last" (1919), slouches deeper into a new America done with its mythic pasts and tidy distinctions between right and wrong.

So consider the film forged in a different kiln, producing not the Grecian urn of tempered poesy but a melting pot of reflexive irony. It hardens as an unknown cypher that explores the schismatic rupture of the postmodern violently succeeding the modern, erupting out of it like pus from a bandaged wound leaving bodies, confusion, incertitude and ambivalence in its wake. From this misshapen mold the film uncannily plays with and parlays blurred boundaries, mixed identities and inexactitude. But it does so not as a linear, Oedipal narrative about these things (a story that begins, happens, ends and mandates its conclusions), but rather by coalescing interactions around the chaotic vortex of a fucked up Mexican drug deal gone wrong. The main event has already happened once the film starts. What we become entangled in are its consequences. Or to say it differently, remaking the film in the foundry of Gregory Ulmer's "textshop" refocuses attention on to a double scene in which the film inscribes a "discourse in a performance" (Ulmer, 1985: 43).

To *speak of* a paracritical reading sculpted out of the film as a visionary, epoch-changing text may seem a theoretical nicety. But it is rather a convenient figure for what the Argentine seer Jorge Luis Borges auratically described as "the deliberate anachronism and the erroneous attribution" (Borges, 1964: 44). To have an avatar of Hassan (there must surely be more than one) *speak* this oxymoronic text makes sense "pataphysically," in a space beyond the rigor of metaphysics. Here he channels the film as if it is a séance fiction, confronting and dismantling binary certainties that don't make sense to old timers who remember a different world from the fuzzy incertitudes of the one to come, or that is already happening around them.

Hassan includes in his 1971 essay "POSTmodernISM" a bibliography of seven key publications that describe "a curious chronology of some Postmodern criticism" – the work is subtitled "Seven Speculations of the Times" (see Hassan, 1972: 45). Critically framing this mosaic of key texts as "postambles" (one Hassan esotericum among many) he concludes we figuratively witness that a "revision of Modernism is slowly taking place," which is "another evidence of Postmodernism" (Hassan, 1967: 46). Capturing this **phrase** hostage and putting it to a semantic and poetic use other than Hassan's (rhetorical rather than bibliographical) frames *No Country For Old Men* as the decline of the old and the shock of a strange new. What follows in Hassan's own words are "some leitmotifs" of that reading (1967: 46). They represent indices of ambivalence, unfamiliarity and devastating violence remixed with the austere "thereness" of an Alain Robbe-Grillet *nouveau roman* about the end of another year and the coming of a revisionary will in the West:

1 *You have followed me here so I can show you this.* Two bookends. Both support the opposing weight of familiar history and an oblique future. The lament of one, B, proper to a weary stoic. He smells change roiling

in the dust, fearing something he doesn't understand. He has seen signs and wonders. Drugs, green hair, bones through noses. He can't stop what's coming. *His story is already over.*

2 *You've constantly avoided my eyes.* C, an unknown Other from nowhere. An impassive chimera whose manners preface unfeeling destruction. *Would you hold still please Sir.* Innocuous words enough. For chaos. They are said again by L. *You hold still now.* Both preface violence. But there is only one death. *Across the same thresholds.*

3 *And what if you were to play first?* He just sells gas. He doesn't understand riddles. Only the rain. Lived here all his life. Now it's time to shut up shop. In the middle of the day. *He had noticed something, a danger.* Perplexed by C and the strange chance he offers. It isn't what it used to be. Oblique. Like a coin mixed with others in your pocket. You don't know where it's been. It has taken its taken time to get here. Not of this place. Or time. *Again I felt that no one understood your words.*

4 *You're raving… I'm tired… let me alone.* A lost opportunity to show mercy. Troubles his sleep. A gesture. Small yet sympathetic. Water to a dying man. *It was you who answered me in the sudden silence.* Too late. And crudely at odds with the fugitive millions in his grasp. Morality between extremes. *A few seconds more, as if others were still hesitating before separating from him.*

5 *You never seemed to be waiting for me. But we kept meeting each other, at each turn, each bush.* Different and alike. More alike than not. Both have troubled limbs. Like Oedipus. *Swollen feet.* Bloodied and bound together by coincidence and circumstance. They bring violence to a land of more gentle temper. C's lack of conscience. L too much. *As if his silhouette.*

6 *He had started the whole thing himself, so that he knew all the possibilities in advance.* L lies in his own blood. Vaguely cruciform across a doorway. Between worlds. To both he is now nothing. *And now you are here where I have brought you.* One timeless like dust. The other precarious like the wind. *He was looking for you. He was coming to you.*

7 *As if his figure, though already grey, already paler, still threatened to reappear.* Wracked by indiscriminate violence. Impatient with its inconvenience he limps into nowhere. *A funny sort of eye.* Indifferent to what casual malice he takes with him into tomorrow. *Perhaps it was an allegory, or something like that.*

Darren Tofts

Hyperreality: Very early in Don DeLillo's deliciously satirical novel *White Noise*, protagonist and narrator Jack Gladney accompanies his friend and colleague Murray Jay Siskind on a daytrip to a tourist attraction in the nearby North American countryside. As they approach the location, signs begin to appear: "THE MOST PHOTOGRAPHED BARN IN AMERICA" (DeLillo, 1986: 12). At the site itself, people mill around taking photos of the barn, while a man in a souvenir kiosk sells postcards and other reproductions of the building.

"No one sees the barn," Murray observes, notwithstanding the fact that dozens of people are presently looking at it. The narrator himself provides no description or depiction of the structure, moreover, presumably because, as Murray insists, "once you've seen the signs about the barn, it becomes impossible to see the barn" (1986: 12). The photographers, therefore, are merely "taking pictures of taking pictures" (1986: 13). And so the *sight seen* can be understood to have been subsumed by the photographic and touristic practices of *sightseeing*, the referent of the photographers' snapshots being less the barn itself, understood as an object that is or was just *there*, prior to the moment of the camera's shutter being pressed, than a particular form of media practice, which one ordinarily understands merely as a means of producing a copy or likeness of such an object. But "[w]e're not here to capture an image," Murray explains; "we're here to maintain one. Every photograph reinforces the aura" (1986: 13). Real-world object and media representation converge as one, in other words, with the barn itself taking on a significance it never had, and could never have had, in the absence of its media-enabled reproduction.

In this way, "the most photographed barn in America," which is just one of several outrageous conceits recounted to hilarious effect in *White Noise*, serves as a perfect illustration of hyperreality – though, see, too, the scene in which a state program called "SIMUVAC," short for "simulated evaucation," uses a *real* emergency, an "airborne toxic event," as a model and an opportunity to rehearse for a *simulated* emergency response exercise scheduled for a subsequent date (DeLillo, 1986: 138–42). That these scenarios are entirely fictional does little to undermine or qualify their explanatory power, moreover. Indeed, their artifice simply makes them all the more fitting as examples in this context, for it is the contemporary primacy of the imitation over the reality that defines hyperreality as analyzed by **Eco** and **Baudrillard**.

For Eco, this analysis takes the form of a pursuit of the "Almost Real" and the "Absolute Fake" – "absolute unreality offered as real presence" (Eco, 1986: 7) – across a long essay called "Travels in Hyperreality," written in 1975. The essay recounts Eco's whirlwind tour of the US "in search of instances where the American imagination demands the real thing and, to attain it, must fabricate the absolute fake; where the boundaries between game and illusion are blurred, the art museum is contaminated by the freak show, and falsehood is enjoyed in a situation of 'fullness', of *horror vacui* [fear of empty space]" (Eco, 1986: 8). In a sometimes overwhelming display of the "excesses" of what might today be described as forms of popular museumology and "edutainment," Eco details dozens of examples of wax museums, art galleries and architectural reconstructions that evince "the conjunction of archaeology and falsification" (1986: 31), "the amalgamation of fake and authentic" (1986: 36), and an "abundance of the reconstructed truth" (1986: 48). In these forms, hyperreality can perhaps be understood with reference to the aesthetic (but also, in a sense, historiographical) technique of realism, by which a cultural text like a painting, a novel or a television show sets out to produce a **representation** of the world that corresponds with our sense of everyday physical and social reality. Central to the technique of realism is less the requirement that the world represented be "believable," in the sense that no physical or moral laws are transgressed – for fantastic or science fictional stories might still adopt the modes of formal or social realism – than the imperative that the representation does not call attention to itself *as* representation. The idea, then, is that a text is written and structured (or filmed and edited, composed and painted, etc.) in such a way that we may look *through* the representation, as it were, to focus on the world thus depicted, without getting distracted by the fact that it *is* a representation we are engaging with – a *sign* of the world (see **semiotics** and **truth**) – rather than the reality of the world itself. But if the success of realism thus lies in forgetting (so to speak) the representation in favor of seeing the world, then what marks the shift from realism to the hyperreal is the forgetting of the world in favor of fetishizing the *representation*, the sign itself: "the sign aims to be the real thing, to abolish the distinction of the reference, the mechanism of replacement" (Eco, 1986: 7).

Perhaps paradigmatic of this shift is the emergence in the 1960s and 1970s of the genre of painting and drawing known as photorealism, to which Eco briefly refers (1986: 7). In such works scenes are reproduced in paints or ink so realistically that they are easily mistaken for photographs. What makes these paintings not merely realistic but hyperrealistic is their depiction of a *more-than-real* by virtue of their aim to pass not for the thing itself, but for *another form of representation*. They *look like* real representations. And, of course, they *are* real representations – just not the representations that they appear to be.

Such is the farrago of real and unreal characterizing the examples that abound in Eco's essay: from waxworks reproductions of Mona Lisa, sitting for a waxwork Leonardo da Vinci (Eco, 1986: 18), through reconstructed European Renaissance houses (1986: 22), to entire "ghost towns" that preserve a mythical past through something akin to a material hallucination (1986: 40–3). While the techniques, processes and effects vary from example to example, Eco's reading of the "studied illusion" of the Knott's Berry Farm in Los Angeles is perhaps exemplary of how the **simulation** must always carry with it a trace of authenticity to produce the hyperreal. At Berry Farm, he writes,

> the whole trick seems to be exposed; the surrounding city context and the iron fencing (as well as the admission ticket) warn us that we are entering not a real city but a toy city. But as we begin walking down the first streets, the studied illusion takes over. First of all, there is the realism of the reconstruction; the dusty stables, the sagging shops, the offices of the sheriff and the telegraph agent, the jail, the saloon are life size and executed with absolute fidelity; the old carriages are covered with dust, the Chinese laundry is dimly lit, all the buildings are more or less practical, and the shops are open, because Berry Farm, like Disneyland, blends the reality of trade with the play of fiction. And if the dry-goods store is fake nineteenth-century and the shopgirl is dressed like a John Ford heroine, the candies [and] the peanuts ... are real and are sold for real dollars ... and the customer finds himself participating in the fantasty because of his own authenticity as a consumer. (Eco, 1986: 41)

Notwithstanding the reference to "fiction" here, hyperreality isn't quite reducible to a confusion of illusion or inauthenticity with (or for) reality, given that it's not always trickery, nor always fakery, let alone falsification, that defines the **essence** of the sign that comes to replace the real. Rather, as fake or fabrication, as illusion or apparition, as reconstruction or imitation, the common thread to all these signs is less their deviation from an authentic original, than simply their status as (faithful) *copy*. It is their *secondariness*, the fact of coming *after* the original – historically, but also logically – that makes them hyperreal. Or, rather, it is the fact of secondariness having *taken the place* of the original that defines the condition of hyperreality. And in the context of expanding processes of replacement that allow a copy to function as the "original" reference point – think here not just of photorealism's reproduction of a photograph, but of the never-ending duplication, **remix** and sharing that today consitute the very workings of the Internet and other **new media** – we are perhaps left wondering whether the real was not already a copy all along.

For this reason, it would be wrong to reduce the hyperreal to a celebration of kitsch or a mass reverence for the fake, let alone to such seeming absurdities as "the most photographed barn in America." And if, as with **Jameson**, Eco's essay betrays a hint of elitist distaste for "American" popular culture, the take offered by Baudrillard, writing at a very similar time to Eco, suggests that the effects of hyperreality extend beyond the practices of representation and consumption that define contemporary cultural tourism. Like Eco, Baudrillard's observations are bound up with reflections on art, culture, representation, not to mention consumer capitalism, with the basic point being that, today, the explanatory and regulative power of "the reality principle" has been surpassed – or subsumed – by the play of simulation:

> The reality principle coincided with a determinate phase of the law of value. Today, the entire system is fluctuating in indeterminacy, all of reality absorbed by the hyperreality of the code and of simulation. It is now a principle of simulation, and not of reality, that regulates social life. The finalities have disappeared; we are now engendered by models. There is no longer such a thing as ideology; there are only simulacra. (Baudrillard, 1988a: 120)

The situation Baudrillard describes here corresponds to the third and latest stage in a historical series of "phases of the law of value." Baudrillard's terms chop and change, but for the sake of convenience these three stages can be designated as the natural, the real and the hyperreal, respectively. The first phase corresponds to an order of metaphysics and natural law, in which "value" is defined in terms of the simple and immediate essence of an object. In Baudrillard's genealogy of the law of value, this first phase is overtaken by "the system of political economy and the law of the commodity," where value is defined in terms of exchange, albeit with a naturally defined "use value" continuing to lead "a kind of phantom existence at the heart of exchange value" (Baudrillard, 1988a: 121). If in the first order of existence we might enjoy a kind of direct connection with things in themselves and form the kind of organic oneness with the world that would allow us simply to intuit the value of a thing, in the second order "Nature" has become veiled – hence our access to it mediated – by a socio-political world of human institutions, attributes and achievements. But while we might thereby lose direct connection to the natural world, we can, by way of our modern human sciences, determine the laws of economy and exchange, the structure of language, the nature of desire, such that we can perceive and understand the *reality* of our human existence, thereby holding out the promise of a form of value that may ground attempts to improve our world, hence ourselves. By the time we enter the order of the code, however, "there is nothing left to ground ourselves on" (Baudrillard, 1988a: 124). Reality is superseded by simulation, and all the certainties offered by "a determinist and objectivist science" are replaced by a "hyperreality of floating values" (1988a: 122).

When captured and presented in such sloganistic fashion, these and other claims made by Baudrillard ("we are now engendered by models") are easily interpreted as a hyperbolic nihilism whose extreme skepticism has lost all contact with reason and reality. Yet in many ways Baudrillard's argument represents merely a generalization of a concept already evidenced by thinkers who are often taken to show a far stronger commitment to "social and historical reality" than many other theorists and writers associated with postmodernism. For instance, four years prior to Baudrillard's first extended discussion of hyperreality (Baudrillard, 1993a [Fr. 1976]), and well before his infamous declaration that "the Gulf War did not take place" (Baudrillard, 1995), Pierre Bourdieu presented a celebrated analysis of the logic and techniques of opinion polling, in which he declared that "public opinion does not exist" (see Bourdieu, 1979 [1972]). Bourdieu's argument is complex and multifaceted, but the upshot is that there is a very real sense in which opinion polls *produce* the opinion they seek to poll, not simply through "biased" questions but also by virtue of the fact that at least some of the people being polled may well have had no opinion on a given issue prior to "being polled" on it.

Three years later, **Foucault**'s highly influential *Discipline and Punish* (1979 [Fr. 1975]) described the constitutive power of what he called "normalizing techniques," by means of which certain regularities – more or less "spontaneous" patterns of social behavior or standard distributions of competence, which have been identified by observation or statistical analysis – are enforced rather as *rules*: "as a minimum threshold, as an average to be respected or as an optimum towards which one must move" (1979: 183). While Foucault's association of these normalizing techniques with the rise of disciplinary society in the late eighteenth century may cast doubt on the neatness of periodicity implied by Baudrillard's "genealogy" of the law of value, both Foucault's and Bourdieu's respective studies arguably illustrate Baudrillard's claim that "we are now engendered by models." In each case, that is, specific human attributes are shown to be produced by a model or standard, insofar as the population measured is then made to conform to the measure.

To the extent that Baudrillard "adds" something to such arguments, that supplement perhaps takes the form of a radical insistence on, hence generalization of, the principle they evidence. For "[n]ow the whole of everyday political, social, historical, economic reality is incorporated into the simulative dimension of hyperrealism" (Baudrillard, 1988a: 146). Accordingly, every attempt to study "the real" today is always already caught up in the play of simulation, its **discourse** inevitably *producing* the real it seeks merely to analyze or observe. Baudrillard's generalization of the point is consistent, moreover, with the "radicalization of all hypotheses" which he proposes as a means of producing the "reversibility" that alone is "fatal" to the terms of the system (1988a: 127). "That each *term* should be ex-*term*inated, that value should be abolished in this revolution of the term against itself – this is the only symbolic violence worthy of the structural violence of the code" (1988a: 127). The very formulation of the "theory" of simulation, in other words, is at the same time the first move in its critique – albeit, not a critique made in the name of some **transcendental signified** or value that is external to the system, nor of any "revolutionary" or "liberatory" agendas grounded in the ideals and language of **modernity**. Such programs amount to little more than "a nostalgiac resurrection of the real in all its forms" (1988a: 124). Indeed, all "these liberations are just transitions toward a generalized manipulation" (1988a: 124), with the result that our conventional ideals and methods of reasoned critique ultimately contribute to the forms of dissimulation and control they would otherwise seek to eliminate.

The radicalization of hyperreality promises, by contrast, not truth but death: "[d]eath is always simultaneously that which awaits us at the system's *term*, and the *extermination* that awaits the system itself" (1988a: 126). Undoubtedly, there's more than a hint of catastrophe, if not apocalypticism in this "hyperlogic of destruction and death," as Baudrillard himself puts it (1988a: 126). It might make for a fitting act of reversal, therefore, to note the secondary, simulative nature of such a logic. For the insistence that "[d]eath should never be interpreted as an actual occurrence in a subject or body, but rather as a *form*, possibly a form of social relation, where the determination of the subject and value disappears" (1988a: 127) places Baudrillard's "hyperlogic" in a lineage that includes some slightly more optimistic, even celebratory antecedents: **Barthes**'s thoughts on "The Death of the Author" (in 1977a [Fr. 1967]), for instance, and Foucault's speculation on the disappearance of "Man" (Foucault, 1970) – not to mention Nietzsche's famous, *life-affirming* pronouncement that "God is dead":

> At hearing the news that "the old god is dead," we philosophers and "free spirits" feel illuminated by a new dawn; our heart overflows with gratitude, amazement, forebodings, expectation – finally the horizon seems clear again, even if not bright … every daring of the lover of knowledge is allowed again. (Nietzsche, 2001: 199; §343)

And so Baudrillard's reported pessimism remains less than convincing, and not because it provides no cause for hope. As *simulation* of cynicism and defeatism, rather, its form of analysis ultimately cannot feign to tell the difference, in truth, between "hope" and "despair." Hence the sense of *conviction* that comes to (re)animate the apparently dead body of critique: "[e]ven the code and the symbolic are terms of simulation – it *must* be possible somehow to retire them, one by one, from discourse" (Baudrillard, 1988a: 127; emphasis added). It's a sense of conviction, then, that strives for its own eventual elimination in the name of a future left open to every possibility that lovers of knowledge may dare think.

Robert Briggs

ABCDEFGHIJKLMNOPQRSTUVWXYZ

J

Jameson, Fredric: *American Marxist cultural critic, born 1934*

Because we are alienated, we are postmodern; and we are alienated because we are subjects under capitalism. This is the broad thrust of Jameson's argument in his influential magnum opus, *Postmodernism, or, The Cultural Logic of Late Capitalism* (1991), developed from an essay published in *New Left Review* in 1984. The argument is not quite that postmodernism *begins* with capitalism, but rather that what might be called capitalism's alienation effect intensifies with each new stage or phase of capitalist history: since our alienation today, in the time of "late" capitalism, according to Jameson, has never been greater, our time is both historically unprecedented (hence *post*modern) and historically inevitable (hence post*modern*). This is to situate **modernism** in Marxist terms as the expression (the cultural superstructure) of the capitalist system (the economic base), a system owed to particular historical conditions associated with the shift in Europe from an agrarian to an industrial economy in the early nineteenth century. Postmodernism is simply the latest expression of that system in its current stage of "late" development.

Jameson adapts his periodic approach to cultural history from the work of German Marxist theorist Ernest Mandel, whose *Late Capitalism* (1999 [Ger. 1972]) posits three broad stages of development: early capitalism spans roughly 1700–1850 in Europe, as industrial capital cultivates domestic markets; the middle period (1850 through to World War II) sees capital flow increasingly from domestic to foreign markets, aided by industrial and

A Dictionary of Postmodernism, First Edition. Niall Lucy.

technological advances; and the so-called late stage, following the end of World War II, corresponds to capital's global fluidity, unrestricted by national border controls. Each economic phase gives rise, for Jameson, to a matching superstructural phase: realism is the cultural dominant of the early-capitalist period; modernism, of the middle phase; and postmodernism, of the late-capitalist present. The local alienation caused by the consumption of goods produced in dark satanic mills thus grew into the postmodern "waning of affect" (Jameson, 1991: 9) that epitomizes the global mass consumption of commodities (goods, styles and images) produced by multinational corporations. This grim state of affairs is captured in the postmodern fascination with a "whole 'degraded' landscape of schlock and kitsch," where the tumbleweeds of style and fashion – "of advertising and motels, of the late show and the grade-B Hollywood film [sic], of so-called **paraliterature**, with its airport paperback categories of the gothic and the romance, the popular biography, the murder mystery, and the science fiction or fantasy novel" – swirl across a cultural wasteland that offers no support for emulating "what a Joyce or a Mahler might have done" (1991: 3).

Jameson came of age as a teenager in the 1950s, when US teens emerged as a new consuming public in the context of post-war prosperity and liberalism (see Hall and Whannel, 1964: 269–312), and yet his *Postmodernism* book is written from the perspective of an outsider, as someone out of joint with the times he writes about and therefore who writes about them only to refute them, a case of the nerd's revenge. Prufrock-like, in other words, Jameson sees in post-war popular culture only an empty "depthlessness" (Jameson, 1991: 8), and not the historically unprecedented and democratizing opportunities it affords new generations to adopt and adapt "looks" and "attitudes" that differ from previous generations, as though something as ephemeral as a "look" should be taken seriously. But the political importance of looking and being looked at in public, as John Hartley reminds us, has a history going back at least to Aristotle's *Politics* (350 BCE), where in order for a public to *be* a public its members must *be seen*:

> there is nothing impoverished about a single glance. According to Aristotle's *Politics*, a democratic polity (i.e. a city state) ought to comprise no more people "than can be seen at a single glance." This is the **dialogic** or messaging element of fashion language, the point of intelligibility towards which a given "look" is intended; a point that always exists *outside* of the body whose look is communicated. What a dress ensemble *means* is therefore not as intended

> or predicted in the wearer's initial choice and arrangement of elements but in *how these are seen* by others. Meanings emerge and change in a socially networked system of active and evolving relationships identified by status-based signaling. That's the message. (Hartley, 2012: 194–5)

Notwithstanding the Aristotelian significance of looking, a "look" is a good example of what Jameson means by the "depthlessness" of postmodern **culture**. Clothes, hairstyles and fashion accessories are all worn on the body's surface, and for Jameson our fascination with appearances, with the way that we and others look, encapsulates the superficial nature of the times we live in. Such a disapproving attitude toward – or simply a distaste for – the popular, however, was far from new by the 1990s; indeed, it's still in vogue, albeit nowadays the scaremongering is less likely to be directed at television, Hollywood and pulp fiction than at the "dangerous" effects of social media and digital technologies (ranging from screen addiction and sleep deprivation to declining literacy standards and easy access to age-inappropriate pleasures and information) on the minds and bodies of the young. In the context of this persistent (and therefore in a sense popular) disapproval of popular culture, Jameson's *Postmodernism* is at least in part a **remix** of Theodor Adorno and Max Horkheimer's *Dialectic of Enlightenment* (2002 [Ger. 1947]), a work that denies authentic meaning and value to what the authors regard as the standardized products of mass culture (movies, comics, fashion, furniture, radio shows, magazines, popular fiction and the like) for being manufactured by industrial means. For Adorno and Horkheimer, we (but of course not they) are deceived by capitalism into consuming "false" goods and pleasures that never satisfy us; and so capitalism, by constructing us *as* consumers, produces both our dissatisfaction *and* the illusion that our fulfillment lies in consuming more and more.

The increasing mechanization of cultural production in the first half of the twentieth century led Adorno and Horkheimer to coin the term "culture industry" to describe what they saw as the process by which commodities (popular culture) came to supplant artifacts (high culture), turning us – but of course not them – into docile consumers. Sometimes, more broadly, the view that culture has been increasingly dumbed down by capitalism since the end of World War I is attributed to the "Frankfurt School," the name given to an informal group of Marxist critics (including Adorno and Horkheimer) associated initially with the Institute for Social Research in Frankfurt, Germany, whose work was influential from around the early

1930s to the mid-1960s (the School moved to New York, via Geneva, when Hitler came to power in 1933, with many members choosing to remain in the US after the Institute was re-established in Frankfurt in the 1950s). But well before Jameson reproduced this view in his *Postmodernism* book its status was being contested by **cultural studies** scholars in Britain – for example in Stuart Hall's *Encoding and Decoding in the Television Discourse* (1973), John Fiske and John Hartley's *Reading Television* (1978), Dick Hebdige's *Subculture: The Meaning of Style* (1979) and Hartley's *Understanding News* (1982) – who saw popular culture not as a problem, but as a question: why is popular culture *popular*? The formulaic Frankfurt School response to this – that capitalism turns us all into stupid, greedy consumers, powerless to resist buying whatever we see advertised and believing everything we watch on television – can't account for why the "culture industry" often *fails* to dupe us. The Hollywood blockbuster that bombs, the bestseller that doesn't sell, the TV extravaganza that doesn't rate, the fast food chain or the glossy magazine that goes bust – these would all be oxymorons, instead of recognizably mundane events, if capitalism or "late" capitalism had control of our desires. A further problem with the Frankfurt School approach lies in its ultimately self-serving distinction between an elite class of clever critics and a lumpen mass of credulous consumers, with the former presuming to teach the culture it both shuns and denounces how to suck eggs.

Such an approach – voiceless, omniscient, scientific – begins by thinking its object of inquiry is indeed objectifiable, and therefore that by careful analysis its atomic features may be identified, described and assessed (see Lucy, 2002). From the outset, then, Jameson was committed to the assumption of a pure and absolute distinction between postmodern culture and the modernist culture it supposedly supplants, each culture constituting a different *system*, and it's not surprising this was well received in the 1990s at a time when the "culture war" in the US was in full swing and the term "postmodernism" – or "**deconstruction**", or simply "theory" – was used in the media and certain parts of the academy as shorthand for a radical, obscurantist attack on reason, common sense and traditional values. The virulent, sometime vitriolic, denunciation of pomo "gibberish" reached its high or low points in the **Sokal affair** (1996) and the front-page *New York Times* obituary for Derrida, in 2004, accusing him of fathering the idea that there is no such thing as "truthfulness" and of duping architects into designing "zigzaggy" buildings (Kandell, 2004; and see **Jencks**). The culture war thus seeded the conditions for a receptive readership – a *market* – to emerge, a market hungry for a plain-speaking critique of the pretensions of postmodern thought, and Jameson's hefty tome was all the more palatable for confirming what many already took "postmodernism" to mean.

Despite the feigned indifference of his "dialectical science," however, Jameson's failure to "get" the culture he claims to be describing ("the grade-B Hollywood film," indeed!) renders his object of inquiry less than unproblematically prior and independent. But it's not only his tin ear that lets him down. In commenting on a Van Gogh painting, *Old Shoes with Laces* (c. 1886), which Heidegger mentions in "The Origin of the Work of Art" (an essay published in 1950 and revised in 1960, based on lectures delivered in the 1930s: see Heidegger, 1971), Jameson fails to paraphrase and thus *to read* Derrida's reading of that essay faithfully, by writing that Derrida "remarks, somewhere, about the Heideggerian *Paar Bauernschuhe* ['pair of shoes'] that the Van Gogh footgear are a heterosexual pair, which allows neither for perversion nor for fetishization" (Jameson, 1991: 8). Yet this – far from it – is decidedly not what Derrida says; indeed he speculates for over a hundred pages in *The Truth in Painting* (1987b) on the implications of Heidegger's inability or refusal to consider that the shoes do *not* comprise a "pair" (since in fact they look like two left shoes). Heidegger can't see the shoes as an "odd" couple, Derrida argues, a homosexual rather than a heterosexual "pair," because he sees them as the *representation* of an *object* in the form of "a pair of peasant shoes" belonging to a woman, a reading or interpretation that returns the shoes to the primordial earth and a certain idea of the maternal (hence the shoes of a peasant woman) and which reinforces Heidegger's association of the *authenticity of being* with all things pre-modern. Heidegger looks past the surface of the painting (and therefore, in a sense, doesn't see the painting at all) to reveal its depth of meaning, a "depth" that is inseparable from his *projection*. In a similar fashion, Lithuanian-born US art historian Meyer Schapiro – who reproaches Heidegger in a 1968 essay for *imagining* that the shoes belong to a peasant woman – insists they belong to Van Gogh himself, as "things inseparable from his body and memorable to his reacting self-awareness" (Meyer, 1994: 140). For Schapiro, Heidegger's error lies "in his projection, which replaces a close attention to the work of art" (1994: 138), but as Derrida points out there are no fixed grounds for distinguishing between these positions, each of which regards the painting as the **representation** simply of a different object (the shoes of a peasant woman, the artist's shoes), no matter how loudly Schapiro might protest that his is not a "projection" – a reading, an interpretation – but rather the unmediated, disinterested art-historical **truth** of the matter (see Lucy, 2010a).

Jameson, too, is interested in the Van Gogh painting only for what it represents, which for him is "the whole object world of agricultural misery, of stark rural poverty, and the whole rudimentary human world of back-breaking peasant toil" (Jameson, 1991: 7). The shoes, then, painted in the modernist era, return the viewer to the immediacy of the world – the "life world" – from which it can be imagined that they came, one of "misery," "poverty" and relentless "toil." By contrast, Andy Warhol's *Diamond Dust Shoes* (1980), which for Jameson typifies postmodern art, depicts but "a random collection of dead objects hanging together on the canvas like so many turnips, as shorn of their earlier life world as the pile of shoes left over from Auschwitz or the remainders and tokens of some incomprehensible and tragic fire in a packed dance hall" (1991: 8). So, on the one hand, Van Gogh's shoes invite hermeneutic completion, allowing viewers to see them as a product of brutal social relations, while on the other Warhol's shoes are mere *fetish* objects (1991: 7) – both in Freud's sense of the fetish as a "substitute" (see Freud, 2001: vol. XXI) for what never was (the mother's phallus) and Marx's sense of "commodity fetishism" (although Marx never used this term) by which, under capitalism, our "fantastic" relationship to things substitutes for authentic social relations between *people* (Marx, 1867: ch.1, §4). The difference if not the **differend** here would thus appear to be between Van Gogh's *representational* shoes and Warhol's simulacra (see **simulation**).

But for modernism and postmodernism to be understood as different cultural *systems*, belonging to different historical periods, the features of one ought not to be applicable to the other. For Jameson's distinction between representation and simulation to hold, there ought to be nothing fetishistic about the Van Gogh shoes; and yet Derrida's point is that it's the suppression of this possibility which enables both Heidegger and Schapiro to debate the identity of the very object that the painting represents – the shoes of a peasant woman *or* the artist's shoes. Both see a pair of shoes (one left, one right) rather than, say, a "perverse" double of the same (two left shoes, perhaps) because the *social use* of shoes is tied to what might be called their hetero-normativity … *and* they see a pair of shoes because they see painting as representational. The very notion of the pair (the pair in general, as it were) "rivets things to use, to 'normal' use," as Derrida puts it (1987b: 332–3), and so the pair occludes the possibility of fetishization:

> It is perhaps in order to exclude the question of a certain uselessness, or of a so-called perverse usage, that Heidegger and Schapiro denied themselves the

> slightest doubt as to the parity or pairedness of these two shoes. They bound them together in order to bind them to the law of normal usage. (Derrida, 1987b: 333)

If, then, Heidegger and Schapiro may be said to fetishize "pairedness," what their fetish substitutes for is a normality that has only ever been imagined or asserted to be real. Even Freud acknowledges that sexual difference – the paired opposition of the masculine and the feminine – is never quite pure and absolute, since for him (in Derrida's words) "bisexual symbolization remains an irrepressible, archaic tendency, going back to childhood" (Derrida, 1987b: 268). Or as Freud himself writes in *The Interpretation of Dreams*: "It is true that the tendency of dreams and of unconscious phantasies to employ the sexual symbols bisexually betrays an archaic characteristic; for in childhood the distinction between the genitals of the two sexes is unknown and the same kind of genitals are attributed to both of them" (Freud, 2010 [Ger. 1899]: 371–2). Sexual identity, in other words, does not come prepackaged, which is true also of the meaning or identity of fetish objects: a shoe, say, may appear to qualify as a prosthetic phallus, but for Freud in the "Symbolism in Dreams" lecture of 1915 (Freud, 2001: vol. IV), as Derrida notes, shoes are "among the symbols of the female genital organs" (Derrida, 1987b: 267). "Could it be," Derrida asks, "that, like a glove turned inside out, the shoe sometimes has the convex 'form' of the foot (penis), and sometimes the concave form enveloping the foot (vagina)?" (1987b: 267). No less than for Heidegger or Schapiro, however, this is not a question for Jameson, who may be said to fetishize a notion of *system* even though, ironically, on the evidence of Derrida's reading of Freud, the fetish resists being systematized. Out of his commitment to a systematic, periodic distinction, then, between the modern and the postmodern, Jameson *must* see the Van Gogh shoes as a pair in order "to displace," as Wes Cecil puts it, "any possibility of an 'unnatural' pairing of two left shoes and thus displace the possibility of the fetish" (Cecil, 1993: 12).

Jameson wants the fetish to belong only to the "system" of postmodern culture. Yet it's clear that the troublesome nature of the Van Gogh shoes cannot be tied to "the law of normal usage," and clearly this raises questions for Jameson's periodicity: what is postmodernism such that one of its so-called distinguishing features may be found to precede "it," to belong in fact to the modernist era that postmodernism is meant to supplant? It's only by repressing this question that Jameson is able to see the Van Gogh and

Warhol paintings as *representations* of contrasting life worlds, with the cultural logic of late capitalism leading to "a new kind of flatness or depthlessness, a new kind of superficiality in the most literal sense" (Jameson, 1991: 8), which, compared to the "'modernist' expressivity" (1991: 9) it replaces, must be understood in terms of loss (hence the postmodern "waning of affect"). But why does Jameson waver here; why the scare quotes around "modernist"? Could it be that he himself is less than fully convinced by his orderly distinction between the systematic cultural features of one historical period and another?

When culture, whether modern or postmodern, is understood merely as the reflection of an economic base (or some other **essence** or foundation), cultural objects must be seen as representational and therefore the differences between objects, media and idioms must be overlooked. There's nothing idiomatic for Jameson about the Van Gogh and Warhol paintings: all that matters is the "expressivity" of the one opposed to the other's "depthlessness" – a position that may confirm his *theory* of cultural production but which also reproduces romantic, value-laden assumptions about the superior quality of a so-called original work of art (such as an oil painting) compared to a synthetic or machinic work, like *Diamond Dust Shoes*, which relies on screen-printing techniques. Surely, though, if it were "depthlessness," or the loss of "expressivity," that Jameson was seeking to illustrate, he need have looked no further than Marcel Duchamp's *Fountain*, the mass-produced urinal that Duchamp was prevented from exhibiting at the Society of Independent Artists' 1917 show in New York. Despite, in a sense, never being seen in public, and regardless of the "original" having been long since lost, *Fountain* (an example of what Duchamp called "readymades") is perhaps the most influential art object of the last century. It was produced or created, however, not at a time when (according to Jameson) "depthlessness" was the dominant cultural mode, but when "expressivity" dominated, a period that Jameson rightly hesitates to call "modernist" since clearly it does not quite belong to history as such. If, in other words, Jameson had been looking for a work that heralded a radical break with the supposed "expressivity" of the Van Gogh painting, surely *Fountain* said it all:

> With Duchamp, thus implicating everything that came before, art turned into the *work* of three functions: signature, event, context. What used to be called the work "itself" could now be seen as more or less incidental to art as such. Does it matter that *Fountain* was a urinal … or that it was *that* urinal?

> Being otherwise indistinguishable from countless manufactured objects of its type, the urinal that Duchamp chose to call *Fountain* (the one that was only ever an instance in a series of any number of identical urinals, and therefore always already no more than *a* urinal) was made over into art in that act of naming. No doubt the artist could have called it *Jet* or *Spray*, or even – perhaps in a moment of aleatory or hallucinatory pre-emption – *Play Station 2*, and the effect would have been the same. What mattered is not that it was named *Fountain*, but that it had a name.
>
> Once named, framed off, as it were, from the series of manufactured readymades from which it had been cut out, the urinal that was *Fountain* was re-messaged. Instead of saying, *Piss in me*, it now said, *Think about me: what am I? What's happening here?* (Briggs and Lucy, 2012b)

Predating Auschwitz, how could *Fountain* have pre-empted the "depthlessness" of Warhol's *Diamond Dust Shoes*? Nor could it matter to Jameson's periodic distinction between the modern and the postmodern, moreover, that the referent of Duchamp's artwork is a urinal and not footwear: the details of the art object are subordinate to the work's historical placement, such that there ought to be an orderly, systematic distinction between the "expressivity" of the modern and the "depthlessness" of the culture that comes after it. In the end, then, because there is nothing Jameson says of a (postmodern) work such as the Warhol painting – which "evidently no longer speaks to us with any of the immediacy of Van Gogh's footgear" and provides not "even a minimal space for the viewer, who confronts it at the turning of a museum corridor or gallery with all the contingency of some inexplicable natural object" (Jameson, 1991: 7) – that he couldn't have said of Duchamp's (modernist) *Fountain*, it would seem that Jameson's insistence on an orderly, systematic distinction between two different sets of cultural features arising from two different capitalist phases simply obscures the fact that he prefers paintings such as *Old Shoes with Laces* to paintings such as *Diamond Dust Shoes*.

Fountain disrupts the neat dichotomy of the "immediacy" of "modernist" art and the "fetishistic" detachment of "postmodern" images from the historical contexts in which they are produced. If, that is to say, detachment – "depthlessness," the "waning of affect," the loss of "expressivity" – may be a feature of a modernist work, how could it be said to define the *system* that is postmodern culture? Or if Jameson's reading of the Warhol painting, as Sven-Erik Rose remarks, "establishes the catastrophic incomprehensibility of 'Auschwitz' as paradigmatic of the way postmodern icons become unmoored, fetishistically severed from their socio-historical totality"

(Rose, 2008: 117), how could Duchamp's urinal be so "fetishistically severed" *ahead* of that "catastrophic incomprehensibility"? There may indeed be something like features we might attribute to something called "postmodernism," but those "features" could not – as the example of *Fountain* attests – be understood as an expression of the cultural logic of late capitalism.

Niall Lucy

Jencks, Charles: *American architectural theorist resident in the UK, author and landscape architect, born 1939*

Jencks famously provided the exact time and date coordinates for the end of **modernism** and – it follows – the commencement of what he calls (with a hyphen) Post-Modernism.

> Happily, it is possible to date the death of Modern Architecture to a precise moment in time. Modern Architecture died in St. Louis, Missouri on July 15, 1972 at 3.32 pm (or thereabouts) when the infamous Pruitt-Igoe scheme, or rather several of its slab blocks, were given the final *coup de grâce* by dynamite. (Jencks, 1977; updated 2002: 9)

The occasion was the ignominious end of the modernist dream of mass housing as a "machine for living." Jencks, who knew what he was talking about, having written an excellent study of *modern* movements in architecture (1973), saw that Saturday afternoon in the Mid-West as significant even though the building was not by Corbusier, Gropius, Mies van der Rohe or any other master of the International Style, but a budget-conscious "tower-and-slab" development (Urban, 2012) by a previously untried American architect called Minoru Yamasaki (more about him later). Nevertheless, it was a massive development, and dynamiting it represented for Jencks the defeat of modern architecture by its users – in this case, public authorities (most of the residents had already left). It was, he wrote (Jencks, 1977/2002: 9), "the first large-scale modernist housing scheme to be *blown up by public demand.*"

Less than 20 years after the Pruitt-Igoe complex was first occupied (in 1954–5), it was demolished. Its entire career bespeaks *post*modernism, not only up to and at the instant of detonation but especially since that moment, insofar as the postmodernism undermines and counters the progressive narrative of modernism, which Pruitt-Igoe certainly does. Indeed, its *petits récits* (see **metanarrative**) are more interesting than its fatal grandiloquence. For a start, as many have pointed out, the demolition process did not actually occur at the "precise moment" designated by Jencks: dynamiting began on March 16, 1972 and the site was not finally cleared until 1976. But that is not surprising, because this was a 57-acre complex of 33 high-rise residential slabs and 4 other buildings, with over 2,800 apartments, accommodating up to 15,000 tenants (Allen and Wendl, 2011). It was dismantled in stages. Nevertheless the *image* of its demise (a widely circulated news item) was very spectacular – "fatal" rather than "banal," in **Baudrillard**'s (1988a) terms. It started an international vogue for "shouting down," as it were, giant public housing developments that had once been the pride of modernism, but were now deemed unfit for human habitation. The latest of these was a plan by the Glasgow Housing Association (privatized successor to the City Council) in Scotland to blow up five towers – once the tallest residential structures in Europe – *live*, during the opening ceremony of the Commonwealth Games in 2014. The plan was shelved after widespread protest, even though two buildings in the Red Road Flats complex had already been dynamited and all the rest were empty except one (not scheduled for demolition) that was used to house asylum seekers. Later it was announced that the presence of asbestos required that the buildings be dismantled over 7 years, rather than in 15 seconds. They will share the banal fate of Quarry Hill in Leeds, England. Built between 1935 and 1941 to house over 3,000 people, it was at the time the largest public housing venture in Britain. Its plans featured – starred, in fact – in a landmark Griersonian documentary film, *Housing Problems* (1935), as the solution to Britain's Victorian slum problem. It duly became a notorious slum in its own right. In 1978, the entire complex was demolished. Quarry Hill's architects had been influenced by socialist housing in Vienna, and by a social housing scheme on the outskirts of Paris called *La Cité de la Muette* (Silent City), completed in 1934, which boasted France's first high-rise residential towers. This pioneering complex (harbinger of the Parisian *banlieue* whose modernist degradation is immortalized in Luc Besson's 2004 film *District B13*; *Banlieue 13* in French) never caught on with tenants either. It was commandeered by the Nazis after the Occupation of France. They found its U-shaped block-and-slab/tower form suitable for a concentration camp. Up to 75,000 Jews and other "undesirables" were interned and 67,000 of them deported by train directly from Drancy (as "Silent City" was now called) to Auschwitz, Sobibór and other death camps. After Liberation the complex lay empty or was used as a barracks until 1976, when the towers (but not the U-shaped "bar" or slab building) were demolished, to the despair of modernist architectural theorists, who lamented its wasted potential (Weddle, n.d.). As Florian Urban (2012: 53–5) put it, Muette/Drancy became a monument not to visionary architecture and industrial *mass housing* but to industrialized *mass murder*: "The former prison now stands like an eerie presage for similar blocks of the postwar era, which their marginalized and impoverished inhabitants often perceive as instruments for lifelong imprisonment" (2012: 55).

This perception was applicable in the case of Pruitt-Igoe, despite its American location away from Nazi atrocities. Nevertheless, its unusual name – and purpose – had its origins in racial segregation. The brief was for two sets of residences: the *Captain Wendell O. Pruitt Homes* and the *William L. Igoe Apartments*. The Pruitt Homes, for African-American tenants, were named after Wendell Pruitt, an air ace who came from St Louis and became a decorated war hero, fighting fascism in Italy. The US military was segregated in World War II, and Pruitt was one of very few Black fighter pilots to see active service, where he and his "wingman" gained fame as the "gruesome twosome" (Wartts, n.d.). The Igoe Apartments, for their part, were named for (white) US Congressman William Igoe (Democrat). His claim to fame was that he had voted against the US declaration of war against Germany in 1917.

When Pruitt-Igoe was first commissioned in 1951, both federal and local authorities practiced segregation:

> Yet in 1954, segregation in public accommodations ended with the Supreme Court's decision in Brown v. the Board of Education. Residents were already living in segregation at the still-incomplete Pruitt and Igoe homes when the St. Louis Housing Authority lifted racial restrictions. Most whites moved out. (Allen and Wendl, 2011)

Nobody admitted at the time that it was not postmodernism but institutional racism, "white flight" to the suburbs, and poor decisions by government that doomed Pruitt-Igoe. The desegregated complex struggled to fill its tenancies, and deterioration of the external environment (stairwells, galleries, elevators, open space) led to vandalism, violence, garbage and "rampant vacancy." Drug dealing and prostitution filled empty spaces; "occupancy rates continued to decline, crime rates climbed, and the most basic building management and maintenance were neglected" (Allen and Wendl, 2011).

As for the architect, Minoru Yamasaki had already washed his hands of it, having told *Architectural Forum* that "I never thought people were that destructive … It's a job I wish I hadn't done" (Bailey, 1965). Blaming the victim, Yamasaki went on to design the World Trade Centre in New York City (1970). He died in 1986, so did not live to see the implosion of a second example of his iconic modernism, the "twin towers," on 9/11.

It is hardly surprising that the St Louis site became the stuff of legend (filmmaker Chad Freidrichs unpicked that in *The Pruitt-Igoe Myth*, in 2011). However, the actual site remains derelict. It was leveled, fenced and abandoned. It still is. Of the original 57-acre site, 33 acres remain undeveloped: "The undeveloped part of the site is marked by several paths … Surrounding these paths … is a large forested area of both deciduous and coniferous trees, shrubs and other plants. … a prairie-like area exists between wooded areas" (Allen, 2011). The winning entry in a 2011–12 competition to imagine new uses for the site came up with an "ecological assembly line" – effectively an urban tree farm with aquaculture, education and recreation on the side (Dunbar and Wang, 2012). However, at the time of writing the site remained undeveloped (but thick with trees).

Charles Jencks saw Pruitt-Igoe as an example of the hubris of International Style architecture. The reality was certainly more complex, because of urban decline (St Louis was depopulating and still is), poverty, racial inequality, and the regulatory, budgetary and political constraints exercised over the project by the authorities responsible for it. Changes were forced on Yamasaki that he apparently fought hard to resist (Bailey, 1965). Nevertheless, in the end he did put up higher, cheaper slabs that mocked his original vision of an airy garden city. Ironically (first sign of postmodernism), that vision has at last returned to the cleared site, but without the architecture.

Meanwhile, Jencks himself could rightly lay claim to first mover advantage in developing the *concept* of postmodern architecture. His book *The Language of Post-Modern Architecture* (1977/2002) established and guided what soon became a dominant topic and some familiar tropes in urban design across the 1980s and 1990s. He introduced the ideas of hybridity, irony, reference back to the past as well as forward to the future, combining modernist universalism with local quotation, relying on what he called "double coding" (high and low **culture**, global and local, etc.). The style strives for communication and reflexivity, playfulness and a human mode of address, unlike the modernist "New Brutalism" beloved of Jencks's own teacher Reyner Banham.

In later editions (2002: 9), Jencks claims that Post-Modernism in architecture is resurgent, returning as a "major movement in the arts" after the turn of the millennium, "in all but name." In other words, it's no longer an architectural language but a social reality.

As for preferring verdant open spaces over hubristic towers, Jencks devoted much of his own talent in later years to the development of landscapes that represent an "architecture of hope" (Jencks and Heathcote, 2010). This refers to a project initiated by Jencks and his wife Maggie Keswick Jencks (1941–95), who lived with breast cancer from 1988, for the "enlightened provision of uplifting environments for cancer care" (Jencks, n.d.). They are part garden, echoing Jencks's own "Garden of Cosmic Speculation" (Jencks, 2003), part day-care center – landscapes and internal spaces "without too much architecture, please" (Jencks and Heathcote, 2010: 94). That's a challenging brief for even postmodern architects, but some of the world's most renowned have donated designs, including Jencks himself, Zaha Hadid, Richard Rogers and Rem Koolhaas. One of postmodernism's poster children, Frank Gehry, designed two centers. He noted that architectural aesthetics were not the first consideration:

> The building I designed in Scotland for Maggie's Centre in Dundee was not designed with her involvement. In fact, it is quite possible she would never have asked me to do one for her since her tastes were at variance with my work. I kept that in mind throughout my design process and threw out a few schemes that at the time I liked better imagining that she would not have liked them. When you know somebody like Maggie you don't want to disappoint her, whether she is alive or not. It turns out that that little Maggie's Centre in Dundee, looking back, was one of the best things I've ever done. (Jencks and Heathcote, 2010)

Instead of representing an authorial vision and damn the consequences, this "new hybrid" version of architecture (Jencks and Heathcote, 2010: 6) embodies Maggie Keswick Jencks's own desire for patients, their families and friends to "build a life beyond cancer," not in a functional or institutional space but in one that creates the right kind of atmosphere. As she put it: "Above all, what matters is not to lose the joy of living in the fear of dying" (Jencks, n.d.). In a book such as this, that version of postmodernism seems reasoned, humane, and overdue.

John Hartley

ABCDEFGHIJK**L**MNOPQRSTUVWXYZ

Lacan, Jacques: *French psychoanalyst and psychoanalytical theorist, 1901–81*

Lacan's work is often described as Freud filtered through the linguistics of Ferdinand de Saussure. Saussure sees the sign as both signifier and signified, with the two separated by the arbitrariness of the conventions that structure any language (see **semiotics**). Lacan, though, takes the further step of insisting that the signified is secondary and no more than an effect of the signifier.

But the signifier is nothing but pure difference, and any signifier is what it is only because of its difference from all the others. This open network of signifiers – the Symbolic – is at the heart of Lacan's thought, whose radicality is to provide a completely novel and far-reaching redescription of the terms of psychoanalysis. It's not difficult to see how this jostling and inchoate differentiality of the Symbolic can function as a framework for Freud's descriptions of the unconscious (see, for example, "The Dissection of the Psychical Personality" in Freud, 2001: vol. XXII). As one of Lacan's best-known aphorisms puts it, "The unconscious is structured like a language" (Lacan, 1993: 167).

Yet Lacan takes a while to get there. His early work is epitomized by the well-known piece on the so-called mirror stage, and the child's first recognition of its image in a mirror. Here, Lacan is still concerned mainly with what he calls the Imaginary. If the Symbolic is a matter of the purely differential, the Imaginary is a matter of identities and likenesses. Where the unconscious is structured like a language, the ego (with which the

A Dictionary of Postmodernism, First Edition. Niall Lucy.

Imaginary is largely concerned) is a hall of mirrors. There is something secondary about both ego and Imaginary. Long before it pays any attention to the mirror, and indeed long before it is even born, the child is always and already immersed in the Symbolic, in ways that it will only come to understand, if it does, in retrospect: spoken to and about, given a name, born into a web of symbolic relations of family, class, language and gender, already the object of desires that are as yet inscrutable to it.

The mirror-stage is probably the best-known aspect of Lacan's work, but it's easy to forget that it's a *false* start. If we find its obvious traces in almost all of his work up until the end of the 1960s (though rarely after that), it's in the sense of an initial hypothesis that didn't work, but whose failure has in true Hegelian fashion opened up the wealth of real questions that are to follow. What the mirror stage describes is the formation of the ego, and the optics of the mirror are those of the *object* reflected in it. The model for the ego is an object, and what that leaves out of play is the entire dimension of subjectivity, and in particular the unconscious dimension for which the Symbolic provides a model. (This is one of the reasons Lacan avoids that commonplace of much psychology, the term "self," carrying as it does so much freight of a personal, internal object.)

The Symbolic becomes Lacan's focus from the first of the 27-year seminar series, *Freud's Papers on Technique*, from 1953–4 (see Lacan, 1991). The ninth seminar (1961–2, see Lacan, 2011), for example, on Identification, begins with a consideration of how the way in which we imagine the ego is based on a misrecognition of our bodily image in the mirror. We might see ourselves as a bounded finite shape, but this irregular sphere is not really even a good description of the body, let alone of the subject. The body's boundaries, after all, are broken and almost fractal in the constant interchanges it must make with the world in order to survive. How much less is this an adequate model for subjectivity, when the breakup of even a bad relationship can be felt not just as a welcome freedom but as the threat of disintegration from within? In this seminar, Lacan begins to develop some of the less familiar topological surfaces he will introduce to do justice to the logic of the subject and its desires and drives: surfaces with only one side and one edge, such as the Möbius strip, or closed surfaces with no inside, like the Klein bottle and the cross-cap. The much-maligned "master-signifier" is not some sort of phallic despot controlling what can or can't be said, but a focal curvature of the Symbolic, like those upholstery buttons (*points de capiton*) that anchor a cushion Lacan, 2006: 681–2. Master-signifiers give a shape and a framework to the Symbolic; their loss is not a liberation, but the chaos of psychosis. They slip and change, frequently: a later seminar (the seventeenth, *The Other Side of Psychoanalysis*, Lacan, 2007) is devoted to the ways in which this happens.

All of this, like the Symbolic itself in this theoretical paradigm, is pre-individual: you don't invent a language, you're born into it. This is why Lacan can insist that psychoanalysis is not a psychology (Lacan, 2006: 672–3): psychology, as it must in order to be a positivistic science, treats the human subject as an object. It's why Freud described psychoanalysis as *meta*psychology: what there must be in order for there to be a human subject (Freud, 2001: vol. XIV). And it is also why when psychoanalysis comes to think the social and cultural (as it does recently with thinkers such as Slavoj **Žižek**), we are no longer in the realm of social psychology, extrapolating out from the individual as though the social and the cultural were nothing more than the sum of a very large number of individuals.

At the same time that Lacan is beginning to formulate the Symbolic, in the early-to-mid 1950s, the Real also becomes a consideration, and one that comes to dominate his later work. The Real is not something primal, the truth behind the Symbolic and the Imaginary. It's what fits into neither: undifferentiated, and thus not any conceivable part of the Symbolic, and impossible to put into any relationship with any object, and thus not any conceivable part of the Imaginary. The Real is an intrusion into our mental maps of the way the world behaves, like the step that's not there when you go downstairs; it affects us not as a revelation of the true state of things, but as trauma or panic, the shock of falling – physically, as we go downstairs, but also through a rent or tear in the Symbolic. It's the unpredictable throw of the dice, the vicissitudes of history and a world, and it comes to take on an increasingly important part in Lacan's thought, not as an outside to the Symbolic and the Real or their untouchable core so much as their necessary incompletenesses and contradictions. Around seminars XIX "*... or worse*" (Lacan, 2010 [Fr. 1971–2]) and XX *On Feminine Sexuality* (Lacan, 1999 [Fr. 1972–3]), sexual difference emerges as such a resistant rock of the Real on which the Symbolic founders: all of those familiar assignations of what's "masculine" and what's "feminine" attest to the repeated failure of the Symbolic to encompass sexual difference, and to the repeated impossibility of all Imaginary dyads in which the two sexes would serenely complement one another's gaze.

At the heart of the subject, then, there is not merely a lack – as there is for the Cartesian *cogito*, where once I've admitted that I can't discount the possibility that any possible given *content* of my thought might be delusion, what I'm left with as indubitable is the bare *form* of that completely empty

I think. Instead, for the Lacanian subject there's the twist of paradox, as Lacan notes in his own Cartesian variations: "I am thinking where I am not, therefore I am where I am not thinking … I think about what I am where I do not think I am thinking" (Lacan, 2006: 430). It's a twist we find elsewhere, in other forms (**Derrida**, **deconstruction**, **Lyotard**, **differend**, **metanarrative**, **truth**, to name only a few other entries), and one that becomes central to Žižek's thinking of **culture**.

Tony Thwaites

Lyotard, Jean-François: *French philosopher, 1924–98*

A prolific writer whose work is an experiment no less in style than thought, Lyotard's ideas can be organized roughly around three successive themes (albeit the "succession" is scrambled when it comes to the publication dates of the English translations): the libidinal (his focus in the early 1970s), the pagan (mid- to late 1970s) and the postmodern (late 1970s and beyond). Disaffected with what he saw as Marxism's totalizing approach to history, Lyotard came to regard social events not as products of large-scale historical structures but of heterogeneous forces and desires. In *Libidinal Economy* (1993 [Fr. 1974]), a book written after the fashion of an avant-garde **modernist** novel that has also been likened to "postmodern porn" (King, 1993/94), he argues that events are outcomes of "intensities" or "affects" akin to those associated by Freud with the libido. This "theoretical fiction" (Lyotard is careful to distinguish his approach from sociology in the standard sense) allows for the transposition of human sexual energy across to human society as a way of thinking about social relations differently, in terms of unrealized or under-developed potentialities that are held in check by official social structures in the form of politics, education, the law and so on. The meaning of social reality is controlled by these structures since they command the ways in which events should be interpreted "correctly," without regard for latent counter-interpretations.

Calling to be read as something other than philosophy, but not as a *non*-philosophical work, *Libidinal Economy* rejects systematic inquiry in favor of anarchic provocation, the point being to reveal that there is no point:

> we do not subordinate our anti-religious, that is to say, anti-capitalist, politics to knowing what the origin of meaning, that is to say, what surplus-value

> really is, not even to know that there is no origin and that it does not lack this or that, but is lacking as an origin, we want and do a dismembered, unaccountable politics, *godless* for politicians, and it is in this way that the *critique* of religion which we rebegin is no longer a critique at all, no longer remains in the *sphere* … of what it critiques, since critique rests in turn on the force of lack, and that *critique is still religion*. (Lyotard, 1993: 6)

The "religiosity" of the belief in Marxist solutions to social inequalities is the target here, the faith in Marx among many French intellectuals having been shaken if not shattered in the aftermath of the de Gaulle administration's defeat of the student-led nationwide revolts of May 1968. (De Gaulle was re-elected in a landslide victory the following month.) Lyotard's assertion of the pointlessness of trying to ground an idea of politics or society in an origin or a center, then, is itself pointed, being owed to a particular historical context out of which fellow Marxist "agnostics" **Deleuze and Guattari** had copyrighted the micropolitics of desire in the first installment of their "capitalism and schizophrenia" project, *Anti-Oedipus* (1983 [Fr. 1972]), written only a couple of years before Lyotard's book. Small wonder he refers to them, along with **Baudrillard**, as his "brothers" in *Libidinal Economy*, a work he later called "my evil book, the book of evilness that everyone writing and thinking is tempted to do" (Lyotard, 1988a: 13). (Note that Lyotard first published *Peregrinations* in English, in 1988. Its French "translation" appeared two years later.)

But if Lyotard was moved by the failure of the May '68 uprisings to reappraise his former commitment to Marxist politics as an effect of blind faith, he certainly didn't think of Marxism as the *only* form of secular religion. Religion, for Lyotard, arises from blind faith in any origin or unitary system, whether it be Marxist theory, representative democracy, the capitalist economy or, of course, God. Thus he sees social injustice as a product of the pious belief in universals, and it is only by breaking faith with such belief that justice may be extended to singular events and incommensurable differences denied the right to speak under a universal law of judgment. Justice is plural and impious, calling not for the righteous application of a universal rule in imitation of a monotheistic religion, but for a "paganism" that calls upon different gods to intervene in different situations: not one rule or a single set of rules, but many. A pagan or a "godless" justice would pass judgment in the absence of criteria, or at least without criteria laid out in advance, having abandoned all faith in the authority of any single story (Marxist, capitalist and so on) to reveal the essence or the underlying structure of the social contract. "Destroy narrative monopolies," Lyotard writes in the dialogue called "Lessons in Paganism," "both as exclusive themes (of parties) and as exclusive pragmatics (exclusive to parties and markets)" (Lyotard, 1989 [Fr. 1977]: 153).

The destruction is undertaken in *The Postmodern Condition: A Report on Knowledge* (1984 [Fr. 1979]), commissioned by the government of Quebec, in which contemporary culture is defined by the loss of faith in **metanarratives** that once served (or may be imputed to have done so, according to an ideal) as the organizing principles of collective social experience. The heterogeneous effects of postmodern language games undermine the power of "narrative monopolies" to explain history and shape the future while remaining oblivious to the **truth** claims of other stories and the different interests they may represent, the exclusion of others forging a consensus that leads to terror. A just society, then, would be governed by *dissensus*, a multiplicity of rules of judgment producing not only greater equity or more tolerance, but also a more diverse spectrum of knowledge.

Lyotard knows, however, that in most cases there is *not* a multiplicity of rules of judgment to appeal to when it comes to resolving a conflict between two or more parties in a dispute, for disputes tend to be decided by rules in the guise of "universals" belonging only to one side. In these instances – of what he calls the **differend** – conflicts cannot be resolved "for lack of a rule of judgment applicable" to all (Lyotard, 1988b [Fr. 1983]: xi). The subtitle of *The Differend: Phrases in Dispute* would appear to nominate language as the source of such irresolution, but for Lyotard a "**phrase**" is broader than simply a linguistic unit of sense or meaning. A phrase is like a move in a game (modeled on the theory of language games developed by Wittgenstein in *Philosophical Investigations* (2001), a key source of Lyotard's thinking in *The Differend* and *The Postmodern Condition*), where a game is defined by the set of rules belonging to it that are not applicable to other games. So while every phrase belongs to a particular "phrase regimen," examples of which include "reasoning, knowing, describing, recounting, questioning, showing, ordering, etc." (Lyotard, 1988b: xii), these regimens are incommensurable with one another: to demand that a phrase from one regimen be accountable to a different regimen is possible, but *only as a demand*. It's for this reason that Lyotard prefers not to offer a definition of "phrase" … because this would mean having to succumb to the demand of the phrase, *Give a definition of "phrase"!* It would mean having to link up to that phrase in a particular way, according to the rules of the phrase regimen of denotation. But the preference not to meet that demand is itself a phrase, which could perhaps be put (no doubt exaggeratedly) as follows: *Denotation is slavery! Multiplicity rules!*

When it comes to phrasing, for Lyotard, the devil is in the links. First, it isn't possible not to phrase and there is no such thing as a "non-phrase" or a "last phrase" (Lyotard, 1988b: xii). Second, anything can be a phrase, including "silence" (1988b: xii). So when a phrase "happens," it poses the question of how to link onto it:

> A phrase "happens." How can it be linked onto? By its rule, a genre of **discourse** supplies a set of possible phrases, each arising from some phrase regimen. Another genre of discourse supplies another set of possible phrases. There is a differend between these two sets (or between the genres that call them forth) because. they are heterogeneous. And linkage must happen "now"; another phrase cannot not happen. (Lyotard, 1988b: xii)

But while linkage is unavoidable, links are not predetermined: it's always possible that a link between this phrase and that one could have been otherwise. While one phrase event (and phrases are events because they *happen*) must lead to another, it cannot determine the regimen of the phrase event that follows: "to link is necessary; how to link is contingent" (1988b: 29).

Differends, however, aren't simply misunderstandings; they don't arise simply from breakdowns in communication. They occur whenever a link results in the failure to present what Lyotard calls a *wrong* understood as "a damage accompanied by the loss of the means to prove the damage" (1988b: 5), where the loss is caused by an inability to establish a link between heterogeneous phrase regimens. Wrongs, as distinct from damages, are *unpresentable*, and this leads to a dilemma:

> Either you are the victim of a wrong, or you are not. If you are not, you are deceived (or lying) in testifying that you are. If you are, since you can bear witness to this wrong, it is not a wrong, and you are deceived (or lying) in testifying that you are the victim of a wrong. Let *p* be: you are the victim of a wrong; *not p*: you are not; *Tp* [true positive]: phrase *p* is true; *Fp* [false positive]: it is false. The argument is: either *p* or *not p*; if *not-p*, then *Fp*; if *p*, then *not-p*, then *Fp*. (Lyotard, 1988b: 5)

Wrongs are therefore incompensable because what they "are" is unpresentable to legal discourse; yet there is often the feeling, after litigation has occurred, a war has ended or a political conflict has been resolved, that justice remains to be done. Such a feeling discloses the differend, in which "something 'asks' to be put into phrases" (Lyotard, 1988b: 13), calling for the invention of new idioms through which to express what cannot yet be phrased. It's our responsibility to testify to that feeling, Lyotard insists, in the name of what exceeds the calculations of the justice system or "the system" generally (as he sometimes likes to put it), and which, like Kant's sublime (1790), goes beyond the limits of available idioms to recognize or represent. Lyotard's "feeling," then, may be said to inaugurate a "weak" organizing principle, barely a principle at all, for a new sense of the political, similar perhaps to **Derrida**'s notion of the "new international" as the unofficial name of a "weak" alliance (without leadership, party or manifesto) whose solidarity is based on nothing more substantial than "a link of affinity, suffering and hope" (Derrida, 1994: 85). This would be a politics unrecognizable to politics as such, concerned not with the **representation** of what is taken to be known already but with the task of finding ways of responding to what is *felt* to be not yet known. "You can't make a political 'program' with it [the differend]," Lyotard writes (1988b: 181), "but you can bear witness to it."

Niall Lucy

Metanarrative: "I don't believe in magic," John Lennon sings with The Plastic Ono Band in the song called "God" (1970), before declaring his disbelief in other spiritual systems and idols from the I-Ching to The Beatles, via Jesus, Elvis and John F. Kennedy. What he believes in instead, all he believes in, is "Yoko and me." "The dream," he sings at the end of the song, the dream of a better world, perhaps, which might be said to have united the counterculture of the 1960s, "is over."

Lennon's "God" could be taken for a pre-emptive summary of **Lyotard**'s *The Postmodern Condition: A Report on Knowledge*, where he famously defines postmodernism by its "incredulity toward metanarratives" or grand unifying systems of belief (1984 [Fr. 1979]: xxiv). Now that we've lost faith in the "big" stories from the past whose promised happy endings in the form of less human misery, greater equality and fewer wars haven't eventuated, we're left only with the alternative of "little" stories (*petits récits*), micro-narratives, to believe in: "Yoko and me." Difference and not consensus is thus the order of the day. "Eclecticism is the degree zero," Lyotard writes, "of contemporary general culture: one listens to reggae, watches a western, eats McDonald's food for lunch and local cuisine for dinner, wears Paris perfume in Tokyo and 'retro' clothes in Hong Kong; knowledge is a matter for TV games" (1984: 76).

Previously, according to Lyotard, knowledge, especially scientific knowledge, served the agreed social function of improving the human condition; and so science was legitimated in the past by its service to the Enlightenment metanarrative of historical progress, "in which the hero of knowledge works

A Dictionary of Postmodernism, First Edition. Niall Lucy.

toward a good ethico-political end – universal peace" (1984: xxiii–iv). This is also the basis of the Marxist metanarrative of a promised egalitarian world to come, a promise that Marxism has not fulfilled. Incredulity toward metanarratives, then, may be accounted for in part as a response to the fact that things have *not* got better. As **Derrida** puts it in *Specters of Marx*, written not long after the first Gulf War: "never before have violence, inequality, exclusion, famine, and thus economic oppression affected as many human beings in the history of the earth and of humanity" (Derrida, 1994 [Fr. 1993]: 85).

Yet metanarratives continue to be invoked, especially by political leaders for the purpose of projecting an image of unified statehood. So, for example, in his second-term inauguration speech on 21 January 2013, US President Obama appealed to a binding sense of national identity defined as a collective "American" belief in the pursuit of happiness and freedom:

> Each time we gather to inaugurate a president, we bear witness to the enduring strength of our Constitution. We affirm the promise of our democracy. We recall that what binds this nation together is not the colors of our skin or the tenets of our faith or the origins of our names. What makes us exceptional – what makes us American – is our allegiance to an idea, articulated in a declaration made more than two centuries ago: "We hold these truths to be self-evident, that all men are created equal, that they are endowed by their Creator with certain unalienable rights, that among these are Life, Liberty, and the pursuit of Happiness." (Obama, 2013)

So powerful would these "**truths**" appear to be, indeed, that there could be nothing (with the exception of the divine proclamation of human rights) to object to here. Who doesn't (or would say they didn't) believe it would not be unequivocally good to have *more* freedom, *more* equality and *more* friendship in the world? Perhaps, then, it isn't metanarratives per se that are the source of general "incredulity" today, but rather the official institutions (governments, corporations, banks, universities and the like) entrusted to act in their name. Banks and corporations, after all, no less than governments and universities, are legitimated by their service to the *social* function of improving the human condition, and are denied legitimation when seen or thought to act from interests regarded as *self*-serving. If "the dream" is now thought to be over, surely the cultural cynicism this expresses is not directed at the ideals that metanarratives might be said to encapsulate, but at the motives of institutions whose self-interests conflict with the collective pursuit of happiness and freedom. Thus the Occupy "movement" is opposed not to the kind of democratic metanarrative invoked by Obama, but instead (according to OccupyWallStreet.org: #ows) to "the corrosive power of major banks and multinational corporations over the democratic process" (Anonymous, n.d.). #ows opposes the self-interests of corporate and other institutions *in the name of* the ideals Obama appeals to. Unsurprisingly, then, the Declaration of the Occupation of New York City by the NYC General Assembly is couched in language very similar to that used by Obama in his second-term inauguration speech:

> As one people, united, we acknowledge the reality: that the future of the human race requires the cooperation of its members; that our system must protect our rights, and upon corruption of that system, it is up to the individuals to protect their own rights, and those of their neighbors; that a democratic government derives its just power from the people, but corporations do not seek consent to extract wealth from the people and the Earth; and that no true democracy is attainable when the process is determined by economic power. We come to you at a time when corporations, which place profit over people, self-interest over justice, and oppression over equality, run our governments. We have peaceably assembled here, as is our right, to let these facts be known. (NYC General Assembly, 2011)

While providing evidence of the continuing currency of the Enlightenment metanarrative of emancipation, the Declaration also gestures to the increasing normalization of environmental concerns on behalf of the future of "the Earth." The popular acceptance, indeed, of scientific truth claims around the impact of global warming suggests that metanarratives are far from bankrupt today, although certainly public confidence in the willingness of authorities to act in the interests of future generations may be low. But whether it's attributed to cultural cynicism or incredulity, the contemporary loss of faith in metanarratives that Lyotard sees as the defining feature of postmodernity has led, he argues, to a general crisis of legitimation in *computerized* society. The ongoing digitization of data and information transforms knowledge into a commodity to be exchanged, in response to which the questions posed by Lyotard in the late 1970s remain pressing:

> Suppose, for example, that a firm such as IBM is authorized to occupy a belt in the earth's orbital field and launch communications satellites or satellites

> housing data banks. Who will have access to them? Who will determine which channels or data are forbidden? The State? Or will the State simply be one user among others? New legal issues will be raised, and with them the question: "who will know?" (Lyotard, 1984: 6)

The "mercantilization of knowledge" (1984: 5) and the question of knowledge ownership rob science and technology research of their legitimation, which for Lyotard used to derive from the assumption that scientific discoveries led to emancipatory social gains and would one day result in the fulfillment of absolute truth. Historically, then, science was seen to be producing more and more knowledge and bringing us closer and closer to global happiness and freedom. But after World War I a general skepticism arose (a mood characteristic of **modernism**) regarding the social benefits of science, and nowadays not even scientists are convinced that science holds the key to truth (see Briggs and Lucy, 2012a). As distinguished American paleontologist and evolutionary biologist Steven Jay Gould put it in 1981, coincidentally around the time of Lyotard's *The Postmodern Condition*:

> Science, since people must do it, is a socially embedded activity. It progresses by hunch, vision, and intuition. Much of its change through time does not record a closer approach to absolute truth, but the alteration of cultural contexts that influence it so strongly. Facts are not pure and unsullied bits of information; culture also influences what we see and how we see it. Theories, moreover, are not inexorable inductions from facts. The most creative theories are often imaginative visions imposed upon facts; the source of imagination is also strongly cultural. (Gould, 1981: 53–4)

By insisting on the "socially embedded" character of scientific activity, Gould comes close to Lyotard's conception of science as a particular kind of language game, a notion drawn from the later work of Wittgenstein (2001). Ideally, that is to say, scientific knowledge offers a pure description of the world as it is, expressed in statements or utterances of a "denotative" nature: *what goes up*, for example, *must come down*. By contrast, what Lyotard calls "narrative knowledge" is prescriptive, consisting of performative statements ("I do"), commands, instructions and requests ("Stop!," "OPEN OTHER END," "Please pass me a drink"). The different language games of science and narrative are incommensurable (the rules of one are not transferrable to the other), and the rules governing each type of game are not self-legitimating but simply the result of an implicit contract among players. While it's possible for a "move" or an utterance to effect a change in the rules ("[t]he most creative theories are often imaginative visions imposed upon facts"), generally the rules constrain what is able to be said and done within any particular game. For a statement to count as scientific it must therefore be denotative and not prescriptive, a distinction roughly attributable to the "speech act" philosophy developed by J. L. Austin in *How to Do Things with Words* (1975 [1955]), because science claims to describe the world and narrative seeks to change it.

Even a realist text offers not a description of the world as such, but the projection of a *possible* world. The "world" of realist cinema, realist painting, the realist novel, realist documentary or whatever is an imagined one, no matter how closely it might seem to resemble the world that science claims to represent, where **representation** is understood as pure, unmediated description. "The only truly false representation," as I'm fond of quoting McKenzie Wark to say, "is the belief in the possibility of true representation" (Wark, 2004: 208). On this view (a variation on what Derrida means by *différance*) there is always some play or movement between a representation and the thing it represents, otherwise the representation would *be* that thing. Thus *différance* – a neographism formed by the silent substitution of an "a" for the letter "e" in the French word *différence* ("to differ" or "to defer") – names the gap within the sign (see **semiotics**) by which meanings are made possible in a practical sense, but which also (to the extent that meanings are thought to be fixed and stable, **transcendental signifieds**) makes them *impossible*. Meaning is an effect of temporal deferral and spatial difference: *X* and *Y* are distinguishable from one another because they don't coexist in the same time and place (see Lucy, 2013a). But since even denotative statements are vulnerable to the movement of differing and deferring, then the threshold between denotatives and prescriptives is at least slightly hazier and less absolute than ideally required for the status of scientific knowledge to be understood as utterly context-independent or objective.

Consider the following denotative statement that once described an aspect of the world as it was known to be: *all swans are white*. It wasn't until the seventeenth century, when Dutch traders sailing for the Spice Islands (part of modern-day Indonesia) were sometimes blown off course and bumped into the Great South Land (Australia), that Europeans discovered otherwise: "downunder," all the swans were black! Yet while the *denotative* status of the original statement remains unaffected by this discovery, what the discovery reveals is not simply that the original statement was false, but also (returning to Gould's point above) that such statements are always "socially embedded." The statement *all swans are white* was never "unmediated" or "decontextual," in other words; and to the extent that it was "scientific" it was also "Eurocentric," a condition which might be said to apply to the European discovery of Australia in general. When Europeans found an antipodean mammal that laid eggs, for example, what else were they to do but name it after a monster? As I've written elsewhere:

> The echidna is different from the hedgehog, after all, and its Australianness resists translation into the languages of Europeans, except as a kind of curiosity – a freak of nature – that helps to define what "Australia" means to others. In its very name, given to the mother of all monsters in Greek mythology, the echidna is marked as a zoological outrage – a mammal that lays eggs! – from within the metaphysics of the natural sciences … [but] … this impossible Australian creature with the European name is "monstrous" only for taking the piss out of a certain taxonomy of living things. In outward appearance the echidna resembles the creature that is called the *hérisson* in French and, in Italian, the *istrice*: a small animal covered in spiky quills, which the English call a hedgehog. So the echidna's "monstrosity" lies in its *difference* from the European "original"; a difference that isn't scientific but cultural through and through. From the echidna's point of view, it's the *hérisson* that is the monster – a mammal that can't lay eggs! (Lucy, 2010b: 118–19)

Despite the condition of im-possibility that *différance* names, however, we can accept that denotative statements are taken to describe pre-existing states of affairs, while prescriptives can be seen to project or produce events that were not in the world beforehand and which may never be (a promise, for example, projects a future event that may or may not happen). But although science plays only one language game (denotation), according to Lyotard, it relies all the same for its legitimation on language games associated with storytelling; on the one hand, scientific research draws on narrative knowledge to justify its funding and explain its findings, and on the other science discredits narrative knowledge for not conforming to the language game of denotation. The worry, then, is that denotation will become the only language game in town as far as official understandings of knowledge go, for which the transformation of what used to be called "scholarship" in the humanities into what is now more or less universally known as "research" offers an example. The hegemony of the scientific language game forces humanities scholars to apply for funds by describing in advance the nature of the pre-existing problem they propose to solve, according to the rules of a game that humanities scholarship doesn't play.

It's important to stress that Lyotard does not argue that narrative knowledge is superior to or more "true" than scientific knowledge. The issue has to do instead with the likely consequences of restricting knowledge to mean only what is allowable from within the language game of science, thus limiting the number of players and discrediting the truth claims of other games. Further concern arises in the context of today's "performance management" regime for which the desired outcome of knowledge is no longer truth, but power:

> The production of proof, which is in principle only part of an argumentation process designed to win agreement from the addressees of scientific messages, thus falls under the control of another language game, in which the goal is no longer truth, but performativity – that is, the best possible input/output equation. The State and/or company must abandon the idealist and humanist narratives of legitimation in order to justify the new goal: in the **discourse** of today's financial backers of research, the only credible goal is power. Scientists, technicians, and instruments are purchased not to find truth, but to augment power. (Lyotard, 1984: 46)

The performativity imperative leads to a regime of "audit culture" and accountability, while the reduction of what qualifies as knowledge to what is produced by a single language game leads to what Lyotard calls "terror." "By terror," he writes, "I mean the efficiency gained by eliminating, or threatening to eliminate, a player from the language game one shares with him"; hence the player's silence or consent is achieved "not because he has been refuted, but because his ability to participate has been threatened" (1984: 63–4). Whatever thus delimits the number of players or the number of games counts as a form of terror, for Lyotard, which is not to argue that the suicide bomber and, say, the modern university are both playing the same language game or that each is playing a different game to exactly the same effect. Since it's clearly not the goal of universities to kidnap or kill staff and students in order to assert the higher authority of the language game of performativity, however, then what does it mean to claim that terror operates by excluding others from this or that game as well as by excluding other games from being played? The answer that Lyotard gives in conversation with Jean-Loup Thébaud in *Just Gaming* is that we must seek, on behalf of an idea of justice, to "maximize as much as possible the multiplication of small narratives" (Lyotard and Thébaud, 1985 [Fr. 1979]: 59) or language games to guard against the domination of allowable moves and outcomes by any single game. "Just" gaming therefore provides others with as much opportunity as possible to play their games, which is why terrorism is unjust for seeking to stop them from doing so. Once the hostages have been killed, they can no longer "play the game of the just and the unjust" (Lyotard and Thébaud, 1985: 67).

Again, the effects of unjust gaming are not identical across all possible forms: players killed by suicide bombers are prevented from speaking "otherwise" far more finally and absolutely than players who might be excluded from access to research funding because their projects are deemed illegitimate for having an inefficient "input/output equation." Countless other comparisons could be made here: the discriminatory effects of first-world sexism, for example, by which women are excluded from becoming players in the unjust language game of patriarchy, are not the same as those of institutional racism in the West and elsewhere, by which the exclusion of non-whites from first-world metanarratives of social identity and nationhood may be said to result in disproportionately high incarceration rates and disproportionately low life expectancies among people of color (certainly these and other shameful indicators are unjustly true of the social experience of Australian Aboriginal people). Lyotard's point, then, is that justice is served by social conversations that maximize participant diversity and narrative multiplicity, so that no one group of players or one set of rules can dominate what is sayable. Contrary to the consensus politics advocated by **Habermas** (1970; 1972), Lyotard's idea of a just society promotes diversity, heterogeneity and *dis*sensus.

But not only the interests of justice would be served by remaining open to the possibility of new moves and new language games arising from such conversations. Knowledge, too, would be expanded and enriched if freed from the "performativity principle," Lyotard argues, since the principle is based on a false conception of society as a rational system modeled after a computer:

> The true goal of the system, the reason it programs itself like a computer, is the optimization of the global relationship between input and output – in other words, performativity. Even when its rules are in the process of changing and innovations are occurring, even when its dysfunctions (such as strikes, crises, unemployment, or political revolutions) inspire hope and lead to belief in an alternative, even then what is actually taking place is only an internal readjustment, and its result can be no more than an increase in the system's "viability." The only alternative to this kind of performance improvement is entropy, or decline. (Lyotard, 1984: 11–12)

The problem with the performativity principle is that it can't account for the "non-algorithmic" or "asystematic" features of the system it seeks both to reproduce and measure. Breakthroughs in knowledge occur not from following prescriptive rules, but often as a result of introducing new moves to existing games or inventing new games altogether, an extemporized approach to knowledge production which applies even to scientific breakthroughs: science, as Gould puts it, "progresses by hunch, vision, and intuition." The progress or advancement of scientific knowledge (as opposed to the routine reproduction of what is known already) proceeds not prescriptively, but (in Lyotard's terms) *paralogically*.

From the Greek *para-* (alongside, against, beyond) + *logos* (reason), what Lyotard calls "paralogy" refers to knowledge arrived at unpredictably, beyond or against reason, by other than straightforwardly rational or standardly methodological means (see also **paraliterature**). Paralogy is thus a far better (more just and more productive) principle of legitimation than performativity, since the latter derives its authority from "the ideology of the 'system,' with its pretensions to totality" (Lyotard, 1984: 65). Hence the limits of a totalizing approach to scientific legitimation are revealed in its narrowing of the range of possible research outcomes (confining these to the repetition of the same) and its misrepresentation of ongoing research activities within an increasingly disparate field:

> Postmodern science – by concerning itself with such things as undecidables, the limits of precise control, conflicts characterized by incomplete information, "*fracta*," catastrophes, and pragmatic paradoxes – is theorizing its own evolution as discontinuous, catastrophic, nonrectifiable and paradoxical. It is changing the meaning of the word *knowledge*, while expressing how such a change can take place. It is producing not the known, but the unknown. And it suggests a mode of legitimation that has nothing to do with maximized performance, but has as its basis difference understood as paralogy. (Lyotard, 1984: 60)

Performativity, then, is aligned with the reproduction of the known; paralogy, with the production of "the unknown." Unleashing the potential of micro-narratives both to proliferate and to effect change, paralogy is closer than performativity to the pragmatics of actual scientific research practices. "The specificity of science," as Lyotard quotes French communications and information technologies scholar Phillippe Breton to say, "is in its unpredictability" (Lyotard, 1984: 100, n. 207).

But unpredictability is not exclusive to science since it is also a general feature of culture, once culture is allowed to be understood as something other than a totalizing "system." Take the example of the Hollywood film industry across the past decade or so, for which the input/output equation could be summarized as follows: minimum narrative variation = maximum box office return. Blockbuster metanarratives have dominated the industry in recent times, the formula for global profitability seeming to lie in the simplicity of the moral contrast between good and bad characters, the high predictability of story arcs and the wow factor associated with CGI-enabled special effects. The *Batman*, *Spiderman*, *Iron Man*, *Star Wars*, *Twilight* and *Harry Potter* franchises are all examples of the type, which isn't to deny that some would-be blockbusters of the period didn't bomb: *Red Planet* (2000), *The Alamo* (2004), *Speed Racer* (2008) and *John Carter* (2012) are among the biggest financial disasters in cinema history, and yet each of these films is more or less faithful to the formula outlined above. Knowing what "worked" in the case of some successful movies (or other cultural productions) doesn't guarantee that the application of that knowledge will lead to success in the future, because culture is not a totalizing system.

Notwithstanding the ultimate unruliness of the input/output equation, however, it's clear that mainstream Hollywood cinema is governed by the performativity principle, and the economics of mass appeal have tended to narrow the range of viable cinematic moves. Television, by contrast, took a paralogical turn with the increased availability of cable licenses in the US in the mid-1990s, as producers targeted a market for narrative innovation among small, mostly middle-class audiences for whom the moral complexities and novelistic story arcs of series ranging from HBO's *The Sopranos* (1999–2007), *The Wire* (2002–8), *Deadwood* (2004–7) and *True Detective* (2014–) to MGM/FX's *Fargo* (2014–) and AMC's *Breaking Bad* (2008–13) and *Mad Men* (2007–15) created enough fan loyalty to compensate for a lack of smash-hit status. Exemplified by the transformation of *Breaking Bad*'s Walter White from mild-mannered high-school chemistry teacher cum reluctant meth cook into badass megalomaniacal drug lord, these and other recent cable series have changed the rules of television. The game is no longer confined to broadcasting variations on more or less the same story to mass audiences, since the narrowcasting of micro-narratives to small, targeted audiences is also proving to be lucrative. Digital technologies and **new media**, meanwhile, have changed the meaning of television as hardware in the form of a receiving set, given that we now watch shows on our laptops, tablets and mobile devices; and the baby boomer experience of scheduled network programming has also become redundant: no longer simply the "small-screen" equivalent of cinema, by which audiences are assembled according to prescribed locations in time and place, television now includes what we watch on DVD and via file downloads at our own discretion.

In Lyotard's terms, then, the production of little narratives by cable television (as against the reproduction of the metanarrative of the Hollywood blockbuster) is an expression of "the quest for paralogy" (Lyotard, 1984: 66) that leads not only to cultural renewal but is also necessary to the improved performance of "the system," protecting it from "its own entropy," since "the novelty of an unexpected 'move' … can supply the system with that increased performativity it forever demands and consumes" (1984: 15). The new utterances of cable television may thus await incorporation into the lingua franca of Hollywood cinema in the future, just as the mainstream music industry's appropriation of the look and sound of **punk** in the late 1970s could be said to have reinvigorated that industry. Yet while examples of paralogical cultural and knowledge production may abound (consider the thriving "indie" music scene in Beijing at present, loosely organized around bands such as Carsick Cars, Hedgehog, Mr Graceless, Birdstriking, Skip Skip Ben Ben and many others), the public's preference for the commercial products of the performativity principle should not be used to justify an avant-gardist attitude of snobbery toward the objects of popular taste and pleasure. Lyotard's point is not, in any case, that metanarratives of consensus appeal to the lowest common denominator, but rather that they limit what it may be possible to know; regarding scientific knowledge, therefore, paralogy is simply a more productive principle of legitimation than performativity. His further point is that paralogy better serves an idea of justice, because no single language game can claim to be in charge of the rules when there are many open-ended little narratives in play. Thus (1984: 67), paralogy "sketches the outline of a politics that would respect both the desire for justice and the desire for the unknown."

Niall Lucy

Minor(itarian): Something said to be minor (a minor league, a minor celebrity, a minor injury, an adolescent) is taken to be lesser in importance, impact or scale than the standard against which it is measured. Minority status is thus a kind of side effect or a supplementary condition, such that women can outnumber men and still be a minority because "man," exemplified by the image of da Vinci's "Vitruvian Man" (1492), stands for the primary subject of human being. But what if minority status wasn't simply an effect of falling short of a norm, a standard or an archetype; what if being minor (or *becoming* minor) were a distinct and positive force in its own right? This is the question **Deleuze and Guattari** pose in *Kafka: Toward a Minor Literature* (1986 [Fr. 1975]), where a minor literature (**paraliterature**, perhaps?) would not be deemed inferior to the canon.

The features of a minor literature, according to Deleuze and Guattari, are threefold: "the deterritorialization of language, the connection of the individual to a political immediacy, and the collective assemblage of enunciation" (1986: 18). By "deterritorialization" they mean a sort of undoing or a decontextualization: an immigrant population, for example, is deterritorialized from its homeland, affording members an opportunity to become someone other than they might have been according to the expectations of their **culture** of origin, which would have predetermined the kind of life they could have led. It follows from this that the more "immigrant" or "multicultural" a nation's population is (think of Australia or the US), the more "free" its people are to choose how they want to live. Historically, though, nations with high immigrant populations tend to identify (through official and popular forms) with a single "mother" country or founding culture – Britain, in Australia's case – as the source of the new nation's values, traditions and way of life. Hence the potentially liberating effects of deterritorialization in Australia have been *reterritorialized* (order has been restored) through Australia's self-representation as a nation steeped in British heritage; indeed, it's the British monarch (Queen Elizabeth II at present) who is Australia's constitutional head of state, the reserve powers of the Crown being vested in the Governor-General of the Commonwealth of Australia as the Queen's representative. So while non-British immigration has helped to deterritorialize Australia's cultural debt to the United Kingdom, creating opportunities for multiple ways of life by undermining or undoing the authority of the British model, the force of that deterritorialization has been curtailed by the monocultural reterritorialization of Australia as a nation forged in the likeness of the UK. Deleuze and Guattari might say that one effect of this, operating not only through the Australian constitution but also across Australian television screens and the mediasphere more generally, is to close off possibilities for living. As Claire Colebrook puts it: "life," for Deleuze, "is not reducible to what has actually been produced, to the world as it has unfolded; for life, when thought properly, is a power or potential to create (and *not* the creation *of* some proper or destined end)" (Colebrook, 2006: 4). If the "Australian" way of life is rooted in British values and traditions, in other words, and the goal of future generations is to reproduce this norm or archetype, then Australians could be only *a people who are* and not, more radically and creatively, "a people to come" (see Colebrook, 2009). Such a people (a people to come) would perhaps be fully deterritorialized, although in practice the processes of deterritorialization and reterritorialization seldom reach an end point (exceptions would include fascist and theocratic states), but instead remain in flux.

All the same, deterritorialization is not exclusively a good or a positive force. The British colonization of Australia in the seventeenth century is an example of "bad" deterritorialization, resulting in the dispossession of Aboriginal people from their homelands and subjecting them to reterritorialization as the assimilated subjects of English laws and the English language. Generally, though, deterritorialization refers to processes aided by technology that enable flows of knowledge, goods and individuals beyond national borders: Facebook, for example, could be said to deterritorialize nation-state citizenship and connect us with others from around the world (see Hartley, Lucy and Briggs, 2013), while the democratizing influence of social media (especially Twitter) in enabling the Arab Spring is now widely acknowledged (see Schroeder, Everton and Shepherd, 2012). What might be called the primal movement or process of deterritorialization, though, is not limited to developments in new technology: "Music," Deleuze and Guattari write in *A Thousand Plateaus* (1987 [Fr. 1980]: 333), "is a deterritorialization of the voice, which becomes less and less tied to language, just as painting is a deterritorialization of the face."

Niall Lucy

Modernism: No less than "postmodernism," the term "modernism" is fraught with controversy. Some see it as defining a set of social, cultural and political ideas coinciding with the European democratic revolutions of 1848 (the so-called Spring of Nations); others see the term as a meaningful description of social attitudes associated with the Jazz Age of the 1920s, where the liberalism of that decade is understood as a reaction to the militarism of

World War I. Further controversy surrounds the meaning and relevance of modernism in the present, with some claiming that modernism is still going strong today (so that postmodernism is just a phase within modernism or **modernity** itself) while others argue that it ended somewhere around the late 1950s with the emergence of teenage popular **culture** and an ever more ironic attitude to authority. Those who see it as ending when postmodernism "began" (in the 1950s or 1960s) are inclined to look back on modernism as an aesthetic movement defined by its nostalgia for a less mechanized or industrial past, which was therefore more authentic, whereas those who regard modernism as a still-active force tend to stress the reformist or progressive nature of modernist ideas, art and social policy (see Nicholls, 1995).

Generally, when "modernism" is taken to refer only to the interests and pursuits of the avant-garde it is thought to be a spent force. On this view, albeit not for **Lyotard**, postmodernism comes *after* modernism. But for those who see it as a more encompassing set of social, cultural and political issues, "modernism" continues to mark our time today as radically different from previous times. Even simply as a cultural movement, though, belonging only to an aesthetic coterie of artists, writers and designers, it can't be said that modernism has had no social or political effects. Certainly it was held to do so by the Third Reich, for example, which regarded modernist art as degenerate. In the infamous *Entartete Kunst* ("Degenerate Art") exhibition in Munich, in 1937, which traveled shortly afterwards across Germany and into Austria, paintings by those who are regarded as modernist masters today (including Picasso, Klee, Chagall, Kandinsky, Munch, Matisse and many others) were shown as examples of the "degeneracy" of modern ideas and values, born of modern racial "impurity." Surprisingly few of the paintings were by Jewish artists, but all were intended to be seen as the deranged expressions of the intellectually and morally depraved. More than three million visitors are estimated to have attended the exhibition, making *Entartete Kunst* the first blockbuster art show of the twentieth century.

What, then, did the Nazis so object to in the paintings? Undoubtedly they were seen as an offense to fascist ideology, calling for a response that was predictably extreme. But while the Nazi propaganda machine took exceptional offense to modernist art, in other ways its attitude was typical of a conservative response to anti-traditional approaches to the question of **representation**. Hitler and Goebbels wanted art to re-present the world according to their ideological view of it, which is to say they wanted it to construct or project that view. They wanted art to be "heroic," in imitation of the ideological belief that the German *volk* shared a common historical destiny and cultural spirit. To this end they favored larger-than-life scenes of strapping, shirtless laborers and farm hands set against idyllic cityscapes and romanticized rural backgrounds, flooded in light. Such art was their realism, compared to which the shattered-mirror effect of a Picasso or the childlike images of a Chagall could be seen only as degenerate and corrupting. A similar ideological aesthetic was enforced through the "socialist realism" program under the Stalinist regime in the Soviet Union at the time, prohibiting representations other than of shiny, happy workers in party-approved domestic, factory and rural tableaux.

While fascist responses to modernist experimentation in the visual arts were extreme, however, it can't be said that a distaste for the new knows no forms of expression in the present. Take the annual controversy surrounding the Turner art prize at the Tate Gallery in London, where the imprimatur of the judging panel rarely meets with popular approval. The winning entry for 2001, for instance, Martin Creed's *The Lights Going On and Off*, was so literalist that, according to one journalist, "many of those who have seen it were unaware that it was anything more than dodgy wiring" (Gibbons, 2001). Yet the judges "loved it for its daring and for driving some traditionalists to apoplexy" (Gibbons, 2001). Opinion is even more greatly divided on the work of another Turner winner, the British artist Damien Hirst, famous internationally for his glass-cased installations of animals suspended in formaldehyde. Still today, then, long after Hitler and Stalin sought to regulate the meaning and purpose of art, it remains a concept open to multiple interpretations.

This wasn't always the case. Rubens and da Vinci, say, were never controversial in the ways that Creed and Hirst are today. Among the many reasons for this, modern systems of transportation and communication play a fundamental role: from the steam train to the Internet, ideas and images became increasingly "global" after about the middle of the nineteenth century. Technologies of telephony, photography, flight and so on gave increasing mobility to ideas, people and representations. But in the context of an ongoing technological revolution, how could a notion of so-called traditional society, or the traditional meaning of art, be sustained? It's the very concept of "tradition," indeed, which modernism might be said to challenge.

Marx was among the first to acknowledge this, through his theory of alienation. The labor system under industrial capitalism which was well established by the mid-nineteenth century, Marx argued (see for example *Wage Labour and Capital*, 2004 [Ger. 1849]), sets workers at a distance from the things they produce, since those things are owned not by workers but by capitalists who buy the workers' labor. Under capitalism, then, workers are employed not as social beings, but as instruments in the service of capitalist production. "Alienated" from themselves and each other as social individuals, workers have value only as a collective labor *force*, which of course Marx understood could be turned back against the capitalist system itself. So in Marx's view modern capitalism changed the so-called traditional idea of work and work relations, to the cost of something like authentic social being. While this is still a powerful political idea (albeit a contested one), a more general sense of social alienation, unrestricted to relations governing capital and wage labor, marks the response of many modernist writers, artists and others to the question of existence in the early part of the twentieth century, especially in the aftermath of the Great War. Suddenly the triumphant wonders of the machine age, which had turned Europe into a slaughterhouse, were made over into instruments of terror, alienation and despair. In the wake of the war's unprecedented death toll, not to mention the traumatic after-effects of the Bosch-like carnage and desolation, modern life had never seemed so medieval.

Hence a despondent sense of individual alienation and social dissolution sets a key tone in many modernist works of the early part of the twentieth century. The T. S. Eliot poems, "The Love Song of J. Alfred Prufrock" (1915) and especially *The Waste Land* (1922), are among the best known of these, but themes of alienation are writ large also in many other works of the period. American writer Sinclair Lewis's 1921 novel *Main Street*, for example, organizes a theme of modern estrangement around some of the disturbing effects of small-town disaffection, especially on women. In the classic 1927 German expressionist film *Metropolis*, by Austrian director Fritz Lang, a similar theme is played out on a grander scale, with estrangement figuring as a brutally literal fact of life for the working underclass of the film's futuristic city. Functioning only as expendable machinic parts and instruments, the workers are confined to a nightmarish, subterranean world of unimaginable drudgery and life-threatening exhaustion, to serve the mysterious interests of those living in the corporate city-state above. Enslaved and out of sight, the workers' relationship to modern metropolitan life is literally one of alienation in the form of being excluded from society.

But while alienation is a strong theme in much of the art of the post-World War I period, the 1920s (for artists and writers alike) was also a time of liberation. American writers like F. Scott Fitzgerald, Gertrude Stein and

Ernest Hemingway, for example, discovered Paris and other European cities, giving them access to ideas and experiences beyond the limits that would have been imposed on them traditionally by virtue of their place of birth, and in turn Europe discovered jazz. In broad social terms, the Jazz Age saw a relaxation of the censoriousness of pre-war, Victorian and Edwardian discourses on sexuality, gender, dress and public comportment. In economic terms the war effort which had ruined Europe's finances gave American capitalism access to new markets, leading first to the worldwide dominance of Hollywood cinema and ultimately to what is now called **globalization**. None of which is to say that the liberalism of the age was entirely without contradiction, or entirely socially progressive. Stein, for instance, despite her exposure to Parisian culture and artistic society, was a supporter of Fascist leader Francisco Franco in the Spanish Civil War of 1936–9 and later of the Nazi-installed Vichy government in France during World War II. For its part Europe was far from consensually comfortable with the spread of American popular culture at the time: a report commissioned by the BBC in 1929, for example, refers to the US culture industry as "the Transatlantic octopus" (cited in Frith, 1983: 103).

Nothing to do with modernism is fixed, then, and it may be that this is all we can use to define it. Compared to previous times, modernism is characterized by a general sense of the unfixity of things. With the appearance of skyscrapers, the traditional idea of what a city should look like changed. The arrival of the steam train changed the time it took traditionally to get from one place to another, which changed again with the development of flight. Car ownership (made possible by mass production) changed the range of what individuals could do and where they could go in a normal day. The Great War changed the idea of traditional warfare, and changed ideas about machinery. Photography and cinema changed ideas about representation, especially in the traditional arts. Following Marx the traditional understanding of relations between capital and labor changed, along with ideas about politics and society. From about the middle of the nineteenth century onward, increasingly rapid change replaced longstanding tradition as the order of the day. As never before, modernists had things to look at and think about – not only planes, trains and automobiles, but also factory assembly lines and mass destruction – which changed ideas about reality.

This is not to deny that some very fixed ideas about such things as art, society, morality, politics and the like are not still powerful today, exemplified by public opposition to the Turner Prize and official support for the war in Iraq. The justification of art (as with the justification of US foreign policy in the Middle East), in other words, continues to rest for some on a bedrock of fixed and stable meanings, as if it were set in stone that the real is always distinguishable from its representations (see **simulation**). By the same token, to suggest that modernists may have thought differently about reality, seeing it perhaps as an effect of perspective or positioning, is not to suggest they did so as a determined consequence of new technologies. It is not as though, after photography and the cinema, modernist artists and writers stopped doing realism altogether, suddenly turning their minds en masse to cubism or surrealism. They didn't get from Dickens to Dada overnight. The point simply is that even if new technologies are inseparable from the very idea of modernism, that idea is not reducible to them or determined by them. Cameras, cars and telephones did not give rise to modernism in a necessary sense, any more than modernism was made inevitable by World War I or the Jazz Age.

But while it's obvious that cameras, cars and telephones were not a part, say, of Shakespeare's world, the role they played in producing modernist ideas about democracy, temporality, subjectivity, reality and the future (which were not a part of Shakespeare's world either) is not so obvious. Nor should we suppose that modernists held unanimous views on a concept like democracy, or any other concept for that matter. Stein's sympathy for fascism is but one example of the fact that modernists were not aligned politically around the left, just as the right-wing leanings of Eliot, Ezra Pound, W. H. Auden and many others show that the post-war political outlook of the avant-garde was far from unanimously liberal-democratic or socially progressive. Around the same time, however, the Bloomsbury Group in London (a loose set of Cambridge University graduates whose most famous members were the writer Virginia Woolf and, in the early years, the economist John Maynard Keynes) preached and practiced liberation in regards to social, aesthetic and sexual matters. In this respect the "Bloomsberries," as they were sometimes called, held views and practiced a lifestyle ahead of their times, albeit for the most part they were not self-consciously activist or political in doing so.

In its earliest phase modernism is associated with a self-conscious rejection of tradition by the new guard (the avant-garde) in the arts generally, but especially among painters (see Greenberg, 1939). The rejection of perspective by Braque and Picasso is the obvious case in point here. But if the repudiation of tradition was very much an acquired taste before World War I, it became more widespread in the 1920s. Many saw the devastation caused by the war as a shocking rebuke of the very idea of tradition itself: if the killing fields of Europe were a product of pre-war traditions of social and political governance, traditional morality and traditional ideas about art – it was these traditions that had to be overthrown and re-made anew. What is the point of realism, for example, after the unimaginable reality of World War I? Who could believe that the old system of traditions, under which millions had lost their lives, was wedded to an idea of historical progress?

So in a sense we might say that the event of World War I (which includes its aftermath) led to a loss of faith in **metanarratives**, which according to Lyotard (1984) is a distinguishing feature of *post*modernism. While some see postmodernism simply as an extension of high modernism, then, it could be said, too, that modernism itself has always been "postmodern," more or less from the start (see **Jameson**, 1991; McHale, 1992). But there need not be any reason for choosing between these seemingly different "social" origins, as it were, in regards either to modernism *or* postmodernism. "Most people," as Lyotard puts it, referring to today, "have lost the nostalgia for the lost narrative" (1984: 41). Stories about when modernism ended or when postmodernism began are not the point, in other words. All such stories rely on a structure of historicization, compelling one periodic force or movement to succeed another in a never-ending continuum of neatly dated origins and terminations. But this nineteenth-century positivist ideal of knowledge is what modernism, let alone postmodernism, can be said to reject (see **Foucault**). Freud's theory of the unconscious, for example, to add to our list of radical breakaways from tradition, posits a disruptive and enabling force of "hidden" desires, repressions and affects as an essential component to any conception of who we are (see *Interpretation of Dreams*, Freud, 2010 [Ger. 1899]). After Freud, therefore, how could we continue to think of ourselves as autonomous, rational subjects?

Needless to say, the point of this entry is no more to *define* modernism than the point of this book is to define postmodernism. Attempts to locate either of these terms historically always seem to encounter as a problem the fact that each stares into the other, as if into a mirror, at certain times and places. Likewise, attempts to separate them according to different sets of ideas or attitudes tend to overlook the many similarities and overlaps between those sets. There is no clear-cut distinction between modernism and postmodernism, in a word, no clear way of deciding when either begins. Very generally speaking, though, "modernism" is taken to refer usually to cultural (and sometimes political) receptions of commodities and technologies associated with the first half of the twentieth century. These fall into two main types: the early to mid phases are characterized by a nostalgia for lost systems of belief and a stumbling search for new systems, while the high modernist phase (which may be indistinguishable from postmodernism) confidently embraces the aesthetic and social possibilities that new forms and technologies of mass production and communication offer. Such confidence is exemplified in the clean lines and modern building materials (concrete, steel and glass) of modernist architecture from the mid-to-late 1920s, which came to be known as the "international style" (see **Jencks**). Famously summing up the logic of that style, one of its leading exponents, Swiss architect Le Corbusier, declared in his influential 1923 book *Vers une architecture* that buildings are "machines for living in" (Corbusier, 2007: 29), and whether that was a modernist or a postmodern thing to say matters very little. What matters is that he could not have said it at just any time in history. Plato, Shakespeare and Kant, for instance, could not have re-imagined buildings as machines, because they did not live in a world of planes, trains and automobiles, let alone one of iPads, laptops and mobile phones. In themselves, these and other commodities and technologies of transport and communication neither define nor determine modern or postmodern culture. Instead, what may be said to distinguish that culture (or those cultures) from classical and neo-classical times alike are the *questions* that such commodities and technologies pose for the very concept of culture itself.

Niall Lucy

Modernity: Depending on which historian you read, the printing press was invented by Johann Gutenberg in Germany or by Laurens Janszoon Coster in the Netherlands somewhere around the 1450s. In fact (according to *Wikipedia*) it was invented in China some four hundred years earlier, although its use there was not widespread and the Chinese version did not include movable type or precision metal dies. Questions of attribution aside, however, the invention of the printing press in Europe in the middle of the fifteenth century is taken usually to mark the start of modernity, which begins therefore with the arrival of a new communications technology.

This is not to say that today's word-processing software is a direct offshoot of fifteenth-century movable type, or that the Internet is descended straight from the printing press. But certainly it seems fair to say that post-medieval history – modernity – is distinguished by expanding systems of information and communication flows, associated with technologies of the printing press, steam power, combustible energy, the telegraph and so on – in a word, by **new media**. The disseminatory force of these and other modern technologies allowed ideas and representations to be extended and reproduced, as well as transformed, across intervals of time and space which the ancient and medieval worlds could not have dreamt of. For the first time in history, then, early moderns had at least in-principle access to ideas, images and information whose purview in a sense was global. But of course this didn't happen straightaway, and indeed it might be said we're waiting for it to happen still (see **Habermas**). As illustrated by the irreconcilably competing ideas, images and information surrounding the present war in Iraq, what is sometimes called the project of modernity has not led to uncontested, universal **truth**. Neither have the effects of technology since the Middle Ages been only beneficial: while modernity can be credited with reducing infant-mortality rates and deaths from childbirth in developed countries, for instance, along with eradicating many diseases, it must also take responsibility for Auschwitz and Hiroshima. For every claim that progressively liberal rights have been won for citizens under modernity there is a counter-claim, in the form of such anti-modern outrages as Abu Grahib or Guantanamo Bay. For all that the project of first-world women's liberation is now well advanced, the starting pistol has yet to be fired in many parts of the third world. For all the undoubted advantages of a modern lifestyle, the environmental damage caused by modern industry is a matter of increasing concern.

The story of modernity is not simply one of progress and **globalization**, but rather of an ongoing tension between progress and catastrophe. From dark satanic mills to unenlightened totalitarianisms of left, right and theocratic persuasions, the history of modernity is rent by anti-modern interests, forces and events. In short, modernity remains far from a universally happening thing.

Niall Lucy

New media: The term "new" media implies some sort of opposition between new and old media, and tends to bring with it certain habits of narrating how media change. If one kind is old and the other is new, then there are likely also to be some opposed qualities that distinguish the old and the new. If the old is hierarchical, centralized, homogeneous, one-way and authoritarian, then the new will be democratic, decentralized, diverse, multilateral and libertarian.

There's a more or less endless literature, mostly dating from the 1990s, that hinges on firstly making the rhetorical gesture of separating old from new, then assigning different qualities to the two media types. Most usually these have been optimistic about the new media, but sometimes the rhetorical structure is reversed, and the new appears as negating some treasured value of old media.

Study of the phenomenon initially described as "new media" has been a gradual process of replacing that neat binary with more supple and enabling languages. In this respect the trajectory of new media studies is not unlike that of postmodern studies.

Discourse around new media was usually only casually grounded in an understanding of technical, economic or cultural aspects of allegedly "new" media. As Alexander Galloway shows in *Protocol* (2003) the Internet can appear to be a democratic, distributed network if examined only in terms of packet-switching protocols that route data. If examined from the point of view of resolving the domain names that people type into their browsers

A Dictionary of Postmodernism, First Edition. Niall Lucy.

into the numerical address codes used by that network of servers, then this "new" media can look very centralized indeed.

Another critical approach to the notion of new media would be to accept that there is indeed something "new," but to question whether the human subjects who interact with this new thing are some kind of a constant in relation to which old and new media can be assessed. Thus Katherine Hayles (1999) argues that cybernetics, computing and information science not only changed media but changed the kind of subjects that interact with this media.

For Lydia Liu (2011) even the critical theories – so often associated with the postmodern – with which some might attempt to critique the category of new media come out of encounters with it. She shows, for example, how the psychoanalytic theories of **Lacan** are in part responses to the then-new quantitative theories of information that arose in the late forties (Shannon and Weaver, 1971).

Given that they were products of research and development funded by the military-industrial complex, the so-called new media based in computation have for David Golumbia (2009) an inbuilt cultural form already, one of hierarchy and control, and thus were doomed in advance to betray the libertarian promise once associated with new media.

That libertarian promise always had a slippery quality. As Wendy Chun (2008) shows, apparently political or cultural values such as "freedom" were gradually reformatted as technical questions of control. Others, such as Jodi Dean (2010) locate the coercive qualities of what new media became more in their subordination to capital. What she calls communicative capitalism "captures" the user as a consumer locked into networks of surveillance and enjoyment.

Some things may indeed have changed, then, as media form moved from the dominance of broadcast techniques and economies onto the Internet and then cellular media. But this requires careful analysis. For Gabriele Pedullà (2012) the distribution of many small screens throughout the time and space of everyday life marks the end of the "black box" viewing experience of the cinema or even the living room with a television, where the architectural and formal properties of the viewing situation enabled film or television itself to command a certain amount of sustained attention.

Not all theorists of new media see the formal properties of the media as the causal factor, however. Borrowing from **Lyotard**, Hiroki Azuma (2001) detects a decline in the effectiveness of **metanarratives** in late twentieth-century Japan, but which resulted in a shift in media reading patterns away from narrative toward what he calls *database consumption*, where what matters are systematic relations between the details, particularly of character design.

Azuma can also be read as responding to the claim by **Jameson** that the replacement of the old Fordist production systems and products with ones based on information and digital technology led to a crisis of **representation**. What for Jameson was a distinctive kind of late capitalism could only be indirectly represented in the cultural logics of postmodern **culture**.

Here the rhetorical structure of discussion of old vs new media and the modern vs the postmodern had a certain similarity. Both imposed a binary and linguistic structure onto questions of historical transformation. In both cases critics could hold up either side of the binary as the privileged one, to be understood as contrasting with its negative pair. Thus writers could be for the new against the old media, or vice versa. Or they could be for the post and against the modern, or vice versa. These binary rhetorical forms could then be aligned with each other: the postmodern could then be the cultural logic not so much of a mutation in capitalism, as it was for Jameson, as the expressive form of new media.

Building explicitly on Jameson, Galloway (2006) attempted a more affirmative way to read the media form and cultural expression in the wake of the postmodern. He identified the computer game as the allegorical cultural form for the era of algorithmic forms of media control. Ian Bogost (2008) built a form of media theory that did not see emerging media forms such as games as particularly different. His non-structuralist approach to interlocking unit-operations of meaning is created out of the study of video games – an archetypal form of new media – but can be applied to traditional literary forms as well.

Where Jameson was inclined to see a foreclosure of politics and struggle in late capitalism, others see it more as changing form. Gabriella Coleman (2014) looks to Anonymous as an example of a distinctive form of Internet-bred activism. McKenzie Wark (2004) sees conflict over the ownership and control of information as one that creates new kinds of class opposition and possibly new class alliances.

Geert Lovink (2011) takes a more pragmatic approach, wisely avoiding the rhetorical grandeur of much new media discourse and focusing instead on the tactics via which those who work in and with today's media might have some control over their working or creative lives. Likewise, Lisa Nakamura (2007) puts more emphasis on the agency of people of color to negotiate the presentation and articulation of identities in online environments. Like Lovink, her view is far from utopian, but it avoids the pitfalls of thinking through binary pairs of terms.

In short, the whole category of new media was in the end a disabling one, which the study of media took some time to undo. There are of course novel phenomena in the domain of media, and perhaps even quite dramatic change, but at every turn the critical study of media has to work both in and against the language of expectations. Not all new media even succeed. The "media archaeology" approach has proven particularly useful in showing how the media familiar to us exist against a background of failed attempts to invent new techniques, forms and cultures (Parikka, 2012).

One version of the postmodern that might be useful for thinking about the new in new media is Lyotard's suggestion that the postmodern comes *before* the modern. Likewise, it would be possible to conceptualize new media as that which comes before old media. Taking a cue from media archaeology, this approach might pay attention not to some definitive binary opposition, but to a process of attempting to elaborate a new media form in and against established ones, some of which stick, many of which don't.

Another way to open up thinking about the question of novelty in media is what Jay David Bolter and Richard Grusin (2000) call *remediation*. Taking a leaf from Marshall McLuhan, they look at how the form of old media becomes the content of new media. For example, when Apple first made computers with a graphic user interface, they remediated images familiar from everyday office life: the desktop, the trash can, the folders, and so on. Aspects of the graphic user interface of computers were subsequently remediated as the content of a new form of interaction on phones and tablets.

Another approach would be to ask not what is new in media but what breaks or interrupts the seemingly seamless and endless web of communication. In other words, to study communication from the point of view of *excommunication* (Galloway, Thacker and Wark, 2013). This approach looks less at the temporal than the spatial axis of media, or in **semiotic** terms at the synchronic rather than the diachronic. What might be key here are the means via which communication incorporates even that with which there can be no communication, whether by way of popular genres like horror or elevated ones such as religious mysticism. This approach dispenses with what it sees as the fetishistic attention to media technology shared by both students of new media and media archaeology.

In sum, the discourse of new media proved both productive and disabling. In popular culture, the theme of repeated novelty lived on past the 1990s, but in media scholarship this theme came under closer scrutiny and from many different angles. Grappling with both alleged and actual novelty in media form even had the effect of changing how past media forms were to be understood. Starting with Lev Manovich (2002), scholars found new objects and new aspects of old objects from the archive that illuminated the evolving form and power of media.

Historians of media found that from the point of view of late twentieth century media culture, certain assumed oppositions within cultural history did not hold. For example, Fred Turner (2008) found not only opposition but also continuity and connection in the romantic opposition to **modernity** of the counter-culture and early computer engineering.

By the second decade of the present century, what had once been new media were hardly even new. Indeed it was the standard, accepted form of media for a generation then entering higher education. Certain technical, economic and cultural features of Internet and cellular-telephony-based media had if anything become an established "old media." While media business might still be committed rhetorically to a language that stressed constant innovation, disruption, creative destruction and so on, this might refer more to surface effects than to media infrastructures and dominant forms.

McKenzie Wark

Paraliterature: The term *paraliterature* has obvious military connotations. But fortuitously such an echo is apt since a *paramilitary* force is unofficial, marginal and unsanctioned by the state. Just as one is composed of unprofessional fighters or civilian volunteers, the regiments of the other may include genres such as science fiction, detective novels, romance stories, comics and other miscellaneous forms of popular culture unlegislated by the ideologues of history, taste and worth. This is the familiar critical alliance of the paraliterary as **minor** writing that doesn't, nor can ever, aspire to inclusion in the historical tradition of *belles lettres*. In an episode of *The Simpsons* (without question the *I Ching* of contemporary popular culture), Bart is busted down to remedial English and his outraged teacher finds him reading a comic book. In a fit of pique she wonders how the discredited object found its way into her booster class for the slow and dim. Once her apoplexy subsides she remembers that it had been used as a teaching aid for demonstrating illiteracy. Order and literary hierarchy is restored in the world of Springfield. *Hic lectionem finit.*

So to apply the subaltern metaphor of the paraliterary to the once sacrosanct tradition of English literature we could describe it (in one of its multiple inflections) as the parachuting of readers beyond contested ideological boundaries, behind what once were iron curtains of fixed and unmoving genres, styles, ideologies, codes, texts and meta-texts. And of course Authors (not authors). Harold Bloom's *The Western Canon: The Books and School of the Ages* (1994) is such a manual, though an elegiac one. Bloom mourns the loss of the unwavering truths and discrimination

A Dictionary of Postmodernism, First Edition. Niall Lucy.

(see **cultural studies**) of the literary humanist canon, which are being hijacked by the shallowness and popularity of literary otherness. For Bloom the untutored, undiscerning and unlearned support of wayward political allegiances like feminism, multiculturalism, black and gay politics is merely a shrill form of "cheerleading" (Bloom, 1994: 7). In other words the usurpers of the canon whom Bloom calls the "School of Resentment" constituted in his mind a despised paraliterature. Literary practitioners and critical supporters of this protestant concept of literary otherness (especially "multiculturalists unlimited," Bloom, 1994: 517) identified *the* canon as narrow, exclusive and in need of being challenged for the historically expedient construct that it *was* (I have thought carefully about this use of the past tense and reflected that it is good). Idealistic in the sense that its assumptions are never questioned, this notion of the canon underpins the formation of what constitutes knowledge and information. Accordingly 25 of the writers in *The Western Canon* are white men predominantly from England and its erstwhile New World. No surprises here – although it is intriguing how Bloom managed to find four women writers to add to their eminent company. Such are the impenetrable vagaries of certitude.

Now jaded irony aside, the critique and dismantling of the so-called "great tradition" of literature in the 1980s amounted to the recognition that paraliterature no longer had to be held captive, straitjacketed in some ghastly ideological Bedlam (Humanism or the Enlightenment two of its more palatable monikers), languishing in abjection with no release date in sight. The postmodern turn that Bloom despises meant difference and something that was broader than the literary. This was a fascination with the disregarded, neglected, impermanent and disposable, popular culture on the badass side of the tracks, hanging around the boundaries of worthy/unworthy, real literature/minor literature, good/bad taste, and so on. So enter the dragon, again. Of course we can't look for dragons beyond representations of them. But what does it mean to be looking for them *outside* an imaginary text such as *Game of Thrones* in which they figure as *mythical* beasts? The persistent and talismanic question "Where are my dragons?" is for Daenerys Targaryen a metaphor for finding a way out of exile and a home, not to mention literally finding her abducted phantasmagorical offspring. But it is also a metaphoric yearning to seek out an impossible ideal, that which is beyond language, "outside-text." The fate of the Khaleesi's wayward and fire-breathing furies presumes a connotative significance *within* the fantasy world of *Game of Thrones*. But also on a street where you live. Flyers with tear-off phone numbers also requesting assistance with finding those same dragons are another. They are referential artifacts that exist in the world outside, but are also parallel with the televisual epiphenomenon (which is not the same as the persistent world that the series presents). That is, the obsession with the televisual spectacle of the imaginary worlds of the Seven Kingdoms outside their representation is an instance of fan culture engaged with the collectability of artifacts, imitating sayings and appropriating other fetishes that transport facets of *another* world into *our* world. I have never been able to acquire a facsimile of Leopold Bloom's sham Crown Derby "moustachecup" from *Ulysses*, but I can wear a House Targaryen bronze talisman necklace or stalk the suburbs wearing the scabbard of Jon Snow. What would Harold think?

If the paraliterary is a form of the subaltern it is also ironically a mode of Bloom's misprision, a practice for finding unexpected and certainly unintended things through misreading. In a 1990 episode of the television show *The Money or the Gun* the Australian comedian and writer Andrew Denton read the pages of "The Simpson Automatic Washing Machine Manual" as if they anticipated and foretold contemporary world events (such as the Gulf War). In Denton's ingenious **remix** he read a bland and utilitarian series of instructions for a household appliance as if they were the quatrains of Nostradamus' sixteenth-century *Les Propheties* (2006 [Fr. 1557]). The apocalyptic warnings that purportedly augured the imminent end of the world in the French apothecary's pages were chillingly echoed in Denton's repeated intoning of the disarming phrase, "the machine stops." In that moment of misreading he simply and deftly transformed a throwaway instance of what Philip K. Dick would have called "kipple" into a millenarian paraliterary text.

Such misreadings do not privilege respective texts in terms of hierarchical, canonical or authoritative importance. The binary either/or that mandates historical differences of cultural worth between the mix of Nostradamus and the remix of Andrew Denton implodes upon release from prison into the utopia of misprision. Wanton and indifferent to who speaks it and when, "The Simpson Automatic Washing Machine Manual" highlights the tenuous, malleable and ultimately ideological membranes that demarcate paratext and text. Tom Phillips and Peter Greenaway's *A TV Dante* came out in 1989; Bloom's elegy for the Western Canon five years later. When he spoke of Dante, up to that point spared the "onslaught" that knocked Shakespeare off his perch, Bloom signaled that it would not be long before the Florentine poet's undoing was imminent and would be just as merciless and abject at the hands of "resenters" such as new historicists of the politically correct left (Bloom, 1994: 76). *A TV Dante* is not mentioned by Bloom, although its multimedia, hybrid video language would clearly not have been to his taste. Imagining what Dr Johnson or George Eliot would make of virtual reality, for instance, he feels heartened by what he knows "would be their ironical, strong refusal of such irrational entertainments" (1994: 517). While smugly reassured by this thought experiment in humanist certitude he wanly concludes that he has little confidence in literary education surviving this latest contagion, no doubt countersigned in the name of the postmodern – a term that didn't detain the attention of Bloom's indexer.

Meanwhile back on planet Earth I received a curious text message on my phone during the writing of this entry. It was for a forthcoming exhibition at the Australian Centre for the Moving Image in Melbourne entitled "Vikings and Dragons." Now "serendipity," as the rock historian Greil Marcus wrote in *Lipstick Traces*, "is where you find it" (Marcus, 1989: 93). Vikings we are familiar with from various kinds of writing (such as the Norse Sagas, the fiction of Terry Pratchett) and other modes of **representation** (film, television, massively multiple-player online games like *Viking Age* or *War of the Vikings*). And we also know that Vikings unlike dragons were corporeal beings in the world, verifiable from relics and remains found in burial middens and historically researched in the **discourses** of anthropology and history. But both Vikings and Dragons coexist powerfully in the world as networks of rich and intimately valued paracultures.

As a testament to the strength of the paraliterature that sustains them it is worth noting (and hardly surprising) that although writing since the early 1970s on matters dragonish, Terry Pratchett, one of the planet's bestselling authors, fails to make the cut in *The Western Canon*. Jorge Luis Borges does, though no mention is made of his interest in Anglo-Saxon or his fascination with the Norsemen and their sagas. He is however reclaimed from his Latin American origins and remade as an honorary member of the Western Canon as the South American Walt Whitman. Thereby Bloom broadens the definition of paraliterature by simply denying anything in the name of the literary that *does not represent* the unimpeachable and apparently universal aesthetic values of the Western tradition. So *vale* professors of hip-hop, MTV, Rap, the ideologues of gender and inadequate Chicano short-story writers (Bloom, 1994: 517). To misread the words of Bloom and a famous Australian resenter of strong patriarchal and nationalist authority, Edward "Ned" Kelly, "such is [the Balkanization of literary] life" (Bloom, 1994: 517). It is still unclear which category of the literary – para, minor or canonical –the "Jerilderie

Letter" represents. And there are no Australian writers included in the 600 pages of *The Western Canon. Australis epistolas nullius.*

Darren Tofts

Phrase: One of the definitive hallmarks of modernity is the subject: one proceeds from a ground and articulates clear and distinct ideas. The "subject" can be the one *who* thinks (the Cartesian subject), *what* one thinks (the subject of this book being postmodernism) or *how* one thinks: using the subject/object structure of sentences in English, for example. One might ask, as many postmodernists did, whether thought needs a subject: do we need to speak in well-formed sentences that are articulated by a distinct "I" who always forms good propositions (S is P)? The late twentieth and twenty-first centuries have been marked by an intensification of "subject technologies": from communication and writing "skills" to information technologies, the hold of grammar over thinking has certainly not weakened.

Postmodern writing, however, was marked not by the proposition but the *phrase*, and this took place in three respects. First, at the level of style many French writers – such as Luce Irigaray, **Derrida**, and **Foucault** (and many others) – often deployed the noun-phrase rather than the sentence in their writings. Rather than speaking from the position of "I think," or saying something about something, phrases were written and left almost as though they were stray objects, as though language operated less as a vehicle for transparent communication and more as a field of disconnected junk that would nevertheless be the milieu in which we think.

Second, many pursued Nietzsche's project of thinking that the subject or "I" was an effect of grammar, and that there was no "doer behind the deed" and that different modes of writing – not tied to grammar – would radicalize thinking and experience beyond human-centered points of view (Nietzsche, 1967). Finally, **Lyotard** argued explicitly for a philosophy of phrases; rather than a coherent and well-organized system that proceeded from premise to conclusion, Lyotard argues for multiple regimes of phrases, such that what counts as true and legitimate has less to do with some primacy of experience that is mediated by language, and more to do with the habits and usages that make up divergent discursive worlds, or what Lyotard refers to as the "**differend**" – a gap that cannot be bridged:

> Why these encounters of phrases of heterogeneous regimen? Differends are born, you say, from these encounters. Can't these contacts be avoided? – That's

> impossible, contact is necessary. First of all, it is necessary to link onto a phrase that happens, (be it by a silence, which is a phrase), there is no possibility of not linking onto it. Second, to link is necessary; how to link is contingent … Genres of discourse determine stakes, they submit phrases from different regimens to a single final finality: the question, the example, the argument, the narration, the exclamation are in rhetoric the heterogeneous means of persuading. It does not follow that the differends between should be eliminated. (Lyotard, 1988b: 29)

Claire Colebrook

Poststructuralism: Often conflated with postmodernism, though the distinction is a useful and cogent one to make. It's a term that is generally used of French thought, or at least French-inspired thought, though it arose not in France but in the US academy, as a way of describing the now influential imports (see Hawkes, 1977), and remains a term for which French thinkers find little use. It's a broad and loose term, one that shouldn't for a moment be taken as naming a common project or object of thought or method of approach shared by all of the thinkers bundled together under that name, as "-ism" words tend to imply. Perhaps the adjectival form *poststructuralist* is more useful: though we can think of structuralism as a cogent project, there is really no such thing as poststructuralism, though there are quite a few areas of thought that it's helpful to think of as poststructural*ist*. There are plenty of guitarists around, but it's not useful to think of them all as exemplifications of something called guitarism.

Around the middle of the twentieth century, Saussure (see **semiotics**) becomes the posthumous founder of a variety of approaches across the humanities, all of which share a broadly semiotic base, under the umbrella of *structuralism*. The French anthropologist Claude Lévi-Strauss, for example, postulates that whatever else they may be, cultural features as disparate as kinship relations, mythologies and food must also work as signs, and thus in have in effect a sort of grammar structuring them.

Structuralist inquiry is thus about how the formal regularities of a system allow well-formed utterances within that system (whether they be a sentence or an alliance among families, the menu in a restaurant or the origin stories a culture tells itself). It won't, however, tell you much about the next level up: how that sentence gets used in social exchanges, say, in the rapid fire of a conversation or **dialogue**, as political mendacity, or as exchanged by lovers. Knowing what the words "I love you" mean in the abstract doesn't help you decide what to do when the words appear anonymously on a piece of paper slipped under your door.

The *post-*, then, represents not so much an attempt to extend the methods of structuralism out to those other levels, as to rethink those "outsides" of structure. What happens when, say, the structural rules are multiple and irreducible, so that there is no single, broader and subsuming set of rules? What arises between genres may be a strictly incalculable **differend**: it never quite leaves the arena of language, but hollows it out, granulates it into what may need to be a case-by-case jurisprudence where the overriding questions are no longer "Is this a systematic or well-formed utterance?" but "How is one to do justice here?" As Lyotard's (1988b) subtitle says, the differend is a matter of "phrases in dispute." With **Derrida** and **deconstruction**, we have the incalculability of effects of what Rodolphe Gasché (1986) calls the infrastructures that are the conditions of possibility of thought and language. Because these infrastructures are logically prior to thought and language (if indeed we can still speak this way about what makes the rigors of logic itself possible), they are not governed by those categories, and so spill out everywhere into all sorts of other articulations. It is not surprising that questions of the ethical and the political figure everywhere in Derrida's work.

Poststructuralist thought is often referred to as part of a broader "linguistic turn" in which philosophy gives its attention to its relations to language. The term comes from a collection of essays edited by the American philosopher Richard Rorty (*The Linguistic Turn*, 1967). It's hard to see Rorty as a poststructuralist for the simple reason that structuralism was never on the agenda in the traditions of American pragmatism and political liberalism from which he comes. (As his own decisive breaks are from analytic philosophy, it would be more accurate to describe him as a post-analytic philosopher.) In many ways, what the "linguistic turn" most accurately describes is not so much the various poststructuralisms as the structuralism from which they break, for which language is indeed the model. With poststructural investigations, we have instead a focus on those aspects that might have been raised by structuralism but nevertheless do not fall within its ambit, or within the linguistic paradigm: the resolutely non-linguistic that is paradoxically at the heart of the linguistic itself.

Tony Thwaites

Punk: The word *punk* has a tangled and dubious history. It may have come from an Algonquin word for rotten wood used as tinder. In American English it meant at various times something that is no good, or someone who is a hoodlum or delinquent, a prostitute, a young man who is sexually available, or who is the sexual property of another man in prison. It was applied to garage band rock and roll in the United States from the early seventies. By the mid-seventies it was applied to both music and related subcultures on both sides of the Atlantic that were loud, raw and seemingly authentic, if not actually so.

American punk is largely associated with scenes in Detroit and New York that produced a loud and abrasive sound, including such bands as The Stooges, The New York Dolls and The Ramones. These remained something of an "underground" sensation (McNeil, 2014). In the UK, punk was not only a musical and subcultural but also a mass-media phenomenon. A "moral panic" was whipped up around the supposedly anti-social antics of punks. Of the bands, the most notable would include The Sex Pistols, The Clash and the all-women band The Slits.

Much to the annoyance of the American punk scene, the British one became a larger than life phenomenon, taken as emblematic of the decline of the post-war British social contract (Savage, 2001). The rather more centralized mass-media and culture industries in the UK quickly transmitted the image of punk across the land, and autonomous punk scenes emerged in many cities, notably Manchester.

After the initial blast of noise, punk mutated into post-punk, a rather more variegated and innovative web of musical styles, scenes, economies and adroit uses of available technologies (Reynolds, 2005). By the mid-eighties, that too was gone.

One influential interpretation of punk saw it as the injection of a kind of sonic and **semiotic** *noise* into the cultural sphere. In this view, punk refused the ideological codes that governed both music and speech and the kinds of class and other domination that such codes enforce.

In *Subculture: The Meaning of Style* (1979), a classic work of **cultural studies**, Dick Hebdige argued that this was an attribute of the work of subcultures. Hebdige studied punk through two lenses. One was critical criminology, which had moved on from seeing subcultures as troubled deviants and delinquents to asking questions about how subcultures constructed themselves both in and against a dominant **culture**. Hebdige combined this with **Barthes** and semiotics more broadly, and looked more closely at the rhetorical tactics subcultures used to repurpose the artifacts and everyday signs of popular culture. For example, British punks repositioned the safety pin as an item of jewelry, making this ordinary object over as a marker of belonging.

Not the least significance of Hebdige's work was its shifting of the work of the negation of capitalist, consumer culture from the working class, as Marxist theory usually had it, to new kinds of social actor, whose interventions were less at the level of the production of things than at the level of the production of signs. Hebdige put punk in a line of succession of post-war British youth subcultures, including the teds and mods and rockers, who had repurposed the signs and artifacts of consumer life, and who practiced a kind of "resistance through rituals" to dominant culture.

While barely acknowledged in Hebdige, this was much more explicitly understood as a **situationist** tactic of *détournement* in the work of Greil Marcus. In his influential book *Lipstick Traces* (1989), Marcus saw continuities between situationist détournement and punk appropriation. What sealed the connection was that Malcolm McLaren, who managed both The New York Dolls in New York and then The Sex Pistols in London, had once been associated with the situationist-inspired sect King Mob.

Others have disputed this view of punk (Home, 1995). This counter-view stresses its low- rather than high-culture origins as a simple and generic kind of working-class expression. This view concentrates more on the scene itself than what was said on its behalf by its various publicists and impresarios, such as McLaren.

Still, particularly once punk had mutated into its various strains of post-punk, it became emblematic of traffic between high and low culture. Many post-punk bands borrowed freely from the history of the avant-gardes of both poetry and visual art. On the other hand artists started to appropriate from the 'zine culture of punk and to form their own bands, sometimes occupying an interstitial location between art and pop.

In the UK this flowed quite naturally from the status of art schools in the post-war period, as they were institutions to which were sent troubled and troubling young people who were too intelligent for a manual trade but not proper material for more elite institutions. A striking number of successful or interesting British bands across the whole post-war period had art school connections (Frith and Home, 1988).

Something analogous can be seen in the career of American artists such as Mike Kelley. From the suburbs of Michigan, in the mid-seventies Kelley was obliquely connected to the Detroit proto-punk scene. He was involved in 'zine making and with the noise band Destroy All Monsters (Rudick, 2011).

He studied at Cal Arts in the late seventies, where he was in the band Poetics. He would go on to a notable career as a fine artist. One of his signature works, which displayed rather worn, grubby and forlorn-looking stuffed animals, was used by the post-punk band Sonic Youth as the cover image for their 1992 album *Dirty*.

There was an ambiguity in Kelley's fine art career, however, and it casts some light not only on the traffic between punk and art, but also on the transition from postmodern art to contemporary art. Kelley's work often drew on popular culture, but always filtered through a kind of aberrant, subcultural experience. It was a translation exercise (see **dialogue**) between two cultural spheres seen as having at least some critical distance from more naked modes of commodification: subculture and fine art.

Such traffic is not uncommon, but it drew heightened attention under the rubric of the postmodern in art, which among other things was sometimes seen as a refusal of a certain high modernist tradition in favor of an infusion of low cultural elements. The critical distance of art might then be renewed via contact with the critical urgency of something like a punk subculture.

The transition from postmodern to contemporary art might then be read as a process of dispensing with the aberrant quality of not just subculture but also art as well. Contemporary art understands itself more as a special kind of commodity for a special consumer, sometimes in continuity with other kinds of luxury goods such as fashion. There would then no longer be an element of punk noise in either subculture or art, as both are quite comfortably assimilated into commodified culture.

The notion that punk had some authentic spirit of negation attached to it in the first place is a view that is not without its dissenters. A cynical view might see it as something that had immediate appeal to the culture industries as it promised to lower costs. Punk emerged at a time when recording and promoting rock and roll bands had become a complex and expensive enterprise. Punk presented itself as a cheaper alternative.

As many punk bands found to their chagrin, signing with "alternative" record labels rather than with the major culture industry conglomerates came with certain disadvantages. Small business is no more inherently honest or reliable than big business, and certainly likely to be less stable and under-capitalized. The autonomous record labels, publications and venues were eventually consolidated again under the control of the big recording companies, booking agencies and so forth. Punk provided no enduring economic alternative to the culture industry.

This was the case not only with music but also with fashion. Particularly in Britain, punk was intimately connected to the fashion industry, and launched the career of Vivienne Westwood. What started as small business and street style was eventually incorporated into high street fashion production.

So while at the level of content punk may have sometimes had an element of transgressive noise, at the level of industrial form it did not deviate all that much from the patterns of development of the culture industries. As in any industry, small concerns outside the habits of the big firms may sometimes make headway with new products, and may sometimes become major players in their own right, as Virgin Records did with successful post-punk pop music such as Culture Club. Others may go out of business, be bought out, or remain marginal, niche business concerns.

In retrospect, then, both Hebdige (1979) and Marcus (1989) may have constructed narratives around punk that tried a bit too hard to connect it to certain **modernist** thematics. They wanted to find something avant-garde at work in punk, and at the same time connected to authentic, dissonant cultural roots. They annexed punk to the story of modernism as a kind of negation of the culture industry product of industrial capitalism. There is a grain of truth in that story.

However, a more postmodern reading might stress not its transgression and authenticity but rather its play with signs and its **simulation** of anger and energy. A close listening to early recordings by The Sex Pistols soon reveals the carefully multi-tracked guitar parts, and the attention paid to getting just the right recorded sound of the energetic vocals of lead singer, Johnny Rotten (John Lydon). The brilliant graphic design of Sex Pistols product by Jamie Reid could be viewed as a kind of **remix** of avant-garde graphic styles, including those of dada and the situationists, which provided some aftertaste of the aura from avant-garde negation but repurposed as product packaging. His famous cover for the Sex Pistols album *Never Mind the Bollocks, Here's the Sex Pistols* perfectly illustrates these qualities.

Ironically enough, even if punk did not have authentic subcultural roots and an avant-garde spirit of negation in its origins, even if it was a simulation and remix of such modernist elements from the beginning, that does not stop it being converted back again from simulation to authentic subculture. Even into the twenty-first century, punk lives on as a global phenomenon where disaffected young people teach themselves to bang out a few chords and make their own world.

For example, in the nineties, riot grrrl appropriated the energy and the simple chord progressions from the American punk scene and gave it a feminist twist (Marcus, 2010). In the UK, the US and elsewhere – including Bali in Indonesia (Baulch, 2007) – one can find Muslim punk bands going back at least to the late seventies. Michael Muhammad Knight later wrote a novel about fictional Muslim punks, *The Taqwacores* (2009; originally published 2003). In a fine example of life imitating art, this in turn inspired the formation of a new wave of Muslim punks. But perhaps the best example of punk living up to its promise of critical negation is the Russian group Pussy Riot, whose public performances against church and state landed some of its members in prison (Pussy Riot, 2012). They might stand as a rare example of the situationist seed in punk actually bearing fruit.

McKenzie Wark

R

Remix: Remix is a specific instance of a reflexive attitude toward and tendency within cultural forms premised on the already said. Re-working the already said presumes an act of creation that is a kind of textual ventriloquism, inhabiting a medium like a spiritual possession. But saying it as you hear it from elsewhere, after **Foucault**, after Beckett, implies that speaking of others speaking is not simply repetition but reiteration (see "What Is an Author?" in Foucault, 1984). Within poststructuralist critical theory the sequence of Foucault quoting Beckett's narrator from the third of his *Texts for Nothing*, asking "What matter who's speaking, someone said what matter who's speaking" (Beckett, 1974: 16), was an incisive anticipation of the "death of the author," authority as a function of **discourse** and not least of all a semantic vanishing of the possessive and self-assured subject of the Enlightenment (Beckett, 1974: 16). Forget Descartes. Think of the "author function" as *that* which speaks (Foucault, 1984).

Foucault quoting Beckett quoting someone quoting. Within the cartography of late-twentieth-century postmodernism in the visual arts and literature remix is a fold-back of noise, a form of echolalia within modernist notions of ingenuity, novelty and inventive panache (hence *post*modernism as not simply that which comes after, but which is implicitly already operating within the principles of the modern novel and its presumptions of transparency, realism and humanism). The illusion of a window on the world is an effect of writing, not architecture. As Foucault (2008) reminded us of Magritte reminding us of the paraphernalia for inhaling tobacco smoke into the body: it is not and will never be a pipe.

A Dictionary of Postmodernism, First Edition. Niall Lucy.

This indifference to the origin of speech acts and who makes them concentrated theoretical attention on to textuality and discourse as codified systems that contributed to the making of subjects through iterative acts of enunciation. Writers such as Raymond Queneau and other members of the experimental movement OULIPO (see **Hassan**) were interested in the formal and rule-governed nature of literary tropes as expressions of grammars, rules and repetitive laws that belong to manuals of style articulated by literary theory, such as genre and form rather than pampered humanist souls courted by the Muse in moments of sublime inspiration. So much for *dolce far niente*. Metafictional novelists, linguists and **poststructuralist** theorists alike premised their various divagations on the Structuralist tenet of competence and performance, our capacity to learn the rules of grammar, the laws of code and iteration then perform them as speech acts. Repeatedly, effortlessly and differently. As if breathing words.

And so I say it again, with a difference. Critical literature devoted to the notion of *re*-turn generally, as well as reflexivity more specifically, recognizes a distinctive postmodern moment of historical temporality (that which emerged after or from within **modernism**), as well as a spatial critique *within* literature itself, of the experimental practices of modernism in the arts and their avant-garde pursuit of stylistic complexity and daring. "Indecent" daring, one could say, of the kind that Virginia Woolf (1924) identified in James Joyce's writing of *Ulysses*, represents one attitude to the dramatic and often violent novelty that stoked the machine of modernism's revolution of the word. So dramatic and unprecedented was Joyce's obsession with "the new" that Woolf likened it to the act of a desperate man smashing a window for fresh air to breathe rather than simply opening it (Woolf, 1924: 24). Terrified of thunderstorms, Joyce was too superstitious to wreak this kind of meteorological violence, but it's a useful figure nonetheless.

As a semiotic index of the so-called "postmodern turn" in the mid-twentieth century the *notion* of remix, before its definitional articulation as *remix*, was ghost-written by the metafictional novelist John Barth. Writing in 1967 of what he called the "literature of exhaustion" he doesn't use the word remix. But he articulates and explains it as a specter inhabiting the literary **culture** of the time. A specter of marks (Derrida, 1994) in advance of its eventual coinage as remix, its attitude and gesture was a reflexive response to the "used-upness of certain possibilities," prevailing forms, styles, genres and even ideologies (Barth, 1967: 29). Remix as an artistic practice emerged out of vibrant do-it-yourself innovation in the projects of the Bronx in New York City in the early 1970s. (Necessary intervention: alternative foundation moments for remix, if ever there can be such a thing as a *foundation*, are identified in relation to previous experimental practices commencing in the 1940s such as *musique concrète*, electronic music and the manipulation of magnetic tape in the "chance operations" of John Cage and David Tudor as well as the cut-ups of Brion Gysin and William S. Burroughs. But these are counter-traditions for another time.) When DJ Kool Herc first manipulated an LP record on a turntable with his hands to isolate the breakbeat he effectively made new sounds and sonic beats from the grooves physically and finitely cut into the vinyl that were not made by him. The idea of remixing the materiality of a physical record concentrated attention on to the DJ as producer or "mixer" rather than a mechanical player of pre-recorded sounds. The generic moniker "turntablism" effectively signified a form of inscription, the re-writing of sonic marks on a technology that was never intended to be re-usable in this way. This practice of re-mixing was not dissimilar to the difference and *différance* of reading a printed page. Both turntablism and *l'écriture* are postmodern reiterations of that most ancient writing technology, the palimpsest.

Such artistic and technological experiment resembled a kind of **Situationist** *détournement*. The fusion of media production and the radical politics of scratching, rubbing and manipulating a record was an analogue of the identity politics associated with the Black Power movement emerging in the United States at the time. The violence of the street, the struggle to find empowerment and a voice occurred at a time when race was politicized and difference was mobilized in response to volatile race politics that legislated it as a social problem to be solved.

The artist and writer Mark Amerika describes the dramatic emergence of the "postproducer" (2011a: 118). This peripatetic wanderer through the words of others emerged out of turntablism as a kind of necessary symptom of the *post-*, or what he calls the "renewable tradition" (2011a: 107). First, *post-* in the sense of temporality as that which comes after working creatively with something previously made (as in digital postproduction in cinema or sampling in Hip-Hop). The creative act (with a nod to Marcel Duchamp's readymades) re-works the material texts of culture from choices made from an ever-expanding, Borges-like infinite library of samples (such as urinals). Remaking and remodeling the already said forms the basis of Amerika's 1996 poetic mantra "surf-sample-manipulate": that is, "surf the culture, sample data and then change that data to meet the specific needs of the narrative" (Amerika, 2011b). Second, artistic practices associated with the utility of digital media are iterative and always on the way to arrival somewhere else. In this sense iteration as repetition/reiteration is an instance of *something-else* implicitly on the way to being remade. When Ornette Coleman shook up the jazz world in 1958 he did so with a debut album talismanically entitled *Something Else!!!!* Dick Higgins's carnivalesque Something Else Press followed in its wake five years later, bringing with it the "swinging crowd" that John Barth riffed off in "The Literature of Exhaustion" in 1967.

Cultural practices such as sampling, the quotation of film style or genre (such as Oliver Stone's *Natural Born Killers* or Quentin Tarantino's *Django Unchained*) make perfect sense in a post-broadcast, networked, **new media** age; a time of reiteration when media and the overwhelming stuff of culture proliferates on unseen servers and information flows as incalculable streams of bits and bytes to be endlessly downloaded and, in the words of a Roxy Music song, remade and remodeled. When tweets are re-tweeted and posts are re-posted the endless cycle of appropriation begins again, like Finn-*again*, midstream in a "commodius vicus of recirculation," yielding difference each time they appear (Joyce, 1975: 1). This logic of generative potential or endless return (like the Möbius strip that is *Finnegans Wake*) in the time of the social network is arguably no better demonstrated than in the ongoing *Downfall* meme; a vernacular practice of re-scripting a key sequence from a middle of the road film about the last days of Adolph Hitler and the Third Reich (*The Downfall*, dir. Oliver Hirschbiegel, 2004). *The Downfall* epiphenomenon is not so much an example of the genre of remix per se, but rather of the potentially endless remixability of any media text that can be distributed through imitation (usually by parody and pastiche) to form a self-referring, participatory network. The idea of variation and distribution in the biological connotation of the word meme is reflected in the repetitive use of the same dramatic, three-minute sequence during which Adolph Hitler (played by Bruno Ganz) is informed of the imminent fall of Berlin and inevitable loss of the war. In such a reflexive ecology it is hardly surprising that the ultimate *mise-en-abîme* of the genre's self-similarity involves Hitler's apoplexy at hearing of *The Downfall* meme itself. Mirrors within mirrors …

But there is nothing exclusively abysmal about such iterative systems. In fact such a code underwrites the fractal geometry of nature that makes topographies, shorelines, leaves or icicles possible. In Benoît Mandelbrot's fractal geometry it accounts for and explains minute transformations of difference within processes of self-similarity, not dissimilar to the bio-evolutionary inflection of the meme articulated by Richard Dawkins. The fractal mechanics of Benoît Mandelbrot may be the key to re-defining the diachronic cultural history of the iterative semiology of remix prior to its synchronic, contemporary grammars (Mandelbrot, 1983: 2).

At the start of Canto 1 of Peter Greenaway's 1989 video adaption of Dante Alighieri's *Inferno*, co-director Tom Phillips declares that "A good old text always is a blank for new things." Speaking of others speaking, **Eco** once famously wrote of the postmodern condition as the inability to speak of love without ironic quotation, to repeat voices and speech acts that precede yours (in novels, plays, aphorisms, common phrases, etc.) (Eco, 2014: 547–9). So with Bruno Ganz, Basil Fawlty and Barbara Cartland in mind, "once again" someone will have mentioned the war.

Darren Tofts

Representation: In the opening line of his 1949 "Lecture On Nothing" John Cage enunciates the problematic presence and confronting absence of both speech and inscription:

> "I am here , and there is nothing to say ."
> (Cage, 1987: 109)

Like measures on a musical stave he punctuates and circumscribes the subject and predicate of a short sentence with three measures of white space. The twentieth century's most eloquent and infuriating poet of silence, Cage lets language *speak* a rupture in the post-Cartesian subject of **modernity**. Turning an inward gaze upon the very act of representing himself Cage is skeptical of the premise that words and breath are organically intimate, causal or certain. This performance of the speech act foregrounds the artifice of words and the systematic ways of putting them together as apparent utterances of the self. Cage may not have anything to say, however something is still being spoken. Cage is not present in or reflected by these words. Nor for that matter am I. He only appears to be speaking of nothing since we share the same codified system for enunciation. This last sentence also implies a presence responsible for it, a presence unseen. Equally then I am not here yet my language is saying something.

Erich Auerbach's formidable study of the "Representation of Reality in Western Literature" (1974) presumes the opposite. In *Mimesis* he asserts that the literary imitation of life evolved from the philosophy and poetry of Plato and Dante, the everyday grittiness of the fiction of Balzac and Stendahl to the *style indirect libre* of Virginia Woolf. Achieved out of such a formidable gestation modern realism "has ever since developed in increasingly rich forms, in keeping with the constantly changing and expanding reality of modern life" (Auerbach, 1974: 554). Having written *Mimesis* in Istanbul in the mid-1940s Auerbach moved to America in 1947. Cage was already there. "He" may not have spoken to Auerbach in person, nor for that matter read him or "spoken" of him in his writing. However their convergence in roughly the same part of the world (Auerbach was teaching in Pennsylvania, Cage in New York) can be appropriated as a rhetorical figure for imminent change. Perhaps without even being aware of this coincidence **Hassan** obscurely inquires *of* it: when "will the Modern period end? Has ever a period waited so long?" (Hassan, 1972: 40). Hassan arrived in America from his native Egypt in 1946 to study electrical engineering at the University of Pennsylvania. In retrospect it would seem that an incipient **discourse** of the *post*modern had been waiting for his attention on arrival in the former British colony.

But this "end" of the modern and the emergence of something new from or after it, perhaps its antithetical Other, is obliquely anticipated in the Epilogue to *Mimesis*. After more than five hundred pages of detailing the "interpretation of reality through literary representation" (Auerbach, 1974: 554), Auerbach's concluding remarks suggest what is to come in the name of an inversion of the mirror's reflection. "With this," Auerbach concludes, "I have said all that I thought the reader would wish me to explain. Nothing now remains but to find him – to find the reader." His modest wish to have a readership for *Mimesis* itself is entrusted to this invisible and unknowable presence upon whom these words may fall. But in retrospect it uncannily announces the death of the author and the birth of the reader, a meta-figure who in any act of reading is trapped in a maze of signs that are no longer transparent. So, again, with a different feeling: "You are about to begin reading Erich Auerbach's new book *Mimesis*."

A rupture in modernity then, prefigured at a time of considerable and varied impatience with the Classical unities of time and space in drama, with fictional authority in writing and an invisible fourth wall in cinema. Accordingly **modernism** did not fail but "reached its limit" (Benjamin, 1991: 63). Philosopher and art theorist Andrew Benjamin argues for this exhaustion not in relation to literature but rather, *inter alia*, the self-portraiture of British artist Lucien Freud that "cannot help but raise the question of its own status" (1991: 61). For Freud pigment is a color used to represent flesh (in this instance Cremnitz white), but he is under no illusions that it is corporeal or mimetic: it is "simply a code" (Benjamin, 1991: 65). But it is in the work of Freud's friend and contemporary Francis Bacon that a more dramatic rejection of the historically sanctioned transparency of representation is articulated. In a strict sense Bacon's images are non-representational. The term "portrait" doesn't make sense in his remediated world of facsimiles since what he paints is rendered not from life but from pre-existing images in books, magazines and photographs. The "presence" that is vital to the logic of representation, as Benjamin observes, is simply avoided (1991: 61). Furthermore Bacon's desire to "deform people into appearance" (Sylvester, 1990: 146) opposes literalness (a representational quality he claimed he could not achieve) in favor of pursing chance and accident to stimulate "sensation without the boredom of its conveyance" (Benjamin, 1991: 65). Bacon's "non-illustrational marks" constituted a break with the optical code of visual representation, another rough trade in his life that irritated or excited the nervous system. Michel Leiris (1983: 13) has aptly described Bacon's practice as a "ludic activity conveying no message," and "a displaced representation breaking the visual routine which obliterates perception" (Leiris, 1983: 26). Like Cage's speech acts a Bacon painting is simply "here." And it has nothing to say.

Deleuze, one of Bacon's most astute critics, described this "logic of sensation" as the drama of a violent immediacy emanating from his canvases. As with the philosophy of Deleuze's peers, contemporary artists such as Bacon "renounced the domain of representation" and instead took its "*conditions*" as their object (Deleuze, 2002: xiii). Deleuze's singular concept to describe this break with the codes and logic of figurative representation is the "figural." A term borrowed from **Lyotard**'s first book, *Discours, Figure* (2011 [Fr. 1971]), it refers to a break within figuration of the dominant anthropomorphic image of the human body. In his violent distortion of form Bacon sought to "unlock the valves of feeling and therefore return the onlooker to life more violently" (Sylvester, 1990: 17). His paintings don't illustrate violence, horror or ecstasy but rather scream and "claw" at the nervous system, a visceral image of tearing and rupture that Samuel Beckett had used of *Endgame* in 1956 to describe its power to lacerate an audience (Beckett, 1962: 183).

This convergence of formalist introspection and stylistic exhaustion rehearses a familiar break in the visual arts away from the modern paradigm of representation. Necessarily selective it nonetheless is consistent with historiographies of postmodernism that locate such moments of change and transition in the middle of the twentieth century. Deleuze, in a passing moment of heterodox bravura, identifies this break as happening much earlier in Christian iconography associated with the crucifixion. "Christianity," Deleuze suggests, "subjected the form, or rather the Figure, to a fundamental deformation." Instead of **essence** and form Deleuze sees the changeable event, accident and an inevitable fall (2002: 100–1). As did Auerbach before him. Nearly a quarter of a century prior to Deleuze's revisionary critique of modern representation, Auerbach concludes his study suggesting that Christian painting of late antiquity and the Middle Ages "differs completely from that of modern realism." He explains this in terms of what he calls *figura* (1974: 555). The figural index of this rupture in the code of modern representation is the grotesquery of "Christ's death-sleep" (1974: 48), in which a sublime anatomically rendered body is disfigured. Bacon's triptych *Three Studies for Figures at the Base of a Crucifixion* was one of his first and most startling renderings of the figural as a distortion of organic form that relates to the human image (Sylvester, 1990: 8). It was painted in 1944.

In *Finnegans Wake*, James Joyce's anticipatory *post*-text of 1939 (Joyce, 1975), there are many reflexive moments of *Wake*-gazing at its own pages. One of the more curious, especially in relation to Deleuze's discussion of the diagram as a "relay" of emergence in Bacon's painting (Deleuze, 2002: 111), points at the time of *this* writing to another anarchist of a postmodern world view: "You is feeling like you was lost in the bush, boy? You says: It is a puling sample jungle of woods" (Joyce, 1975: 112). Who knows which "woods" of "alphybettyformed verbage" (1975: 183) Joyce had in mind. But contrapuntally my reading of Joyce's anticipation of an "ideal reader suffering from an ideal insomnia" (1975: 120) brings to mind one Lebbeus Woods, the twentieth century's anarchist of experimental architecture.

If the 1940s mark a temporal rupture in the modern paradigm of representation, the 1990s converged the materiality of lived experience and cyberspace. Here the somatic immediacy of presence within the built environment converged seamlessly with the notional and immaterial time-spaces of ambient networks; what Woods described as the "electronic instrumentation of speed-of-light communications" (Woods, 1996: 286) – an anticipation of the miraculous that sounds very dated and unremarkable to contemporary ears. Impatient with "old logical chains" that bound the intrinsic and mathematical abstraction of architecture to human habitation, Woods coined the neologism "freespace" in part to reflect this convergence of analogue and digital modes of experience (1996: 285). De-emphasizing the functionality of domicility as the a priori purpose of architectural design (see **Jencks**), freespace demands the "invention of new ways of occupying space [and] new types of activities" possible within it (1996: 286). It is also a speculative environment designed for survival in cities having experienced disasters, ravaged by war or unified after segregation (such as the Berlin and Zagreb *Free-Zone* projects of 1990 and 1991 respectively). Freespaces were conceived beyond representation as heterarchical and potential concepts of space (heterarchy here meaning a fusion of metaphysical states such as human and machine in Donna Haraway's cyborg (1990a; 1991) and the nomadic, itinerant figure of **Deleuze and Guattari**'s "*transhumant*" artisan (Deleuze and Guattari, 1987: 409)). While there may be "no there, there" (as in William Gibson's oracular cyberspace), freespaces are projective and anticipatory, rhizomic "lines of flight" (Deleuze and Guattari, 1987: 277) that postulate non-Euclidean design in which the very notion of space is inextricably bound up with the ambient and consensual topographies of virtual networks.

The word "representation" is notable by its absence in Woods's "The Question of Space."

Darren Tofts

Ronell, Avital: *American philosopher of knowledge, literary and feminist theorist, born 1952*

Ronell is singular among postmodern theorists in (at least) two respects. First, she does not begin with "a" theory in the grand sense of establishing an ontology or foundation from which to analyze events or topics. There is no equivalent to **Foucault**'s "power," **Derrida**'s "writing," **Deleuze**'s "difference" or **Lyotard**'s "intensity" in her work. And even though these writers multiplied terms, they nevertheless began with some way of thinking about difference as such. She cannot easily be labeled "a" feminist (although her work has profoundly interrogated the politics of desire), and she cannot be thought of as a Derridean or Deleuzean, even though her mode of thinking and writing is inspired by thinking or writing and difference as productive and inhuman forces for disturbance. Instead, Ronnell's work is manifestly characterized by a series of interventions in seemingly peripheral topics: stupidity (Ronell, 2002), testing (2005), crack (2004a) or a phone call (1989). She is set apart from the "master thinkers" of late twentieth-century thought who tackled capitalism, metaphysics and power by delimiting systemic workings and providing some way of conceptualizing limits. She is singular, then, in not being a theorist in the manifest sense of offering *a theory*.

Second, and relatedly, Ronell is singular in the way in which a series of "topics" are treated *as singularities*. Something is singular if it occupies a threshold, or if its existence is not extensive (taking up space) but intensive (producing distances, delays, disparate fields). Rather than a theory that precedes and governs the study of an object, Ronell begins from rogue singularities: certain events, forces or "things" – when examined – start not to look like delimitable things at all, and tend to destroy the stable fabric of thinking. What results is *theory*: not in the sense of "a" theory that is some explanatory system that precedes and organizes how one examines the world, but theory as an untethered or disrupted event of thinking. If theory derives from *theoria* or looking, and has tended to be associated with a history of thinking that operates from a distance, then Ronell's work is theory because whatever she looks at creates a rupture in the syntax that has previously tended to organize and synthesize our thinking and experience. The distance of theory is not that of a detached observer who has magisterial distance and mastery of what she surveys, but a distance or gap in thinking.

This mode of singular theorizing – where what is looked at tears thinking apart – is most evident in her work on stupidity (Ronell, 2002). Stupidity is not an error that can be corrected; it is not a simple mistake, lie or dissimulation. Rather, there is always something inert and immobile (and unmasterable) within thinking. If, for example, we write with the supreme confidence that there is a **truth** to the world and that it can (with honesty and good will) be faithfully conveyed and circulated we are blind to the languages, technologies, assumptions, habits and practices that enable us to think and know. In this respect Ronell's work on stupidity operates as a form of rumination or immersion in the noise of the technologies through which we think (including writing) without claiming any pure or transcendent mastery. In *The Telephone Book* (1989) this tendency or necessity of thought being invaded and forced from outside is explored through the motif of the call; on the one hand when we pick up the telephone we cannot determine in advance what we will hear – there can be no control or pure rationality of information of what we come to hear – and yet, at the same time, the call is always *for us*, and we are nothing other than all the voices that assail us. Even not answering (or not reading) is a form of answering. Unlike the notion of a contained book that has a meaning that we can (at least in some delusional moments) grasp once and for all, a telephone book is composed from numbers that may at any time become voices to which we have to respond.

Rather, then, than see texts and technology as parasitic – or as the way in which truth and information happen to be conveyed – what is ultimately given or true is a world of text and technics from which various calls, tests, problems, truths and messages seem to emerge. When we read it is as if the voice were there all along, waiting for us to hear its message; but it would be more accurate (or less stupid) to say that it is the relay of messages, and all the texts, tests and signs that assail us, that opens some space for thinking. Thinking is not the elimination of what tests or confuses us; thinking occurs when what appears to be apparent or what appears to be tried and tested, tests us, or calls us, or compels us to re-read and re-think just one more time.

Ronell's chosen events through which she thinks and theorizes are always double: there is the stupidity of simple error, where one imagines that in a good world we would all be upright thinkers without stupidity, and then there is Ronell's theoretical stupidity that embraces the irreducible gaps in thinking – here stupidity is what makes thinking possible. There is also the test of postmodernity, where we demand that everything be tested, and we see testing as a form of rationality and mastery, and then there is Ronell's ongoing experience of being tested, of nothing being settled once and for all, and of experience as that which tests us. There is one notion of the phone call – with technology acting as an accidental and external means – and then there is the conception of the telephone book, where texts as such – all texts – may call us, even if they are written from the past. When the text is read, it seems to be calling us, as if from the future. Reading is never a closed book, which brings us to "crack" or that irrational and seemingly peripheral addiction that always requires one more hit. Against a model of knowledge as acquisition, in which we flourish by means of increased and ongoing understanding, one might see the war on drugs, or the desire to eliminate those substances that deflect us from becoming who we ought to be, or who we properly are, as a war on addiction, a war on a form of stupidity, testing and endless calling that is (ultimately) literary.

Claire Colebrook

Semiotics: Associated with the work of Swiss linguist Ferdinand de Saussure (1857–1913), "semiotics" (or, in Continental Europe, "semiology") refers to the study or the science of signs. Saussure himself focused on the study of signs in language, but he understood that his work had implications for the study of signs in the broadest sense:

> It is … possible to conceive of a science *which studies the role of signs as part of social life*. It would form part of social psychology, and hence of general psychology. We shall call it *semiology* (from the Greek *semeîon*, "sign"). It would investigate the nature of signs and the laws governing them. Since it does not yet exist, one cannot say for certain that it will exist. But it has a right to exist, a place ready for it in advance. Linguistics is only one branch of this general science. The laws which semiology will discover will be laws applicable in linguistics, and linguistics will thus be assigned to a clearly defined place in the field of human knowledge. (Saussure, 1974: 16)

He projects his general theory on the basis of arguing that all signs (linguistic or otherwise) comprise two parts: the *signifier* (the quasi-material form) and the *signified* (the idea or mental image to which the signifier gestures). Saussure's radical insight was to see that the relationship between these two parts is arbitrary or conventional.

There is therefore no determined relation between a sign and its *referent*, the idea or thing to which a sign refers and which is ideally independent of

A Dictionary of Postmodernism, First Edition. Niall Lucy.

semiosis (see **representation**). For Saussure, indeed, the referent was entirely independent of the sign, a point well made by Judith Williamson: "Saussure says that with the word H-O-R-S-E, where the concept of horse is what is signified, the referent is what kicks you" (Williamson, 1978: 20). We'll come to the exceptions in a moment, but, in general, signs don't re-present things as they "are" in the world already; they gesture to or posit them. As Saussure puts it, "in language" – and the principle applies to any sign system – "there are only differences *without positive terms*" (Saussure, 1974: 120). So, for instance, *dog* differs from *log, hog, bog* and so forth, and also from *wolf, pig, cat* (not to mention from *trouble* or *beleaguer*). It's because of this system or network of differences that the signifier "dog" can refer to "a domestic animal that barks" (the signified), where the relationship between the two parts of this sign is, in principle, arbitrary and, in practice, conventional. There is no in-principle reason why the signifier "cat," say, couldn't signify "a domestic animal that barks"; it's simply by informal agreement among the members of the sign-using community of English speakers that the animal who makes the sound "woof woof" is referred to as a "dog." Other sign-using communities use a different signifier: *chien* (French), *cane* (Italian), *anjing* (Indonesian), 狗 (Mandarin). This isn't to suppose, however, that the signified of *dog* was always "there" in the world already, waiting on a signifier, so that it's only at the level of the signifier that differences between languages occur. The complex structure of differential relations within which signs are held means that signifieds aren't straightforwardly translatable from one language into another, as if according to an algorithm; if they were, Google Translate would be a universal language. Signifieds, then, are not pre-existing.

Think of a dragon, for example. Because the signified belongs to the sign and not to nature, we can identify the features of this mythical creature (winged, reptilian, fire-breathing) in the same way as we do those of a dog, a creature (but not a signified) that does belong to nature (see **culture**). The referent of the sign *dragon*, in other words, is not independent of semiosis ... but neither is the referent of the sign *dog*. That's the import of the necessarily dyadic structure of the sign: signifieds do not come first and are never independent of the system of differences within which they can be exchanged by members of particular sign-using communities. While this holds true for signs in general, Saussure recognized that in some cases (which he called "symbols") the signifier–signified relationship is not entirely arbitrary and the sign is thus *motivated* by its referent:

> The fundamental principle of the arbitrary nature of the linguistic sign does not prevent us from distinguishing in any language between what is intrinsically arbitrary – that is, unmotivated – and what is only relatively arbitrary. Not all signs are absolutely arbitrary. In some cases, there are factors which allow us to recognize different degrees of arbitrariness, although never to discard the notion entirely. *The sign may be motivated to a certain extent.* (Saussure, 1974: 131)

The classic example of linguistic symbols is onomatopoeic words, which are motivated to varying degrees: "woof," "meow," "moo," "ouch," "thump," "screech," "murmur" and so on. But while the relationship between each of these and its referent is less than absolutely arbitrary, this doesn't mean that "woof," say, *is* the sound that dogs make or that "buzz" is identical to the sound produced by bees. Onomatopoeic words (symbols) don't *bring* nature into language, as it were, any more than photography (realist photography) opens a direct passage from signification straight to the real. While certainly a photo or a drawing of a tree is symbolic in the Saussurean sense, being a more motivated sign than the word *tree* (or *pohon* in Indonesian, etc.), any symbol of a tree would still be a representation of something that doesn't quite exist outside of language or signifying systems in general. There is no such thing in the world, that is to say, as "tree" (or "dog," "man," "nation" and the like), since "tree" is a hypostatic concept belonging to signification and not to nature. Any candidate instance of that concept (including a symbolic sign in the form of a drawing or a photograph) would thus be representational and not an instance of the thing itself.

Saussure's theory of the fundamentally arbitrary structure of the sign is perhaps the most influential idea of the twentieth century, leading to the development of structuralism in Europe and thereafter to its "scandalous" uptake in the UK and the US (see Lucy, 2002) in the 1960s and 1970s, as well as to the emergence of **poststructuralism** and (British) **cultural studies** around that time (see also **dialogue** for an alternative approach to signification). As for postmodernism, the notion of the gap within the sign underpins the view that cultural meanings and values are not immutable but historical, and since they're historical they must be perfectible; hence the accusation (see the **Sokal affair**) that postmodernists believe that "there is no such thing as truth," though there appears to be no record of anyone ever saying such a thing. Postmodernism, then, may be seen to have extended Saussure's ideas in the direction not of science but of ethics, as witnessed (not always directly) in the work of **Lyotard**, **Baudrillard** and **Deleuze and Guattari**.

Saussure's *Course in General Linguistics* (1974) was written up posthumously from lecture notes taken by his students before World War I. It was not until after World War II that his approach to language generated much of the theorizing upon which structuralism, poststructuralism, **deconstruction** and postmodernism came to be based, influencing the work of "founding" figures in the 1950s and 1960s. Saussure's approach to semiotics shaped postmodern thinking by installing *difference* as the fundamental attribute of language, such that the meaning of any one sign could only be described in terms of its difference from others in the system. This simple idea, that something *is* only what its potential others *are not*, proved productive across numerous knowledge domains, including anthropology (Lévi-Strauss), literary criticism (**Barthes**) and philosophy (**Derrida**).

Semiotics provided Continental philosophy with a new way to think about existing problems, particularly the nature of subjectivity, objectivity and the representation of the real. As a result, it gained a foundational place in the emerging fields of communication, media, cultural studies and literary theory. By the 1980s Saussure had become a "set text" in more senses of the term than one. From Saussure (and his followers) we derive many of the paired terms that have become familiar in semiotics: synchronic and diachronic; langue and parole; denotation and connotation; signifier and signified; paradigm and syntagm.

Saussure's formula promised to provide a simple "algorithm" (as it were) to account for the rules of sense making. At the same time it dethroned the idea that things in themselves (e.g. words) bore any intrinsic meaning, or that speakers of a language (subjects) had control over what and how their utterances would mean. That assumption had earlier been ridiculed by Lewis Carroll as what we may call "the Humpty Dumpty delusion":

> "When I use a word," Humpty Dumpty said, in rather a scornful tone, "it means just what I choose it to mean – neither more nor less."
>
> "The question is," said Alice, "whether you *can* make words mean so many different things." (Carroll, 1872: 72)

Equally delusional is the idea that certain signs are "natural" – determined by their intrinsic or objective properties, as in *naturalism*, which flowered in drama and painting and thence cinema, as well as in science, over the course of the twentieth century.

The political appropriation of the idea that meanings were natural, and language a transparent window onto the real, was picked apart by Barthes in *Mythologies* (1972). He used Saussurean linguistics to demonstrate the way that a naturalistic sign (say, a news photograph of a black boy saluting a French flag) may connote ideological meanings (say, patriotism and imperialism), which he called "myth." Meanings turned out to be constructed, but not according to the individual will or whim of users. In a relational system with abstract rules or codes, no object (such as a sign) could be said to have inherent or immutable meaning; and no subject could legislate what their utterances should mean. Meanings depended on positionality in an essentially abstract system of difference.

This idea refocused critical and philosophical attention from the *subject* to the *system* (Baudrillard, 1988a: 198), while maintaining skepticism toward the powers, motives and intentions of *users*. From such a structural vantage point, it seemed possible to explain all kinds of human mentifact, including kinship and economics as well as communication. The anthropologist Claude Lévi-Strauss especially argued that the same rules applied to the circulation of values in apparently very different systems: he thought that the rules governing how *women* (kinship and marriage), *money* (economics) and *meanings* (communication) are circulated and exchanged are structural transformations of one another (i.e. a universal rule).

In a Saussurean system, individual concepts can only be defined negatively, by reference to what they are not: "raw" can only mean what it does in opposition to "cooked," "edible" to "inedible," "marriageable" to "unmarriageable" … and so on. The same item or sign may appear on either side of any binary, because the *rules* of edibility have nothing to do with the taste of an individual diner or the intrinsic (nutritional) value of a creature, such that dogs, cats and insects, for instance, are widely (but not universally) regarded as inedible. Culture makes the choices.

Because arbitrary signs are unmotivated by nature or subject, their polarity can be reversed, which enables a politics of signification – negative connotations can be reversed to positive. Revalorizing such binary terms as "black" and "female" (as opposed to "white" and "male") became the political program of structuralist criticism, based on the politics of difference and subjectivity – identity itself was seen as socially constructed.

At the same time, the release of the sign from the shackles of realist referentiality led to a new interest in (and tolerance for) *excesses* of signification. Sign systems were understood as being productive in their own right. Pleasure, play, and even *jouissance* (ecstasy) became proper topics for study (see **Barthes**). Constructivism extended beyond the social, to more concrete examples: postmodern *buildings* betrayed an excess of signification, divorced from functionality and given over to playful exorbitance (see **Jencks**). Meanings multiplied, and the **remix** triumphed. The idea that there may be a general human capacity for making meaningful distinctions at the level of systems and rules, relatively unconstrained by real*ism*, was an exciting alternative to the positivism, behaviorism and empiricism of the times, which, simply by insisting on observation, experience and experiment (as opposed to theory, for instance), seemed to be *naturalizing* inequality, for in an unequal society, inequality is certainly empirically evident. Such sciences sought to convert social semiosis into observable individual behavior, but in the process ascribed to "human nature" attributes and actions that were all too clearly historical, ideological and political (see **differend**). At the same time external guarantees of truth were subjected to "creative destruction": duplicity, disorder and excess seemed to unfix the order of things. You couldn't tell truth from its opposites – fiction, propaganda, lies, insignificance (see **Eco**; **truth**). Representation lost its *representative* status: it could no longer speak for everyone. Realism had ruled the roost for too long, with too many unspoken assumptions and ideologies that rendered empiricism, positivism, behaviorism and methodological individualism increasingly suspect, especially when these approaches were put to instrumental use, with science the servant of power, and power (via President Eisenhower's "military-industrial complex") the main investor in science. Armed with Saussurean difference, postmodern theory stood outside scientific realism, but from there was able to critique it. If a blast of Derridean doubt, Barthesian "play of difference" and Lyotard's differend were able to undermine the foundations of this edifice, then perhaps its truths were not so self-evident as its proponents had supposed.

Niall Lucy and John Hartley

Simulation: Postmodern culture (or what **Lyotard** calls the postmodern condition), according to **Baudrillard**, is characterized by the simulated nature of reality. The real is no longer what existed prior to its **representations**, but is in fact *preceded* by a process through which signs and images are made over into simulacra. Baudrillard names this process "simulation," although the term is also used synonymously with "simulacrum" (and its plural, "simulacra"), thus naming both a process and the product of that process.

He sees the process in broad historical terms as corresponding to the following phases, whereby the sign

- reflects reality
- masks and perverts reality
- masks the absence of reality
- bears no relation whatsoever to reality: pure simulacrum.

(See Baudrillard, 1983: 11)

The first sign (the sign of "good appearance") is associated with premodern times; the second (the sign of "evil appearance") with the Renaissance; the third (the sign that "*plays at being* an appearance") with **modernity**, beginning with the industrial revolution; and the fourth, which is no longer a sign at all, with postmodernity (Baudrillard, 1983: 11–12). But the totalizing lack of historical or sociological evidence for the successive phases of the sign's increasing recursivity raises a problem for Baudrillard's theory, the millennial cynicism of which might be seen to match its technological determinism.

For Mark Poster, though, the strength of Baudrillard's theory is that it is a "*historical* theory of sign structures," overcoming the "weakness" of the ahistorical formalism of **semiotics** (Poster, "Introduction," in Baudrillard, 1988a: 4, emphasis added). Thus, once upon a time, signs were understood to represent their referents in good faith; then, during the Renaissance, they began to function more abstractly (as metonyms, for example, of monarchy); and later still, with the advent of photographic technology in the nineteenth century, signs imitated reality so well that they began to replace it. The replacement process was complete, turning signs into simulacra or simulations, when the media and thereafter the Internet became inseparable from everyday life by the end of the last century. Brian Massumi nicely summarizes the Baudrillardian perspective on the current scene as follows:

> There is a seductive image of contemporary culture circulating today. Our world, Jean Baudrillard tells us, has been launched into hyperspace in a kind of postmodern apocalypse. The airless atmosphere has asphyxiated the referent, leaving us satellites in aimless orbit around an empty center. We breathe an ether of floating images that no longer bear a relation to any reality whatsoever. That, according to Baudrillard, is simulation: the substitution of signs of the real for the real. In **hyperreality**, signs no longer represent or refer to an external model. They stand for nothing but themselves, and refer only to other signs. (Massumi, 1987: 90)

Baudrillard attributes this rather dire state of affairs to the media as a kind of global simulation machine for reproducing "floating images" that call on us not for a response, but for our seduction. The media "fabricate non-communication – this is what characterizes them," he writes, "if one agrees to define communication as an exchange, as a reciprocal space of a speech and a response" (Baudrillard, 1981: 169). In this bleak environment, what could the postmodern be if not the postlapsarian?

The apocalyptic tone of Baudrillard's media theory echoes, perhaps, the pessimism of the Frankfurt School (see **Jameson**) and Guy Debord's **situationist** theory of "the spectacle" (a concept he defines as "a social relation among people, mediated by images") as "the common ground of the deceived gaze and of false consciousness" in post-industrial society (Debord, 1994: thesis 3 and 4). But the lament for the sign's "fall" into simulation, its communicative function supposedly hollowed out by media technologies, forgets that the proposed singular feature of post-modern signs (that they "refer only to other signs") is in fact a condition of signs in general. What **Lacan**, for instance, calls "the incessant sliding of the signified under the signifier" (Lacan, 2006: 154) typifies a **post-structuralist** approach to meaning (see also **semiotics**), which contends that every signified is always another signifier: hence the signified of "cat" – *small fluffy animal that purrs* – is a chain of signifiers, each link ("small", "fluffy", etc.) giving on to a "signified" in the form of another chain of signifiers ("small": *of less than average size*; and so on). For Lacan, the lesson of Saussure's *Course in General Linguistics* (1974 [Fr. 1916]) is that "no signification can be sustained other than by reference to another signification" (Lacan, 2006: 150). But this is not to say that we are denied all possibility of meaningful exchange with one another; indeed, Lacan insists that "incessant sliding" is halted when the signified is sometimes stitched to the signifier after the fashion of a quilting point or *point de caption*, literally an upholstery button that prevents the stuffing from moving around inside a cushion or a mattress: "this is the point at which the signified and the signifier are knotted together, between the still floating mass of meanings that are actually circulating" (Lacan, 1993: 267). The sign's structural instability, in other words, warrants neither a hermeneutic free-for-all nor an "anything goes" approach to meaning. Similarly, the notorious claim by **Derrida** that "*[t]here is nothing outside of the text*" (1976: 158) doesn't commit **deconstruction** to holding that there is no such thing as truth, but simply that truth is never to be found outside a context or beyond mediation (see Lucy, 2004: 142–4).

The ideas and positions attributed to the Frankfurt School and others in the previous paragraph were all in circulation prior to the English publication of Baudrillard's *Simulations* in 1983 (based on essays in French from 1977 and 1981). *Dialectic of Enlightenment* by leading Frankfurt School figures Adorno and Horkheimer first appeared in 1944 (Adorno and Horkeimer, 2002); Debord's *The Society of the Spectacle* and Derrida's *Of Grammatology* in 1967 (see Debord, 1994; Derrida, 1976); and Lacan's "The Agency of the Letter in the Unconscious" and "The Quilting Point" derive from seminars given in 1957 and 1955–6 respectively (see Lacan, 1993; 2006). This is not to accuse Baudrillard of plagiarism, but certainly if there's something "new" about his theory of simulation it can't be that it introduces the idea that signification is recursive or the view that mass society is "fallen." As Derrida writes, however, barely a page after making the seemingly totalizing claim that there's nothing outside the text:

> If it seems to us in principle impossible to separate, through interpretation or commentary, the signified from the signifier ... we nevertheless believe that this impossibility is historically articulated. It does not limit attempts at deciphering in the same way, to the same degree, and according to the same rules. (Derrida, 1976: 159)

The formal condition of the inseparability of the signified from the signifier thus needs to be accounted for in particular contexts, according to the different historical articulations of that condition. On this view, what may be new about simulation is that it names the times.

The oft-cited example Baudrillard gives of a perfect simulation machine today (when he was writing in the 1970s) is Disneyland, which functions to disguise the hyperreality of American culture at large:

> Disneyland is there in order to conceal the fact that it is the "real" country, all of "real" America, which *is* Disneyland (just as prisons are there to conceal the fact that it is the social in its entirety, in its banal omnipresence, which is carceral). Disneyland is presented as imaginary in order to make us believe that the rest is real, when in fact all of Los Angeles and the America surrounding it are no longer real, but of the order of the hyperreal and of simulation. It is no longer a question of a false representation of reality (ideology), but of concealing the fact that the real is no longer real, and thus of saving the reality principle. (Baudrillard, 1983: 25)

The explicit unreality of Disneyland serves to make the world beyond it seem real, but for Baudrillard there *is* no outside-Disneyland and therefore no "real" against which to measure the "not real." It's not as though the mediated experience of a perfect childhood offered by Disneyland could be set against the unmediated space of culture at large, since contemporary culture is both mediated and mediatized through and through. There's no outside the media, as it were, or no outside mediation, for Baudrillard, which might also be taken for a summary of Derrida's later work (see Lucy, 2011). In Derrida's case, though, contemporary forms of mediation, rather than instigating a fundamental shift in the nature of reality as such, would be simply the historical articulation of a particular mode or instance of the signified's inseparability from the signifier.

On this account, simulation would not be entirely new. The sign's makeover into the simulacrum presumes that hyperreality succeeds a former time when the real was distinguishable from its copies. But if, in this "former" time, the sign was characterized by the inseparability of the signified from the signifier, as it is today, then perhaps what we are faced with now is not a choice between the real and the imaginary, but, as Massumi (1987) puts it, "between two modes of simulation." One mode (which might be historicized as "earlier," although it may also continue to be in operation) would be "normative, regularizing, and reproductive" and we would recognize this mode as the one that "goes by the name of 'reality'" (Massumi, 1987): what we call reality is the product of a particular mode of simulation.

The other mode, the one that produces hyperreality, "turns against the entire system of resemblance and replication" (1987: 94). This is what we call art, according to Massumi (following **Deleuze and Guattari**), but where "art" is understood in general terms *as a mode of simulation* (the mode that perhaps declares itself as such) and not as a particular aesthetic practice or object. Hence the Platonic separation of simulation from representation (Plato, 360 BCE: 236 a–d), Deleuze argues, privileges an idea of the "good" appearance in order to preserve a distinction between original and copy. Plato gives the example of a colossal statue whose proportions are not found in nature, thereby producing rather than reproducing an image for contemplation; an image that doesn't resemble an original, but which is in itself a semblance or a phantasm. Such an image (the simulacrum) is dangerous, Plato says, because it threatens the natural order of things by which originals precede their likenesses. But for Deleuze, in an essay first published in 1967, the situation is very different:

> The simulacrum is not degraded copy, rather it contains a positive power which negates *both original and copy, both model and reproduction.* Of the at least two divergent series interiorized in the simulacrum, neither can be assigned as original or as copy … Similarity and resemblance now have as their **essence** only the condition of being simulated, that is, of expressing the operation of the simulacrum. (Deleuze, 1983: 53)

The point for Deleuze is to "overthrow Platonism," a whole system of thought and values founded on a distinction between essences and appearances, but nonetheless a system sustained by a certain mode of simulation. In contrast to Baudrillard, for whom simulacra are fallen or degraded images that remain within the Platonic system of good and bad appearances, albeit as traces of a "lost" reality, simulation for Deleuze is a positive force that opens the possibility of a future freed from the logic of representation, a logic governing our conception of a world founded on the distinction between essence and appearance. "The goal," he writes, "is the subversion of this world" (1983: 53).

Deleuze gives the examples of *Finnegans Wake* and Pop Art, but simulations are not simply the result of avant-garde textual practices; they are also an effect of what lies in the eye of the beholder. Indeed, this was a crucial aspect of the simulacrum for Plato, who understood that the disproportions of the colossal statue were the source of its beauty to onlookers. "From the beginning, then," as Michael Camille (1996: 32) remarks, "the simulacrum involved not just image makers but also their viewers." It was the possibility that a sign's meaning might not be absolute but contextual, the possibility that there is no outside the text, that Plato sought to banish in distinguishing simulation from representation; for Plato, a viewer's "position" ought not to determine whether an appearance should be judged good or bad. The educational approach known as critical literacy (often derided as postmodern "relativism") might thus be seen as a move toward the overthrowing of Platonism in its insistence on the role of reader- or viewer-positioning in the production of textual meaning (see Lucy, 2010b, 33–53). The idea that a work of literature, for example, is not reducible to a representation of (authorial, national, cultural, historical or other) experience opens a breach in the system of "resemblance and replication" by which the current order of things feigns to appear natural.

Or consider the American West. Consistent with what Deleuze calls "the established order of representations" (1983: 56), the West might be said to have its good appearances in historical accounts of the period (in which signified and signifier are thought to be "knotted together"), assuming "the West" has anything to do with periodicity, while other versions of nineteenth-century frontier America would be judged by their degree of resemblance to those appearances. Thus the Quentin Tarantino film *Django Unchained* (2012) could be dismissed for simulating a West that never was according to the history books. As noted in many reviews, however, the film's referents are less historical than cinematic, especially the mid-1960s "Django" series of Spaghetti Westerns starring Franco Nero (knowingly cast in the Tarantino film and thanked for his "friendly participation") and 1975 big-budget Hollywood blaxploitation movie *Mandingo*. In its simulation of a West that doesn't quite belong to history, if not also in what one reviewer refers to enthusiastically as the film's "comic book" dimensions (Bradshaw, 2013), *Django Unchained* quotes a discontinuous series of Western simulations going back at least to Buffalo Bill's Wild West Show, various incarnations of which toured eastern America, England and Europe for 30 years (1883–1913). The film could be criticized on historical grounds, then, only if it were seen to *fabricate* the real, Deleuze being careful to distinguish fabrication (the "artificial," the "factitious") from simulation on the basis of the former's *false* claim to faithfully represent something posited as prior to it (Deleuze, 1983: 56). Narratives of Holocaust denial would be a good example of this. Deliberate (as it were, ideological) *mis*representation is therefore not at all what Deleuze means by simulation. But since *Django Unchained* makes no claim to reproduce events outside the text of cinematic history (its ecstatic artifice signifying the opposite of documentary realism), criticism of the film on historical grounds could only reaffirm the authority of a system that presumes to represent the natural order of things – the very system, it might be said, whose authority the film refuses. From which we may conclude that Baudrillard's "simulation" is Deleuze's "fabrication,"â risking the possibility that a Baudrillardian reading of contemporary culture could be nothing but, in Massumi's (1987) words, "one long lament."

Niall Lucy

Situationism: The Situationist International was an avant-garde movement that lasted from 1957 to 1972 and included the work of Guy Debord , Ivan Chtcheglov, Asger Jorn, Constant Nieuwenhuys, Michèle Bernstein, Jacqueline De Jong and Raoul Vaneigem among others (Wark, 2011). It was a continuation of the succession of avant-garde movements of the early to mid-twentieth century, such as the futurists, constructivists, dada, and the surrealists (Vaneigem, 2001). It was perhaps the last avant-garde, given that one of the defining features of the postmodern is that it allegedly rendered not just any particular avant-garde, but the whole category of the avant-garde, obsolete. Ironically, one of the ways of arguing this later proposition comes from the writings of the Situationist International itself.

Avant-gardes claim to be in advance of current aesthetic and social forms, and to point toward future states that are at least possible transformations of the present. In this sense they are an advance guard of **modernism**. They participate in the kind of time that for **Jameson** at least can be thought of as modern time, where future states are qualitatively different from past ones (Jameson, 2013). But as the Situationists would argue, the advance of commodification into everyday life could erase the possibility of historical time itself.

The Situationist International came up with several innovative strategies, and as with most of the historical avant-gardes, these were somewhat more than mere aesthetic innovations. They were propositions about changing life itself. The first of these is a cluster of practices and concepts to do with urban space.

Their practice of *dérive*, a kind of wandering, was a way of detecting the ambiences of urban spaces as they might be experienced outside of the division of the space of the city between the places and times of work and leisure. The practice of *dérive* yielded a psychogeography, a way of mapping the ambiences of the city, finding in the everyday experience of the city hints of how to build another kind of city for another kind of life. The Situationists used *dérive* to find clues as to how to imagine what the city could be like after the abolition of wage labor and the freeing of all of time and space for, as they put it, "less mediocre games" (Wark, 2011: 7–45).

It was through a version of *dérive* that Jameson would later come up with his influential version of the category of postmodernism. His most famous essay on the topic opens with him wandering around the Bonaventure Hotel in Los Angeles. What he found there was the dialectical opposite of the kind of urban space the Situationists aspired to build.

Lacking the means to build cities, the Situationists transformed the one thing that was available to them: the means of communication. The key practice here is *détournement*, based on a reading of the nineteenth-century poet the Comte de Lautréamont. It was well known that in his short work the *Poesies* Lautréamont had plagiarized and modified famous maxims from Pascal and others. In the 1950s it turned out that Lautréamont's masterpiece, *Les Chants de Maldoror* (1965 [Fr. 1868–9]), contained huge chunks of plagiarized material, including a fantastic and "poetic" description of a flock of starlings that was actually lifted from a natural history textbook. Rather than make excuses for Lautréamont, the Situationists fully embraced this strategy of copying and transforming past cultural material, treating all of culture as a commons, free of private property (McDonnough, 2007: 13–53).

When the post-war building boom started to destroy the old urban districts the Situationists favored, their practice of *dérive* fell out of favor in the group, and they began to take an interest in a more total critique, borrowing from non-Stalinist Marxism. Yet *détournement* remained a key practice. The best-known Situationist work, Guy Debord's *The Society of the Spectacle*, contains chunks of Hegel, Marx, Freud and many other writers, both major and minor (Debord, 1994 [Fr. 1967]). It became famous in retrospect as the text that best captured the revolutionary mood of 1968, when students occupied their universities and workers occupied their factories in France. Insurrection seemed to be in the air in many places around the world, from Amsterdam to Prague to Mexico City.

For Debord, everyday life appears as a vast accumulation of spectacles. The spectacle is the result of a declension from being into having and of having into appearing. The images that appear to populate the social world are extrusions from the world of production, and present what has already been produced as if it was the sum total of all that could ever be desired. That which is alienated from the worker as producer, her potential agency and power in and on the world, is returned to her as consumer in the form of a seemingly endless parade of things.

This is not a theory of media so much as a theory of how a certain stage of capitalism became thoroughly mediated. Debord builds on (and also influenced) the work of the Hegelian-Marxist sociologist Henri Lefebvre, who in his *Critique of Everyday Life* (2014 [Fr. vol 1. 1947; vol 2. 1961; vol 3. 1981) argued that, with the defeat of French colonialism in Algeria, capitalism was turning toward a colonization of the everyday life in the metropolitan centers. As such, Lefebvre, Debord and the Situationist International are part of a history of open-ended, adaptive, non-Stalinist Marxist theory which tried to understand capitalism as that dynamic, self-cannibalizing system whose effects Marx captured in his famous phrase "all that is solid melts into air, all that is sacred is profaned."

For Debord, the spectacle was a product of the historical development of capitalism, but one that erased its own historical qualities. If capitalist production makes all of time quantifiable, then capitalist spectacle likewise renders the time of consumption and everyday life as one of the endless repetition of equivalent, and hence equally valueless, images. The spectacle replaces the time of history with the time of fashion. Its emblematic social figure is not the great statesman but the fashion model, who embodies not what can be done but what can be consumed.

In the spectacle, everything is subordinated to private property, including time, desire and everyday life. But Debord still thought it possible to puncture this afflatus of the commodity. Boredom, the refusal of work, the refusal of spectacular desires, could all be avenues back to historical thought and action. Hence the key category in *The Society of the Spectacle* is not spectacle, but *détournement*, which becomes the active and collaborative re-appropriation of everything that the spectacle alienates from the worker-consumer. This appeared to many at the time to be exactly what was at stake in the strikes, occupations and street-barricades that erupted in 1968.

But 1968 was in the end the presage to a time of defeat for radical movements. Jean Baudrillard's influential theory of **simulation** appears then as a reworking of Situationist spectacle, but without the sense of it being a false world that could be shucked off to reveal the true one. In Baudrillard, there is no return from appearing and having – commodified everyday life – back to true being. There is only a going-forward, an acceleration of simulation. Here his writing of the 1970s was typical of a species of radicalism which no longer believed that capitalism could be negated by some force that resisted it, but could only be accelerated toward its end and supersession by another form of life. The 1970s work of **Lyotard**, **Deleuze and Guattari** had aspects of this postmodern reworking of the kind of position Debord had articulated in the 1960s (Plant, 1992).

The postmodern might appear then as the spectacle perfected, where its erasure of the time of historical action becomes all but complete. Revolts may yet break out, but no longer have the capacity to challenge the totality. After the defeat of 1968, Debord dissolved the Situationist International, and went into a kind of internal exile. He translated his distinctive practice of *détournement* into some powerful works of cinema, in particular the 1973 film version of *The Society of the Spectacle* (Debord, 2005), and what may be his masterpiece, the 1978 film *In Girum Imus Nocte Et Consumimir Igni*. He also wrote his *Commentary on the Society of the Spectacle* (2001 [Fr. 1988]), noting how the spectacle itself was changing form; and his brilliant, most personal work, *Panegyric, Volumes 1 and 2* (Debord, 2004 [Fr. 1989; 1997]). Ironically enough, he would in the twenty-first century be declared by the French government to be a national cultural treasure, completing the absorption into the spectacle in the most piquant manner.

By then, both the word "spectacle" and a rather less reflective and critical version of "détournement" had become commonplaces. The Situationist International became part of the canon of art history. Debord would be dutifully name-checked in media studies. His books would be reprinted for the theory-market. The works of other members and associates of the Situationist International would be rediscovered. The Situationist style of vituperation would become a standard one among the kinds of unoriginal "pro-situ" groups of exactly the kind he always despised, but shorn of its distinctive wit.

A more interesting legacy might be the attempts not at scholarly quotation or cranky repetition but at reimagining a total critique of postmodern life. To pick just two examples, one might point to the work of the Critical Art Ensemble in the United States and the *Tiqqun* journal and its affiliates and descendants in France (Holmes, 2012; Tiqqun, 2010; 2012). In both cases, these groups attempted to restate the whole project, forging new languages and practices.

And in both cases, this led to high-profile court cases. Steve Kurtz of Critical Art Ensemble was charged with "bioterrorism." Julien Coupat always denied authorship of the incendiary texts of *Tiqqun* and its apparent descendant, *The Invisible Committee* (2009; 2015). Nevertheless he was accused of belonging to an "anarcho-autonomist sect" and of plotting sabotage. In neither case were such charges proven in court.

Between these extreme forms of refusal and the easy assimilation of the Situationists into the **remix** of spectacle itself are a wide range of critical practices, by artists, activists, hackers and others which freely *détourn* from the Situationist archive. What they might have in common is a project of locating forms of agency in and against the totality of commodified life that some call the postmodern. Some aim to negate and arrest it, others to affirm and accelerate it (Noys, 2014). But if there is an enduring legacy of the Situationist International, it is one of mostly group projects for combining theory and practice for remaking the world.

The group took their name from a term developed by Sartre, for whom a "situation" is what mediates between my free consciousness and the dead materiality of the world (Sartre, 1984: 619–707). The Situationist project was one of constructing situations, which refused the dualism of Sartre's thought, and sought rather the co-creation of new and less boring worlds. Perhaps the key thing their work still transmits is this daring to make worlds. They denied that there was any Situation*ism* (Knabb, 2007: 51). It was an evolving set of strategies rather than a doctrine. That sense of daring to commit to strategies for making situations for more interesting games lives on.

McKenzie Wark

Sokal affair

Alan Sokal: *Alan Sokal is an American physicist and mathematician, born 1955*

One of the more pointed ironies of the so-called Sokal Affair or Sokal Hoax, is that that it is actually a great illustration of one of the key arguments of postmodern theory. Sokal may have intended to show that postmodern theory, particularly regarding science, is bogus, but the affair is a good example of what **Lyotard** called a **differend**, which is an argument that cannot be resolved because the parties to it make statements of different kinds, which follow different rules and make different kinds of **truth** claims (Lyotard, 1988b).

But let's start with the facts of the case. In its spring/summer issue of 1996, the journal *Social Text* published "Transgressing the Boundaries: Towards a Transformative Hermeneutics of Quantum Gravity" by Alan Sokal. When it came out, Sokal claimed in the May 1996 issue of *Lingua Franca* that his article was in his view a "hoax" (see Lingua Franca, 2000).

This led to a flurry of publications, in both the academic and the popular press, a good deal of which sided with Sokal. In this view, Sokal had succeeded in exposing postmodern theory as making false claims about science, claims that were treated as authoritative when authored by prominent humanities professors, but never subjected to rigorous review or refutation.

It needs to be pointed out, however, that *Social Text* was not at that time a peer-reviewed journal. It was what has been called a "journal of tendency," exploring new ideas, rather than a "journal of record" (Ahluwalia and Miller, 2005). It may also be of relevance that the editors had requested changes to Sokal's article, which he had refused to make. These facts may be relevant to the question of the difference between what kinds of statement, and what kinds of claims Sokal and *Social Text* thought they were communicating.

This is where the affair takes on the coloring of a differend. Sokal acted as if his statements made truth claims, and hence their publication showed that *Social Text* was unable to test and verify such truth claims. But *Social Text* thought Sokal was making not truth claims but ethical claims, in the sense of not being claims about the facts – in this case about what quantum gravity *is* – but about how quantum gravity *ought* to be interpreted. In rather crude terms, it is a difference between what Sokal might claim to know and what he might believe is a basis for ethical action.

Hence the editors seem genuinely shocked that Sokal made false claims, and viewed his actions as unethical. What could be more unethical than to knowingly make false claims about one's own ethics? But from Sokal's point of view, even this sort of response by the editors helped prove the point that *Social Text* was not subjecting truth claims to some procedure of verification. If seen as a journal publishing truth claims, Sokal is correct and *Social Text* is at fault. If seen as a journal publishing ethical claims, then *Social Text* is right and Sokal has acted unethically. Hence it has the character of Lyotard's differend.

From the point of view of those who disdain all things postmodern, it gets worse. It is not as if there can be a neat separation between kinds of statements, the kinds of claims they make, and the forms of adjudication of such claims. In this case, there is a certain slippery quality on both sides. *Social Text* does not seem to have questioned its own ability to assess ethical statements that might yet depend on truth claims about the sciences. Sokal could indeed be seen as correct in criticizing the cavalier approach of that journal to matters rather beyond its ken.

But there are weaknesses on the "winning" side too. The means by which Sokal made his point were by claiming to have proven a truth claim. Yet he attempted to publish his text in only one journal, and one which moreover was not peer reviewed. This was not an experiment with a control, nor did it produce enough data points to show any sort of statistical probability. Sokal's supporters quickly generalized his one instance of a hoax to "postmodern theory" in general, making exactly the kind of ungrounded truth claim they supposedly criticized.

Moreover, if one of Sokal's points is that *Social Text* published such texts based on the authority of high-ranking professors, then this applies also to his own claim that the text was in some sense not what it seems. It was simply taken on Sokal's authority that the text's claims could not be justified.

If the test is one of whether a kind of academic discourse can be fooled into publishing claims that are not defensible as truth claims, then the unfortunate effect of such a test might be to also invalidate many fields that claim to be actual sciences. In many fields, even prominent journals have been obliged to withdraw papers which subsequently turn out to be at best unproven and at worst fraudulent. The withdrawal of scientific papers is common enough that there is a website devoted to it – retractionwatch.com.

There may be a range of motivations among the authors whose papers are withdrawn, from honest error to haste to fraud, to the rather rare cases (like Sokal) of intentional hoax. But still, if there is a Sokal test of a truth-claim assessment procedure, it is hard to see why it would not apply to at least some of these cases too. Authorship is a slippery and perhaps not entirely conscious activity, with many motivations. Here yet another supposedly postmodern theme seems to be in play: that sense, derived from Nietzsche, of **discourse** as a kind of combat, a will to power, in which all of the rhetorical arts might be deployed.

In short, if Sokal meant to disprove "postmodern theory," he may inadvertently have shown its utility. But once again the crucial thing is the kind of statements and their test. What the Sokal affair shows is that certain concepts about how what Lyotard called "language games" work might actually be quite useful, but useful in the sense of understanding how language works, not useful for understanding things in the world other than language that language might attempt to describe.

It was not quite his intention, but Sokal did quite rightly end up showing that there could be an unhelpful slippage between statements about language and statements about the world to which language refers. This certainly seems to have happened in the instance of *Social Text* and his contribution to it. But it is yet another irony here that this might call for more, rather than less, attention to language. One that might, however, lead to a certain pulling-back from the precipice of a total critique of scientific truth claims on the part of scholars from the humanities.

If one studies language, it is likely that one will think language very important; if one studies some non-language object then it is likely one will think language rather less important. A more useful reading of the Sokal affair than the one that actually transpired might be to get those who study the language arts to pay more attention to how other modes of knowledge actually work.

If one of the features of the postmodern turn was supposed to be attention to differences, then one difference that was rather ignored was the different kinds of history, **culture**, techniques and procedures of the sciences. It may be the case that a humanist scholar could read what scientists do as just another kind of storytelling, but as Donna Haraway pointed out, science is a form of *constrained* storytelling, shaped by a number of powerful limits other than the structural possibilities of language and the kinds of meaning and power such language might bear (Haraway, 1990b: 366).

On the other hand, there was more to the Sokal affair, and the so-called "science wars" around it, than the allegedly postmodern claim that there is nothing outside language. Many historians and anthropologists studying science since the twentieth century take its truth-claim procedures very seriously, and were in some sense "pro-science" (Biagioli, 1999). And yet they were not simply prepared to take scientists at their word, based just on their authority, that they were in possession of an absolute and foolproof method for making truth claims. Indeed what might have been part of the motivation behind attacks on "postmodernism" was an attempt to preserve scientific authority in the public realm from legitimate and even in a broad sense "scientific" scrutiny of the basis of such claims.

It must be remembered that the twentieth century was both the era of great scientific advances such as the polio vaccine, but also the century of the atom bomb, and of Rachel Carson's exposé of the effects of pesticides such as DDT in her book *Silent Spring* (1962). This gave rise to several strands of the critique of science. A more properly Marxist one, with roots among great leftist scientists of the interwar period, such as J. B. S. Haldane, Joseph Needham and in particular J. D. Bernal, stressed the cooption and corruption of science by capital, militarism and obscurantist political movements such as fascism (Werskey, 1978).

But there was a more general line of critique, with roots in a certain poetic and nostalgic romanticism, which rejected the scientific and technical endeavor altogether. Heidegger's "The Question Concerning Technology" was an influential statement of such a position (Heidegger, 2013). The Cold War attack on the Western left greatly reduced the influence of the former line of critique, while encouraging the latter, which in popular form amounted to a kind of moralistic hand-wringing about the fate of "man" (Greif, 2015).

To the extent that there was a postmodern critique of science, it tended to draw more on the latter tendency than the former, and to combine it instead with powerful tools for looking at language. This had its roots in Levi-Strauss's influential work in structuralist anthropology (see, for example, Levi-Strauss, 1963; 1969), which worked from the anti-colonialist position that all cultures were equally "modern," and which was skeptical of the unilateral imposition of Western enlightenment on supposedly "backward" peoples (Levi-Strauss, 2012). But the Cold War silencing of positions that were pro-science but critical of its applications and institutional frame left a noticeable gap in the field of positions that might have contended in a more constructive way over the power of science to make truth claims and at the same time of the limits of those claims.

This becomes particularly pressing in the twenty-first-century context, where a powerful version of the anti-science argument is deployed to attack the scientific evidence for climate change (Oreskes and Conway, 2010). While it was certainly not the intention of "postmodern" critiques of science to lend succor to climate change deniers and their powerful backers in, for example, the fossil fuel industries, to some extent that has indeed come to pass. One can implicate the sciences in the development of technologies of war and environmental degradation, but at the same time it is in large part owing to scientific methods and institutions that one can make truth claims to the effect that climate change really is happening.

If the Sokal affair rather confirmed the utility of Lyotard's line of thought in *The Differend* (1988b), it is another matter with his more famous book, *The Postmodern Condition* (1984). That book, written as a sort of parody of a government report about the state of higher education, contends that knowledge no longer rests on either of the "grand recits" or **metanarratives** about **modernity**. One of these was enlightenment; the other was liberation. Knowledge, he thought, became more a matter of "parology" (1984: 60), a game played for purely formal stakes, internal to each discourse, not grounded in a larger goal beyond. That might of course be thought of as a fairly accurate description of what is actually going on in today's academia. But whether that is what ought to be the end purpose of knowledge in the era of climate change is of course quite a different matter.

Ironically, in setting out to close the door to the interpretive practices associated with the postmodern, the Sokal Affair rather opened itself up to them. Indeed, the matter could still be seen as an open one. For example, Sokal's actual text might lend itself to further scrutiny as an example of what the **Situationists** called "détournement", in the sense that Sokal cobbled it together by borrowing phrases and terms then popular in humanities discourse. As such, it exposes the unoriginality of all such language games, regardless of the field in which they play.

McKenzie Wark

Transcendental signified: You know those times when you're having an argument or debate with someone, or a group of people, about some issue or event – whether voting in democratic nations should be compulsory, or whether animals can think as such; or perhaps something seemingly less consequential or philosophical, like the meaning of a film or book, whether the governess in Henry James's *The Turn of the Screw* (1898) actually sees ghosts or is just mad, say (see Lucy, 1997: 128–30) – and one of participants in the debate makes a point that puts an end to disagreement, just stops the argument dead, not only because everyone instantly understands what that person means but also because they can see that the point made is unquestionably right, absolutely spot on …? What's more, having heard the point, you and your fellow discussants – and everyone else who heard it or comes to hear of it – remain forever convinced by it, never having cause to doubt its **truth** or to feel that there might be more to consider about the situation …?

As fanciful as this scenario sounds, it has more or less remained the dream of philosophy since Plato, who sought to arrive at an understanding of the fundamental forms or ideals defining the nature and meaning of existence through the Socratic method of **dialogue**. The thought of a fully formed, self-sustaining and eternal idea or meaning that can ground knowledge and bring the play of interpretation (understood up to this point therefore as *mis*interpretation) to an end – that is the dream of what **Derrida** sometimes calls the "transcendental signified": "a *concept signified in and of itself*, a concept simply present for thought, independent of a relationship to language, that is of a relationship to a system of signifiers" (Derrida, 1981: 19).

A Dictionary of Postmodernism, First Edition. Niall Lucy.

Across the course of the history of philosophy, this philosophical ideal has taken different forms and been given different names – being, **essence**, the cogito, Absolute Spirit, the material conditions of production – such that we might say of "the transcendental signified" (deliberately retaining the quotation marks here) something very similar to what Derrida famously said of his "différance": it "lends itself to a certain number of nonsynonymous substitutions" (Derrida, 1982: 12). It's an ideal that resonates, moreover, in contexts beyond philosophy, such as in (or as) the notion of a defined and definitive "authorial intent" that lies beneath or behind a poem, an argument, a philosophical treatise, ready to be revealed by a reading that remains "faithful" to the text "itself."

Of course, for philosophy (and not just philosophy) the transcendental signified isn't a dream or fantasy. On the contrary, it's the realist thing in (or out of) the world! It's that epistemological or ontological bedrock upon which, according to this mode of thinking, we may build our certain knowledge of everything that is beautiful and good and true – knowledge which, having been "grounded" as such, takes on in turn the stability, universality and timelessness of its metaphysical foundation. If participants in a debate (including philosophers) continue to disagree, to argue over the truth or fail to see reason, therefore, it's because one or more (or all) of them remains blind either to some flaw in their reasoning or to some unjustified assumption, which once exposed can allow truth to prevail (see **differend**). What gets in the way of consensus, then, is always some form of ignorance, prejudice or fallacy, where these obstacles are understood (ideally) not as insults or statements of character flaws but as candidates for correction and improvement on the path to truth and a more enlightened world. All that's really needed is some seriously smart thinking to lead the way.

In contrast – but not quite in opposition – to this view, Derrida suggests not only that the thought of a transcendental signified is something more like a transcendental "illusion" (in the Kantian sense; see Derrida, 1981: 33), but also that the history of philosophy itself has demonstrated this point time and again. **Semiotics** has played a large role in making the point too, although, for Derrida, Saussure's rigorous distinction between the signifier and the signified ultimately succumbs to the illusion: "from the moment that one questions the possibility of such a transcendental signified, and that one recognizes that every signified is also in the position of a signifier, the distinction between signified and signifier becomes problematical at its root" (Derrida, 1981: 20). This is not to say that there simply *is* no difference between the signifier and the signified, hence no hope for meaning or truth. It's more that, simply, the signs of truth can never entirely shed their signifiers, their "outer" "clothing," to become pure and simple signifieds. Meaning and truth "appear," that is, not (quite) transcendentally and ideally, but (also) contextually and materially, remaining marked and in a sense constituted by the materiality of their signifiers, shaped by the context of their statement and re-statement. To the extent that such contexts remain open to ongoing reflection – as **Habermas** (1987), as much as Derrida, has effectively argued, despite the former's general antipathy toward the latter – the *significance* of truth, language and **representation** continues to await its future renewal and transformation.

Robert Briggs

Truth:

Always historicize!

Frederic Jameson, epigraph to The Political Unconscious

We all know, apparently, that for something called "postmodernism" there is no such thing as truth. We've been told it often enough, not by so-called postmodernists as by those for whom postmodernism is a whipping boy. Lucy (2010b) and Lucy and Mickler (2006) have been indefatigable and bemused chroniclers of this. As they point out (in *The War on Democracy*), it's hard to see just where it might come from in any of the considerable range of the writings of the usual suspects: **Derrida**, **Lacan**, **Deleuze**, **Lyotard**, Alain Badiou … All of them spend a lot of time taking the term very seriously indeed, as indispensable to intellectual and political activity alike rather than something to be dismissed as the consensual hallucination of fools (Lucy, 2010b; Lucy and Mickler, 2006). It is like the phrases "Elementary, my dear Watson," and "Play it again, Sam," which never seem to have existed as first-degree utterances made by the ones to whom they're variously attributed, but have grown out of and proliferated in the thickets of commentary.

And of course, to take the idea of truth seriously involves recognition of its very difficulty, its aporetics, even – dare we say it, without giving an inch to the boy-whippers? – its *impossibility*. To see truth as being in an important sense impossible is not at all the same thing as a declaration that truth doesn't exist. It's (more interestingly) to say that there is a contradiction at its heart *without which* it would not exist. (See the discussion of the supplement in the entry on **Derrida**.) Impossibility is not so much a denial of existence as the mark of a certain very important mode in which certain categories have their existence.

Let's consider that claim, "There is no such thing as truth," on its own terms. Let's do it not in order to debunk it, but to see what this oddly rootless statement can tell us about truth – this statement that gets repeatedly attributed to an entire group of utterly disparate writers in none of whose work it has ever appeared, but which is repeatedly held, by other writers who repeatedly appear to have read very little of that work, to be at the heart of a shared philosophy, summing it up.

Most obviously, the very statement "There is no such thing as truth" is itself a truth claim. To have any purchase at all, it has to claim some truth, and some general truth at that. It isn't even enough to posit that as the single excusable exception needed in order to get a thoroughgoing relativism off the ground because, in its exceptionalism, what "There is no such thing as truth" claims is a universality, even if a negative one. There is no such thing as truth, it says, anywhere, except necessarily and problematically in this one place, this exception that completely contradicts the rule that there's no such thing as truth, but without which there's not even any possible conception of that rule. Truth floods back in: negative, to be sure, but universal and unavoidable. And it's a peculiarly empty truth: it doesn't say *this* or *that* particular content is universally true, it's just the empty formal demand that's necessary if a particular utterance is to make sense. Truth is not so much a lack as a sort of uncontrollable excess, an essential instability in the system. Truth emerges as what Derrida calls an *undecidable*: which is not to say as a place at which no decision can or should be made, but the place at which a decision *must* be made, because without that decision nothing proceeds.

There's the same fold at work here in **Jameson**'s famous epigraph to *The Political Unconscious* (1981): "Always historicize!" One historicizes, *always*: the one thing that is itself not subjected to the vicissitudes of historicization is the act of historicizing. The point is not that Jameson is wrong, but that he is not interested in the implications of that fold for his project.

There is another dimension to this, too. In the ninth of his seminars, Lacan (2011 [Fr. 1961–2]) talks about a similar statement, the famous Cretan liar paradox, "I am lying," and argues that it's too quick a conclusion to draw that it's just self-contradictory (I am lying, therefore this statement is a lie and I'm telling the truth after all, therefore I'm lying, therefore I'm telling the truth, and so on and so on). That would be to stick to the sheer content of it, what's said, and to ignore a vital dimension of any utterance, the *fact* of utterance, the act of saying it. I can, after all, tell what is strictly speaking, from the point of view of the content, truth itself, but do that in order to lie and deceive in the act of utterance. Former US President Bill Clinton's famous denial in the Lewinsky affair, "I did not have sexual relations with that woman," is one such example. It's meant to be categorically true if we take "have sexual relations" in a narrow sense of genital contact and penetration, but it's said in order to dismiss the wide range of undoubtedly sexual and erotic activities that did take place. One can tell the truth in order to lie. That's the suspicion behind the punchline in a joke Freud tells, about two enemies together on a train:

> "If you say you're going to Cracow, you want me to believe you're going to Lemberg. But I know in fact you're going to Cracow. So why are you lying to me?" (Freud, 2001: vol. VIII)

More interesting, though, is the other possibility: it may be that even in the act of willful lying, one does not know when one is telling the truth – what little tics and unconscious tells beyond control are giving the game away even as one speaks. I am lying, but I have absolutely no idea of just where and how I may despite myself be telling the truth in my most intricate and careful lie. The act of saying it works against what is actually said. Where the first instance is that of the conscious calculation of just what I can say that is strictly true but will end up deceiving, in the second things escape my calculation. I lie, I tell the truth, both at once, each informing the other. I am lying.

We find this very often in certain claims made about metalanguage, language about language. Certain "metafictional" novels, for example, play freely with the idea that they are not just representations of the world but novels. This is often called postmodern, though it's hardly new. It was, after all, one of the first great European novels, *Don Quixote*, that played with the idea that you'd be a fool to believe what you read in novels (and at the same time tied that knot tighter by making the claim *in* a novel). To say nothing of *Tristram Shandy*. It's more accurate to say that any act of language involves the metalingual. The conversational reminder "You know what I mean?" asks for comment or reassurance on what's gone before, and from its first sentence *Pride and Prejudice* brings with it the entire genre of the marriage plot.

The claim that much theory of metafiction makes is based largely on the straw figure that there are some sorts of fiction that *don't* have these characteristics, or that ignore these features and invite the reader to ignore them too.

(But what reader really does ever ignore that they are reading a novel, in the full knowledge of its fictiveness?) A supposed "traditional" novel, then, claims to know, to tell the truth. The "metafictional" novel, on the other hand, so the claim goes (see for example Hutcheon, 1988: 105–23), *knows that it's not telling the truth* – and in doing so, on the rebound, lays claim to knowing a further more modest truth of its own, even if that should be no more than the knowledge of its own limits. It lays claim to a superior honesty and integrity that refuses any attempts to deceive. (But then when *did* fiction deceive, when its claim is not "I am speaking the truth" but "All this is a fiction"?)

Moreover, could that claim be truly separable from the disavowal that's inescapable in any first-person utterance of the form, "I am honest"? It's not that there is no honesty in the world, but that there must always be a stake in the claim, and the extent of that stake can never be calculated by the parties involved. What that amounts to is that the metafictional claim, "I know I'm not speaking the whole truth," has the structure of Freud's Cracow–Lemberg joke: "You say you're not speaking the whole truth in order to make me think that on another level you are in fact being honest with me and telling me the truth. But I know that you're not telling the truth anyway. So why are you lying to me?"

If the truth of an utterance has this paradoxical structure (see **Eco**), then isn't the negative in the wrong place in that proposition that I know I'm not telling the truth? Isn't it more that truth is such that I can't know when I *am* speaking it? Even in the middle of my most calculated lie, I can never be sure that some aspect of what I'm saying isn't just giving the game away. There is a truth, and it's there on the surface, perhaps plainly or even painfully there to read, but just what it is and the full extent of its implications is not something I can calculate and guarantee beforehand. We produce truth whether or not we acknowledge it, and our knowledge of the truth we've produced is often late and after the event.

It's this constitutive impossibility of truth that we find in all sorts of ways throughout much of what's often seen as postmodern thought: see, for example, Derrida, Lacan, **Žižek**. What that constitutive impossibility means is not the fatuous relativism that "there is no such thing as truth." On the contrary: there's a discomforting excess of it, as it everywhere exceeds our calculations and our accounting.

Tony Thwaites

ABCDEFGHIJKLMNOPQRSTUVWXY**Z**

Žižek, Slavoj: *Slovenian philosopher, cultural critic and psychoanalytic theorist, born 1949*

If **Lacan** is Freud reinterpreted in the wake of Saussure, Žižek reads Lacan not only as the single most important figure in psychoanalysis since Freud, but as a major philosopher in the Continental and specifically Hegelian traditions, and the basis for a significant rethinking of much classical political theory, especially theories of ideology.

For Žižek, if we are to take psychoanalysis and its logic of the unconscious seriously, it can be little more than naïve to think of ideology as a sort of "false consciousness" to be dispelled by the conscious clarity of demystification. That claim "I am aware" is all too easily nothing more than sophisticated ruse: for Žižek, the basic structure of disavowal is "I know [that such-and-such is really the case], but nevertheless [I behave as if it weren't]" (Žižek, 1989: 18; 2001: 126; 2002: 241–5; 2012: 120, 679–80 – to name only a few). The essential twist that is at the heart of the Lacanian subject now becomes the heart of the social relation too. The great "superego imperatives," as he calls them (Žižek, 2000), of postmodern late capitalist liberal democracies are thus not the simple injunctions and prohibitions beloved of dystopian fiction from *1984* (Orwell, 1993 [1949]) to *Deliverance* (Dickey, 1970) ("Do this," "Don't do this," "Be this," "Don't be this"), but the folds of double binds one can neither obey nor disobey: "Be yourself!" "Think for yourself!" or, more simply, "Enjoy!"

A Dictionary of Postmodernism, First Edition. Niall Lucy.

And here we reach a fold at the very end of this book too. For Žižek, the postmodern is simply the name for what we have when the "dialectic of the Law and its inherent transgression is given an additional twist: transgression is more and more directly enjoined by the Law itself" (2008: 29). When one attempts to dissolve the Law, to *declare* it dissolved, does not that declaration itself become the Law? "There are no more grand narratives" becomes the one **metanarrative** left on the shelves, the one that makes all the others redundant. What it authorizes and makes necessary is the proliferation of small narratives among which there can only be **differends**, and in which the social relation is reduced to a matter of the proliferation of multiple and conflicting rights. For Žižek, the postmodern is a mirror of the superego injunctions of capitalism itself, from advertising ("Where do you want to go today?" "Just do it") to Margaret Thatcher's declaration that "There is no such thing as society." In the place of the master-signifier, we have instead the ferocity of the superego imperative, which never lets go in its irresolvability.

Tony Thwaites

References

Adorno, T. (2008) *Lectures on Negative Dialectics: Fragments of a Lecture Course 1965/1966*. Ed. R. Tiedemann. Trans. R. Livingstone. Cambridge: Polity Press.

Adorno, T. and M. Horkheimer (2002) *Dialectic of Enlightenment: Philosophical Fragments*. Trans. E. Jephcott. Stanford: Stanford University Press.

Ahluwalia, P. and T. Miller (2005) "Editorial Note: Journal of Tendency/Journal of Record." *Social Identities: Journal for the Study of Race, Nation and Culture*, 11(2), 87–8.

Allen, M. (2011) "Before and After Pruitt Igoe." Pruitt Igoe Now. Accessible at: http://www.pruittigoenow.org/before-and-after/.

Allen, M. and N. Wendl (2011) "The Unmentioned Modern Landscape." Pruitt Igoe Now. Accessible at: http://www.pruittigoenow.org/the-unmentioned-modern-landscape/.

Amerika, M. (2011a) *Remix the Book*. Minneapolis: University of Minnesota Press.

Amerika, M. (2011b) "Surf-Sample-Manipulate: The Pseudo-Autobiography of A Work-In-Progress." Professor VJ. Accessible at: http://professorvj.blogspot.com.au/2011_06_19_archive.html.

Anonymous (n.d.) "About." OccupyWallStreet.org. Accessible at: http://occupywallst.org/about/.

Aristotle (350 BCE). *Politics*. Trans. B. Jowett. *The Internet Classics Archive*. Accessible at: http://classics.mit.edu/Aristotle/politics.html.

Armitage, J. (2000) "Beyond Postmodernism? Paul Virilio's Hypermodern Cultural Theory." *CTheory*. Accessible at: http://www.ctheory.net/articles.aspx?id=133.

Auerbach, E. (1974) *Mimesis: The Representation of Reality in Western Literature*. Trans. W. Trask. Princeton: Princeton University Press.

A Dictionary of Postmodernism, First Edition. Niall Lucy.

Austin, J. (1975) *How to Do Things with Words*, 3rd edn. Ed. J. Urmson and M. Sbisà. Cambridge, MA: Harvard University Press.

Azuma H. (2001) *Otaku: Japan's Database Animals*. Minneapolis: University of Minnesota Press.

Bailey, J. (1965) "The Case History of a Failure." *Architectural Forum*. Accessible at: https://courses.the-bac.edu/Spring2014/PROGRAMMINGTM685-7685/Week1/PruittIgoe-CasehistoryofaFailure-fromARCHITECTURALFORUM.pdf.

Bakhtin, M. (1981) *The Dialogic Imagination*. Austin: University of Texas Press.

Bakhtin, M. (1984) *Problems of Dostoevsky's Poetics*. Minneapolis: University of Minnesota Press.

Barth, J. (1967) "The Literature of Exhaustion." *The Atlantic*, 220(2), 29–34.

Barthes, R. (1967) *Elements of Semiology*. Trans. A. Lavers and C. Smith. London: Jonathan Cape.

Barthes, R. (1970) *S/Z*. Trans. R. Miller. New York: Hill and Wang.

Barthes, R. (1972) *Mythologies*. Trans. A. Lavers. London: Granada.

Barthes, R. (1975) *The Pleasure of the Text*. Trans. R. Miller. New York: Hill and Wang.

Barthes, R. (1977a) *Image – Music – Text*. Ed. and trans. S. Heath. London: Fontana.

Barthes, R. (1977b) *Roland Barthes*. Trans. R. Howard. New York: Macmillan.

Barthes, R. (1978) *A Lover's Discourse: Fragments*. Trans. R. Howard. New York: Farrar, Straus and Giroux.

Barthes, R. (1981) *Camera Lucida: Reflections on Photography*. Trans. R. Howard. New York: Hill and Wang.

Barthes, R. (1985) *The Fashion System*. Trans. M. Ward and R. Howard. London: Jonathan Cape.

Baudrillard, J. (1981) *For a Critique of the Political Economy of the Sign*. Trans. C. Levin. St Louis: Telos Press.

Baudrillard, J. (1983) *Simulations*. Trans. P. Foss, P. Patton and P. Beitchman. New York: Semiotext(e).

Baudrillard, J. (1988a) *Selected Writings*. Ed. and Int. M. Poster. Cambridge: Polity Press.

Baudrillard, J. (1988b) *The Ecstasy of Communication*. Trans. B. and C. Schutze. New York: Semiotext(e).

Baudrillard, J. (1990) *Seduction*. Trans. B. Singer. New York: St Martin's Press.

Baudrillard, J. (1993a) *Symbolic Exchange and Death*. London: Sage.

Baudrillard, J. (1993b) *The Transparency of Evil: Essays on Extreme Phenomena*. Trans. James Benedict. London: Verso.

Baudrillard, J. (1995) *The Gulf War Did Not Take Place*. Trans. P. Patton. Bloomington: Indiana University Press.

Baudrillard, J. (2000) *The Vital Illusion*. Ed. J. Witwer. New York: Columbia University Press.

Baudrillard, J. (2001) *Impossible Exchange*. Trans. C. Turner. London: Verso.

Baudrillard, J. (2003) *The Spirit of Terrorism and Other Essays*, new edn. London: Verso.

Baulch, E. (2007) *Making Scenes: Reggae, Punk, and Death Metal in 1990s Bali*. Durham, NC: Duke University Press.

BBC (2003) *The Cambridge Spies*. Accessible at: http://www.bbc.co.uk/history/historic_figures/spies_cambridge.shtml; and http://www.bbc.co.uk/history/worldwars/coldwar/cambridge_spies_01.shtml.

BBC Films (1992) *The Last Romantics*. Accessible at: http://www.imdb.com/title/tt0102276/.

Beckett, S. (1962) "Letter to Alan Schneider, June 21, 1956." In *The Village Voice Reader*, ed. D. Wolf and E. Fancher. Garden City, NY: Doubleday, 183.

Beckett, S. (1974) *Texts for Nothing*. London: Calder & Boyars.

Benjamin, A. (1991) *Art, Mimesis and the Avant-Garde: Aspects of a Philosophy of Difference*. London: Routledge.

Bennett, T. (2003) *Formalism and Marxism*, 2nd edn. London: Routledge.

Bhabha, H. (1994) *The Location of Culture*. London: Routledge.

Biagioli, M. (ed.) (1999) *The Science Studies Reader*. New York: Routledge.

Bloom, H. (1994) *The Western Canon: The Books and School of the Ages*. New York: Harcourt Brace & Co.

Bogost, I. (2008) *Unit Operations: An Approach to Videogame Criticism*. Cambridge, MA: MIT Press.

Bolter, J. and R. Grusin (2000) *Remediation: Understanding New Media*. Cambridge, MA: MIT Press.

Bonner, F., S. McKay and A. McKee (2001) "On the Beach." *Continuum: Journal of Media & Cultural Studies*, 15(3), 270–4.

Borges, J. L. (1964) *Labyrinths. Selected Stories and Other Writings*. Ed. D. Yates and Ja. Irby. New York: New Directions.

Bourdieu, P. (1979) "Public Opinion Does Not Exist." In *Communication and Class Struggle, Vol. I: Capitalism, Imperialism*, ed. Armand Mattelart and Seth Siegelaub. New York: International General, 124–30.

Bradshaw, P. (2013) "[Review of] *Django Unchained*." *The Guardian*, January 18. Accessible at: http://www.guardian.co.uk/film/2013/jan/17/django-unchained-review.

Brandist, C. (n.d.) "The Bakhtin Circle." *Internet Encyclopedia of Philosophy*. Accessible at: http://www.iep.utm.edu/bakhtin/.

Briggs, R. and N. Lucy (2012a) "Art as Research?" *Ctrl-Z: New Media Philosophy*, 2(December). Accessible at: http://www.ctrl-z.net.au//journal?slug=briggs-lucy-art-as-research.

Briggs, R. and N. Lucy (2012b) "Frame #1 – ones & zeroes, light & shade (dimensions: 4, easter eggs: 3)." *Ctrl-Z: New Media Philosophy*, 1 (July). Accessible at: http://www.ctrl-z.net.au//journal?slug=briggs-lucy-frame.

Burgess, A. (1967) *A Clockwork Orange*. London: Heinemann.

Burgess, A. (1989) "A Conspiracy to Rule the World." *The New York Times*, October 15. Accessible at: http://www.nytimes.com/1989/10/15/books/a-conspiracy-to-rule-the-world.html.

Burgess, A. (1992) *A Mouthful of Air*. London: Hutchinson.

Butler, J. (1990) *Gender Trouble: Feminism and the Subversion of Identity*. New York: Routledge.

Cage, J. (1987) "Lecture on Nothing." In *Silence: Lectures and Writings*. London: Marion Boyars, 109–26.

Camille, M. (1996) "Simulacrum." In *Critical Terms for Art History*, ed. R. Nelson and R. Shiff. Chicago: University of Chicago Press, 31–44.

Caputo, J. D. (1997) *Deconstruction in a Nutshell: A Conversation with Jacques Derrida*. New York: Fordham University Press.

Carr, W. (n.d.) "Anthony Burgess on Low-Life Language." The International Anthony Burgess Foundation Blog. Accessible at: http://www.anthonyburgess.org/?mediablog=anthony-burgess-on-low-life-language.

Carroll, L. (1872) *Through the Looking-Glass*. Accessible at: http://gutenberg.readingroo.ms/1/12/12-h/12-h.htm.

Carson, R. (1962) *Silent Spring*. Boston: Houghton Mifflin.

Castells, M. (1996) *The Rise of Network Society*. Oxford: Blackwell.

Cecil, W. (1993) "[Review of] Fredric Jameson, *Postmodernism, or, The Cultural Logic of Late-Capitalism*." *Surfaces*, 3, 12.

Chun, W. H-K. (2008) *Control and Freedom: Power and Paranoia in the Age of Fiber Optics*. Cambridge, MA: MIT Press.

Colebrook, C. (2006) *Deleuze: A Guide for the Perplexed*. London: Continuum.

Colebrook, C. (2009) "The Singularity of The Triffids." In *Vagabond Holes: David McComb and The Triffids*, ed. C. Coughran and N. Lucy. Fremantle, WA: Fremantle Press, 303–14.

Coleman, G. (2014) *Hacker, Hoaxer, Whistleblower, Spy: The Many Faces of Anonymous*. Brooklyn, NY: Verso.

Corbusier, Le [C-É. Jeanneret-Gris] (2007) *Toward an Architecture*. Trans. J. Goodman. Los Angeles: Getty Research Institute.

Dalgliesh, B. (2013) "Globalisation and Mondialisation." *Fast Capital*, 10(1). Accessible at: http://www.uta.edu/huma/agger/fastcapitalism/10_1/dalgliesh10_1.html.

Dawkins, R. (1998) "Postmodernism Disrobed." *Nature* 394 (July), 141–3.

Dean, J. (2010) *Blog Theory: Feedback and Capture in the Circuits of Drive*. Cambridge: Polity Press.

Debord, G. (1994) *The Society of the Spectacle*. New York: Zone Books.

Debord, G. (2001) *Comments on the Society of the Spectacle*. London: Verso.

Debord, G. (2004) *Panegyric: Volumes 1 and 2*. London: Verso.

Debord, G. (2005) *Complete Cinematic Works: Scripts, Stills, Documents*. Edinburgh: AK Press.

Deleuze, G. (1983) "Plato and the Simulacrum." Trans. R. Krauss. *October*, 27 (Winter), 45–56.

Deleuze, G. (2002) *Francis Bacon: The Logic of Sensation*. Trans. D. Smith. Minneapolis: University of Minnesota Press.

Deleuze, G. and F. Guattari (1983) *Anti-Oedipus: Capitalism and Schizophrenia*. Trans. R. Hurley, M. Seem and H. Lane. Minneapolis: University of Minnesota Press.

Deleuze, G. and F. Guattari (1986) *Kafka: Toward a Minor Literature*. Trans. D. Polan. Minneapolis: University of Minnesota Press.

Deleuze, G. and F. Guattari (1987) *A Thousand Plateaus: Capitalism and Schizophrenia*. Trans. B. Massumi. Minneapolis MN: University of Minnesota Press.

Deleuze, G. and F. Guattari (1994) *What Is Philosophy?* Trans. H. Tomlinson and G. Burchill. London: Verso.

DeLillo, D. (1986) *White Noise*. Picador: London.

De Man, P. (1996) *Aesthetic Ideology*. Ed. A. Warminski. Minneapolis: University of Minnesota Press.

Derrida, J. (1976) *Of Grammatology*. Trans. G. C. Spivak. Baltimore: Johns Hopkins University Press.

Derrida, J. (1978) *Writing and Difference*. Trans. A. Bass. Chicago: University of Chicago Press.

Derrida, J. (1981) *Positions*. Trans. A. Bass. London: Athlone.

Derrida, J. (1982) *Margins of Philosophy*. Chicago: University of Chicago Press.

Derrida, J. (1985) "Letter to a Japanese Friend." In *Derrida and Difference*, ed. D. Wood and R. Bernasconi. Warwick, CT: Parousia Press, 1–5.

Derrida, J. (1987a) *The Post Card: From Socrates to Freud and Beyond*. Trans. A. Bass. Chicago: University of Chicago Press.

Derrida, J. (1987b) *The Truth in Painting*. Trans. G. Bennington and I. McLeod. Chicago: University of Chicago Press.

Derrida, J. (1990) *Glas*. Trans. J. P. Leavey Jr. and R. Yand. Lincoln: University of Nebraska Press.

Derrida, J. (1992) *Given Time, Vol. I: Counterfeit Money*. Trans. P. Kamuf. Chicago: University of Chicago Press.

Derrida, J. (1994) *Specters of Marx: The State of the Debt, the Work of Mourning, and the New International*. Trans. P. Kamuf. New York: Routledge.

Derrida, J. (1995) *The Gift of Death*. Trans. D. Wills. Chicago: University of Chicago Press.

Derrida, J. (1999) *Adieu to Emmanuel Levinas*. Trans. P-A. Brault and M. Naas. Stanford: Stanford University Press.

Derrida, J. (2000) *Of Hospitality: Anne Dufourmantelle Invites Jacques Derrida to Respond*. Trans. R. Bowlby. Stanford: Stanford University Press.

Derrida, J. (2001) *The Work of Mourning*. Ed. and trans. P-A. Brault and M. Naas. Chicago: University of Chicago Press.

Derrida, J. (2003) *On Cosmopolitanism and Forgiveness*. Trans. M. Dooley and M. Hughes. London: Routledge.

Derrida, J. (2005) *Paper Machine*. Trans. R. Bowlby. Stanford: Stanford University Press.

Derrida, J. (2008) *The Animal That Therefore I Am*. Ed. Marie-Louise Mallet. Trans. D. Wills. New York: Fordham University Press.

Derrida, J. (2009) *The Beast and the Sovereign*, vol. I. Ed. M. Lisse, M-L. Mallet and G. Michaud. Trans. G. Bennington. Chicago: University of Chicago Press.

Derrida, J. (2011) *The Beast and the Sovereign*, vol. II. Ed. M. Lisse, M-L. Mallet and G. Michaud. Trans. G. Bennington. Chicago: University of Chicago Press.

Descartes, R. (1999) *Discourse on Method and Related Writings*. Ed. D. Clarke. Harmondsworth: Penguin.

Dickey, J. (1970) *Deliverance*. New York: Delta.

Dingee, W. (2011) "Fifteen Questions with Umberto Eco." *The Harvard Crimson Magazine*, November 17. Accessible at: http://www.thecrimson.com/article/2011/11/17/umberto-writer-interview/.

Dunbar, H. and X. Wang (2012) "St. Louis Ecological Production Line." Pruitt Igoe Now. Accessible at: http://www.pruittigoenow.org/projects/winners/1-st-louis-ecological-production-line/.

Dutton, D. (1992) "Umberto Eco on Interpretation." *Philosophy and Literature*, 16, 432–37. Accessible at: http://www.denisdutton.com/eco_review.htm.

Eagleton, T. (1983) *Literary Theory: An Introduction*. Oxford: Blackwell.

Eco, U. (1972) "Towards a Semiotic Inquiry into the Television Message." Trans. Paola Splendore. *Working Papers in Cultural Studies*, 3, 103–21.

Eco, U. (1976) *A Theory of Semiotics*. Bloomington: Indiana University Press.

Eco, U. (1984) *The Role of the Reader: Explorations in the Semiotics of Texts*. Bloomington: Indiana University Press.

Eco, U. (1986) *Travels in Hyperreality*. Trans. W. Weaver. London: Picador.

Eco, U. (1989) *Foucault's Pendulum*. London: Secker & Warburg.

Eco, U. (1992) *Interpretation and Overinterpretation*. Cambridge: Cambridge University Press.

Eco, U. (1993) *Misreadings*. New York: Mariner Books.

Eco, U. (2014) *The Name of the Rose* and *Postscript to The Name of The Rose*. New York: Mariner Books.

Eisenhower, President D. (1961) "Farewell Address." Accessible at: http://www.eisenhower.archives.gov/research/online_documents/farewell_address/Reading_Copy.pdf.

Eliot, T. S. (1915) "The Love Song of J. Alfred Prufrock." Accessible at: http://www.gutenberg.org/etext/1459.

Eliot, T. S. (1922) *The Waste Land*. Accessible at: http://www.gutenberg.org/etext/1321.

Eliot, T. S. (1923) "Ulysses, Order, and Myth." Accessible at: http://people.virginia.edu/~jdk3t/eliotulysses.htm.

Farndale, N. (2005) "Heavyweight Champion." *The Telegraph*, May 24. Accessible at: http://www.telegraph.co.uk/culture/books/3642577/Heavyweight-champion.html.

Fiske, J. (1983) "Surfalism and Sandiotics: The Beach in Oz Popular Culture." *Australian Journal of Cultural Studies*, 1(2), 120–49.

Fiske, J. and J. Hartley (1978) *Reading Television*. London: Methuen. 2nd edn 2003, Routledge.

Fiske, J., B. Hodge and G. Turner (1987) *Myths of Oz: Reading Australian Popular Culture*. Sydney: Allen & Unwin.

Flew, T. (2014) "Six Theories of Neoliberalism." *Thesis Eleven* 122(1), 49–71.

Foucault, M. (1967) *Madness and Civilization: A History of Insanity in the Age of Reason*. Trans. R. Howard. London: Tavistock.

Foucault, M. (1970) *The Order of Things: An Archaeology of the Human Sciences*. London: Tavistock.

Foucault, M. (1972) *The Archaeology of Knowledge*. Trans. A. M. Sheridan Smith. London: Tavistock.

Foucault, M. (1973) *The Birth of the Clinic: An Archaeology of Medical Perception*. Trans. A. M. Sheridan Smith. London: Tavistock.

Foucault, M. (1979) *Discipline and Punish: The Birth of the Prison*. Trans. A. Sheridan. Harmondsworth: Penguin.

Foucault, M. (1980) *The History of Sexuality, Vol. I: An Introduction*. Trans. R. Hurley. New York: Vintage Books.

Foucault, M. (1982) "The subject and power." In *Michel Foucault: Beyond Structuralism and Hermeneutics*. Ed. H. L. Dreyfus and P. Rabinow. Chicago: University of Chicago Press, 208–26.

Foucault, M. (1984) *The Foucault Reader*. Ed. P Rabinow. London: Penguin.

Foucault, M. (1985) *The History of Sexuality, Vol. II: The Use of Pleasure*. Trans. R. Hurley. New York: Vintage Books.

Foucault, M. (1988) *The History of Sexuality, Vol. III: The Care of the Self*. Trans. R. Hurley. New York: Vintage Books.

Foucault, M. (1991) "Governmentality." In *The Foucault Effect: Studies in Governmentality*, ed. G. Burchell, C. Gordon and P. Miller. Chicago: University of Chicago Press, 87–104.

Foucault, M. (2008) *This is Not a Pipe*. Trans. J. Harkness. Berkeley: University of California Press.

Freud, S. (2001) *The Standard Edition of the Complete Psychological Works of Sigmund Freud*. Ed. and trans. J. Strachey, in collaboration with Anna Freud, assisted by Alix Strachey and Alan Tyson, 24 vols [Reprint]. London: Vintage.

Freud, S. (2010) *The Interpretation of Dreams*. Ed. and trans. J. Strachey. New York: Basic Books.

Frith, S. (1983) "The Pleasures of the Hearth: The Making of BBC Light Entertainment." In *Formations of Pleasure*, ed. Formations Collective. London: Routledge & Kegan Paul, 101–23.

Frith, S. and H. Home (1988) *Art into Pop*. London: Methuen.

Galloway, A. (2003) *Protocol: How Control Exists After Decentralization*. Cambridge, MA: MIT Press

Galloway, A. (2006) *Gaming: Essays on Algorithmic Culture*. Minneapolis: University of Minnesota Press.

Galloway, A., E. Thacker and McK. Wark (2013) *Excommunication: Three Inquiries in Media and Mediation*. Chicago: University of Chicago Press.

Gasché, R. (1986) *The Tain of the Mirror: Derrida and the Philosophy of Reflection*. Cambridge, MA: Harvard University Press.

Gaskell, E. (1987) *Cranford*. New York: Marshall Cavendish.

Gibbons, F. (2001) "Judges Switched On as Turner Prize Goes to the Creed of Nothingness." *The Guardian*, December 10. Accessible at: http://www.guardian.co.uk/uk/2001/dec/10/20yearsoftheturnerprize.turnerprize2001.

Gibson, M. (2001) "Myths of Oz Cultural Studies: The Australian Beach and "English" Ordinariness." *Continuum: Journal of Media & Cultural Studies*, 15(3), 275–88.

Gibson, M. (2007) *Culture and Power: A History of Cultural Studies*. Oxford: Berg.

Golumbia, D. (2009) *The Cultural Logic of Computation*. Cambridge, MA: Harvard University Press.

Gould, S. J. (1981) *The Mismeasure of Man*. New York: W.W. Norton.

Greenberg, C. (1939) "Avant-Garde and Kitsch." *Partisan Review* 6(5), 34–49.

Greif, M. (2015) *The Age of the Crisis of Man: Thought and Fiction in America 1933–1973*. Princeton: Princeton University Press.

Habermas, J. (1970) *Toward a Rational Society*. Trans. J. J. Shapiro. Boston: Beacon.

Habermas, J. (1972) *Knowledge and Human Interests*. Trans J. J. Shapiro. London: Heinemann.

Habermas, J. (1987) *The Philosophical Discourse of Modernity: Twelve Lectures*. Trans F. Lawrence. Cambridge, MA: MIT Press.

Habermas, J. (1988). *Legitimation Crisis*. Trans. T. McCarthy. Cambridge: Polity Press.

Habermas, J. (1992) *Postmetaphysical Thinking: Philosophical Essays*. Trans. W. M. Hohengarten. Cambridge, MA: MIT Press.

Habermas, J. (1996) *Between Facts and Norms: Contributions to a Discourse Theory of Law and Democracy*. Trans. W. Rehg. Cambridge, MA: MIT Press.

Habermas, J. (1997) "Modernity: An Unfinished Project." In *Habermas and the Unfinished Project of Modernity: Critical Essays on The philosophical Discourse of Modernity*, ed. M. Passerin d"Entrèves and S. Benhabib. Cambridge, MA: MIT Press, 38–55.

Hall, S. (1973) "Encoding and Decoding in the Television Discourse." Centre for Contemporary Cultural Studies, University of Birmingham, *CCCS Stencilled Paper* no. 7.

Hall, S. (2007) "Richard Hoggart, *The Uses of Literacy* and the Cultural Turn." *International Journal of Cultural Studies*, 10(1), 39–49.

Hall, S. and P. Whannel (1964) *The Popular Arts*. London: Hutchinson.

Haraway, D. (1990a) "A Manifesto For Cyborgs: Science, Technology, and Socialist Feminism in the 1980s." In *Feminism/Postmodernism*, ed. L. Nicholson. New York: Routledge, 190–233.

Haraway, D. (1990b) *Primate Visions: Gender, Race and Nature in the World of Modern Science*. New York: Routledge.

Haraway, D. (1991) *Simians, Cyborgs, and Women: The Reinvention of Nature*. New York: Routledge.

Hartley, J. (1982) *Understanding News*. London: Methuen.

Hartley, J. (2012) *Digital Futures for Cultural Studies and Media Studies*. Oxford: Wiley-Blackwell.

Hartley, J. and J. Green (2006) "The Public Sphere on the Beach." *European Journal of Cultural Studies*, 9(3), 341–63.

Hartley, J., N. Lucy and R. Briggs (2013) "DIY John Curtin: Uncertain Futures for Heritage and Citizenship in the Era of Digital Friends and Foes." *International Journal of Cultural Studies*, 16(6), 557–77.

Harvey, David (1989) *The Condition of Postmodernity*. Oxford: Blackwell.

Hassan, I. (1967) *The Literature of Silence: Henry Miller and Samuel Beckett*. New York: Alfred A. Knopf.

Hassan, I. (1972) *Paracriticisms: Seven Speculations of the Times*. Champaign: University of Illinois Press.

Hassan, I. (1982) *The Dismemberment of Orpheus: Towards a Postmodern Literature*. Madison: University of Wisconsin Press.

Hassan, I. (1987) *The Postmodern Turn: Essays in Postmodern Theory and Culture*. Columbus: Ohio State University Press.

Hawkes, T. (1977) *Structuralism and Semiotics*. London: Routledge.

Hayles, K. (1999) *How We Became Posthuman: Virtual Bodies in Cybernetics, Literature, and Informatics*. Chicago: University of Chicago Press.

Hebdige, D. (1979) *Subculture: The Meaning of Style*. London: Methuen.

Heidegger, M. (1971) "The Origin of the Work of Art." In *Poetry, Language, Thought*. Trans. A. Hofstadter. New York: Harper and Row, 15–87.

Heidegger, M. (2013) *The Question Concerning Technology and Other Essays*. New York: Harper.

Hoffmeyer, J. (1996) *Signs of Meaning in the Universe*. Bloomington: Indiana University Press.

Hoffmeyer, J. (2010) "A Biosemiotic Approach to the Question of Meaning." *Zygon* 45(2), 367–90.

Holmes, B. (2012) *Critical Art Ensemble: Disturbances*. London: Four Corners Books.

Home, S. (1995) *Cranked Up Really High: Genre Theory and Punk Rock*. London: Codex.

Huffington Post (2011) "George Soros Responds To Glenn Beck, Fox News Attacks." February 19. Accessible at: http://www.huffingtonpost.com/2011/02/19/george-soros-glenn-beck-fox-news_n_825489.html.

Hunter, I. (2006) "The History of Theory." *Critical Inquiry* 32(4), 78–112.

Hutcheon, L. (1988) *The Poetics of Postmodernism: History, Theory, Fiction*. New York: Routledge.

Hyde, L. (1998) *Trickster Makes This World: Mischief, Myth, and Art*. New York: Farrar, Strauss and Giroux; UK: Canongate Books, Edinburgh, 2008.

Invisible Committee (2009) *The Coming Insurrection*. Los Angeles: Semiotext(e).

Invisible Committee (2015) *To Our Friends*. Los Angeles: Semiotext(e).

Irwin, G. and C. Walrond (2012) "When was New Zealand first settled?" *Te Ara – The Encyclopedia of New Zealand*. Accessible at: http://www.TeAra.govt.nz/en/when-was-new-zealand-first-settled.

Jaggi, M. (2002) "Signs of the times." *Guardian Online*, October 12. Acessible at: http://www.theguardian.com/books/2002/oct/12/fiction.academicexperts.

James, H. (1898). *The Turn of the Screw*. Available at: http://www.gutenberg.org/ebooks/209.

Jameson, F. (1972) *The Prison-House of Language: A Critical Account of Structuralism and Russian Formalism*. Princeton: Princeton University Press.

Jameson, F. (1981) *The Political Unconscious: Narrative as a Socially Symbolic Act*. London: Methuen.

Jameson, F. (1991) *Postmodernism, or, The Cultural Logic of Late-Capitalism*. Durham, NC: Duke University Press.

Jameson, F. (2013) *A Singular Modernity*. London: Verso.

Jencks, C. (1973) *Modern Movements in Architecture*. New York: Anchor Press.

Jencks, C. (1977/2002) *The Language of Post-Modern Architecture*. London: Academy Editions; New York: Rizzoli. Reissued 2002 as: *The New Paradigm in Architecture: The Language of Post-Modernism*. New Haven: Yale University Press.

Jencks, C. (2003) *The Garden of Cosmic Speculation*. London: Frances Lincoln.

Jencks, C. (n.d.) "Maggie's Centres." CharlesJencks.com. Accessible at: http://www.charlesjencks.com/#!maggie%27s-centres.

Jencks, C. and E. Heathcote (2010) *The Architecture of Hope: Maggie's Cancer Caring Centres*. London: Frances Lincoln.

Joyce, J. (1975) *Finnegans Wake*. London: Faber & Faber.

Kandell, J. (2004) "Jacques Derrida, Abstruse Theorist, Dies at 74." *The New York Times*, October 10. Accessible at: http://www.nytimes.com/2004/10/10/obituaries/10derrida.html.

Kant, I. (1784) "Answering the Question: What is Enlightenment?." Trans. D. F. Ferrer, 2013. Accessible at: https://archive.org/details/AnswerTheQuestionWhatIsEnlightenment.

Kant, I. (1785) *Fundamental Principles of the Metaphysic of Morals*. Trans. T. K. Abbott. Available at: http://eserver.org/philosophy/kant/metaphys-of-morals.txt.

Kant, I. (1790) *The Critique of Judgement*. Trans. J. C. Meredith, 2004. Accessible at: http://ebooks.adelaide.edu.au/k/kant/immanuel/k16j/index.html.

King, P. (1993/4) "Postmodernist Porn [review of Jean-François Lyotard, *Libidinal Economy*]." *Philosophy Now*, 8 (Winter). Accessible at: http://philosophynow.org/issues/8/Postmodernist_Porn.

Knabb, K. (ed.) (2007) *Situationist International Anthology*. Berkeley: Public Secrets.

Knight, M. M. (2009) *The Taqwacores*. New York: Soft Skull Press.

Kull, K. (1998) "On Semiosis, Umwelt, and Semiosphere." *Semiotica*, 120(3/4), 299–310. Accessible at: http://www.zbi.ee/~kalevi/jesphohp.htm.

Lacan, J. (1991) *The Seminar of Jacques Lacan, Book I: Freud's Papers on Technique, 1953–54*. Ed. J-A. Miller. Trans. J. Forrester. New York: Norton.

Lacan, J. (1993) *The Seminar of Jacques Lacan, Book III: The Psychoses, 1955–56*. Ed. J-A. Miller. Trans. R. Grigg. New York: Norton.

Lacan, J. (1999) *The Seminar of Jacques Lacan, Book XX: On Feminine Sexuality; The Limits of Love and Knowledge, 1972–73*. Ed. J-A. Miller. Trans. B. Fink. New York: Norton, 1999.

Lacan, J. (2006) *Ecrits: The First Complete Edition in English*. Trans. B. Fink with H. Fink and R. Grigg. New York: Norton.

Lacan, J. (2007) *The Seminar of Jacques Lacan, Book XVII: The Other Side of Psychoananlysis, 1969–70*. Ed. J-A. Miller. Trans. R. Grigg. New York: Norton.

Lacan, J. (2010) *The Seminar of Jacques Lacan, Book XIX: ... Or Worse, 1971–72*. Trans. Cormac Gallagher. Accessible at: http://www.lacaninireland.com/web/wp-content/uploads/2010/06/Book-19-Ou-pire-Or-worse.pdf.

Lacan, J. (2011) *The Seminar of Jacques Lacan, Book IX: Identification, 1961–62*. Trans. Cormac Gallagher. Accessible at: http://www.lacaninireland.com/web/wp-content/uploads/2010/06/Seminar-IX-Amended-Iby-MCL-7.NOV_.20111.pdf.

Lautréamont, C. de (1965) *Les Chants de Maldoror*. Trans. G. Wernham. New York: New Directions.

Lee, R. E. (2003) *Life and Times of Cultural Studies: The Politics and Transformation of the Structure of Knowledge*. Durham, NC: Duke University Press.

Lee, R. E. (2010) *Knowledge Matters: The Structures of Knowledge and the Crisis of the Modern World-system*. St. Lucia, UQP; New Brunswick NJ: Transaction.

Lefebvre, H. (2014) *The Critique of Everyday Life*. London: Verso.

Leiris, M. (1983) *Francis Bacon: Full Face and in Profile*. Oxford: Phaidon.
Lévi-Strauss, C. (1963) *Structural Anthropology*. Trans. C. Jacobson and B. G. Schoepf. New York: Doubleday Anchor Books.
Lévi-Strauss, C. (1969) *The Elementary Structures of Kinship*. Trans. J. Bell, J. von Sturmer and R. Needham. London: Eyre and Spottiswoode.
Levi-Strauss, C. (2012) *Tristes Tropiques*. New York: Penguin.
Levinas, E. (1969) *Totality and Infinity: An Essay on Exteriority*. Trans. A Lingis. Pittsburgh: Duquesne University Press.
Levinas, E. (1998) *Otherwise than Being, or Beyond Essence*. Trans. A. Lingis. Pittsburgh: Duquesne University Press.
Levinson, M. (2006) *The Box: How the Shipping Container Made the World Smaller and the World Economy Bigger*. Princeton: Princeton University Press.
Levitt, T. (1983) "The Globalization of Markets." *Harvard Business Review*, May. Accessible at: https://hbr.org/1983/05/the-globalization-of-markets.
Lewis, S. (1920) *Main Street*. Accessible at: http://www.gutenberg.org/etext/543.
Lingua Franca (ed.) (2000) *The Sokal Hoax: The Sham That Shook The Academy*. Lincoln: Bison Books.
Liu, L. (2011) *The Freudian Robot: Digital Media and the Future of the Unconscious*. Chicago: University of Chicago Press.
Lotman, Y. (1990) *Universe of the Mind: A Semiotic Theory of Culture*. Bloomington: Indiana University Press.
Lotman, Y. (2009) *Culture and Explosion*. Berlin: Mouton De Gruyter.
Lovink, G. (2011) *Networks Without a Cause: A Critique of Social Media*. Cambridge: Polity Press.
Lucy, N. (1997) *Postmodern Literary Theory: An Introduction*. Oxford: Blackwell.
Lucy, N. (2002) "Structuralism and the Structuralist Controversy." In *The Edinburgh Encyclopedia of Modern Criticism and Theory*, ed. J. Wolfreys. Edinburgh: Edinburgh University Press, 743–50.
Lucy, N. (2004) *A Derrida Dictionary*. Oxford: Blackwell.
Lucy, N. (2010a) "Art, Criticism & Philosophy: The Case of Van Gogh's Shoes." *The International Journal of the Arts in Society* 4(6), 183–92.
Lucy, N. (2010b) *Pomo Oz: Fear and Loathing Downunder*. Fremantle, WA: Fremantle Press.
Lucy, N. (2011) "From Text to Media." *Vlak: Contemporary Poetics and the Arts*, 2, 16–19.
Lucy, N. (2013a) "*Différance*." In *Vocabulary for the Study of Religion*, ed. R. Segal and K. von Stuckrad. Leiden: Brill.
Lucy, N. (2013b) "The Acropolis of the Dragon." *VLAK: Contemporary Poetics and the Arts*, 3 (October).
Lucy, N. and S. Mickler (2006) *The War on Democracy: Conservative Opinion in the Australian Press*. Nedlands, WA: University of Western Australia Press.
Luhmann, N. (1991) "What is Communication?" *Communication Theory*. 10, 251–9.

Luhmann, N. (2012) *Theory of Society*, vol. I. Stanford: Stanford University Press.
Luhmann, N. (2013) *Introduction to Systems Theory*. Cambridge: Polity Press.
Lyotard, J-F. (1984) *The Postmodern Condition: A Report on Knowledge*. Trans. G. Bennington and B. Massumi. Manchester: Manchester University Press.
Lyotard, J-F. (1988a) *Peregrinations: Law, Form, Event*. New York: Columbia University Press.
Lyotard, J-F. (1988b) *The Differend: Phrases in Dispute*. Trans. G. van den Abbeele. Minneapolis: University of Minnesota Press.
Lyotard, J-F. (1989) "Lessons in Paganism." In *The Lyotard Reader*, ed. A. Benjamin. Oxford: Blackwell, 122–54.
Lyotard, J-F. (1993) *Libidinal Economy*. Trans. I. H. Grant. Indiana: Indiana University Press.
Lyotard, J-F. (2011) *Discourse, Figure*. Trans. A. Hudek and M. Lydon. Minneapolis: University of Minnesota Press.
Lyotard, J-F. and J-L. Thébaud (1985) *Just Gaming*. Trans. W. Godzich. Minneapolis: University of Minnesota Press.
Mandel, E. (1999) *Late Capitalism*. Trans. J. de Bres. London: Verso.
Mandelbrot, B. (1983) *The Fractal Geometry of Nature*. New York: W. H. Freeman & Co.
Manovich, L. (2002) *The Language of New Media*. Cambridge, MA: MIT Press.
Marcus, G. (1989) *Lipstick Traces: A Secret History of the Twentieth Century*. London: Secker & Warburg.
Marcus, S. (2010) *Girls to the Front: The True Story of the Riot Grrrl Revolution*. New York: Harper Collins.
Marx, K. (1845) *The German Ideology*. Accessible at: https://www.marxists.org/archive/marx/works/1845/german-ideology/ch01b.htm.
Marx, K. (1867) *Capital: A Critique of Political Economy*, vol. I. Ed. F. Engels and E. Untermann. Trans. S. Moore and E. Aveling, 1906. Accessible at: http://www.econlib.org/library/YPDBooks/Marx/mrxCpA.html.
Marx, K. (2004) *Wage Labour and Capital*. Trans. J. L. Joynes. Montana: Kessinger.
Massumi, B. (1987) "Realer than Real: The Simulacrum According to Deleuze and Guattari." *Copyright*, 1, 90–7. Accessible at: http://www.brianmassumi.com/textes/REALER%20THAN%20REAL.pdf.
McCloskey, D. (2006) *The Bourgeois Virtues: Ethics for an Age of Commerce*. Chicago: University of Chicago Press.
McCloskey, D. (2010) *Bourgeois Dignity: Why Economics Can't Explain the Modern World*. Chicago: University of Chicago Press.
McCloskey, D. (forthcoming) *Bourgeois Equality: How Betterment Became Ethical, 1600–1848, and Then Suspect*. Chicago: University of Chicago Press. Exordium available: http://www.deirdremccloskey.org/docs/pdf/McCloskeyExordiumAugust2014.pdf.
McDonnough, T. (2007) *"The Beautiful Language of My Century": Reinventing the Language of Contestation in Postwar France*. Cambridge, MA: MIT Press.

McHale, B. (1992) *Constructing Postmodernism*. London: Routledge.
McLuhan, M. and Q. Fiore (1967) *The Medium is the Massage: An Inventory of Effects*. New York: Bantam Books.
McNeil, L. (2014) *Please Kill Me: The Uncensored Oral History of Punk*. New York: Grove Press.
Miller, J. H. (1987) *The Ethics of Reading: Kant, de Man, Eliot, Trollope, James, and Benjamin*. New York: Columbia University Press.
Mitford, N. (1956) *Noblesse Oblige: An Enquiry Into the Identifiable Characteristics of the English Aristocracy*. London: Hamish Hamilton.
Morris, M. (1992) "On the Beach." In *Cultural Studies*, ed. L. Grossberg *et al.* New York: Routledge, 450–78.
Morris, M. (1998) *Too Soon, Too Late: History in Popular Culture*. Bloomington: Indiana University Press.
Nabokov, V. (1955) *Lolita*. New York: G. P. Putnam's Sons.
Nakamura, L. (2007) *Digitizing Race: Visual Cultures of the Internet*. Minneapolis: University of Minnesota Press.
Nicholls, P. (1995) *Modernisms: A Literary Guide*. Berkeley: University of California Press.
Nietzsche, F. (1967) *On the Genealogy of Morals, and Ecce Homo*. Trans. Walter Kaufmann and R. J. Hollingdale. New York: Vintage.
Nietzsche, F. (2001) *The Gay Science, with a Prelude in German Rhymes and an Appendix of Songs*. Ed. Bernard Williams. Trans. William Weaver. Cambridge: Cambridge University Press.
Norris, C. (1992) *Uncritical Theory: Postmodernism, Intellectuals, and the Gulf War*. Amherst: University of Massachusetts Press.
Nostradamus, M. (2006) *Nostradamus: The Complete Prophecies of Michel Nostradamus*. Minneapolis: Filiquarian Publishing LLC.
Noys, B. (2014) *Malign Velocities: Accelerationism and Capitalism*. Winchester: Zero Books.
NYC General Assembly (2011) "Declaration of the Occupation of New York City." Accessible at: http://www.nycga.net/resources/documents/declaration/.
Obama, President B. (2013) "President Barack Obama's [Second] Inaugural Address: Full Text." *The Guardian*, January 21. Accessible at: http://www.guardian.co.uk/world/2013/jan/21/barack-obama-2013-inaugural-address.
Oreskes, N. and E. Conway (2010) *Merchants of Doubt*. London: Bloomsbury.
Orwell, G. (1946) "Politics and the English Language." *Horizon* 13(76), 252–65. Accessible at: https://ebooks.adelaide.edu.au/o/orwell/george/o79p/.
Orwell, G. (1993) *Nineteen Eighty-four*. London: Compact Books.
Parikka, J. (2012) *What is Media Archaeology?* Cambridge: Polity Press.
Pedullà, G. (2012) *In Broad Daylight: Movies and Spectators After Cinema*. London: Verso.
Peeters, B. (2013) *Derrida: A Biography*. Trans. A. Brown. Cambridge: Polity Press.

Plant, S. (1992) *The Most Radical Gesture: The Situationist International in a Postmodern Age*. London: Routledge.

Plato (ca. 360 BCE *Sophist*. Trans. B. Jowett. Accessible at: http://classics.mit.edu/Plato/sophist.html.

Plato (ca. 380 BCE) *The Republic*. Trans. B. Jowett, 2014. Accessible at: http://ebooks.adelaide.edu.au/p/plato/p71r/.

Poole, S. (2000) "Meet the David Bowie of Philosophy." *The Guardian*, March 14. Accessible at: http://www.guardian.co.uk/books/2000/mar/14/artsfeatures.davidbowie.

Pussy Riot (2012) *A Punk Prayer*. New York: Feminist Press.

Quiller-Couch, A. (1916) *On the Art of Writing*. Cambridge: Cambridge University Press. Accessible at: https://archive.org/details/onartofwriting00quiluoft.

Quiller-Couch Memorial (2011). Cornwall: Truro Cathedral. Accessible at: http://commons.wikimedia.org/wiki/File:Quiller_couch_memorial.JPG.

Raban, J. (1974) *Soft City*. London: Harvill Press.

Reed, W. L. (1987) "The Problem of Cervantes in Bakhtin's Poetics." *Cervantes: Bulletin of the Cervantes Society of America* 7(2), 29–37. Accessible at: http://www.h-net.org/~cervant/csa/articf87/reed.htm.

Reiss, T. J. (1982) *The Discourse of Modernism*. Ithaca: Cornell University Press.

Reynolds, S. (2005) *Rip It Up And Start Again: Postpunk 1978–1984*. London: Faber.

Rhodes, N. (1998) "From rhetoric to criticism." In *The Scottish Invention of English Literature*, ed. R. Crawford. Cambridge: Cambridge University Press, 22–36.

Ronell, A. (1989) *The Telephone Book: Technology, Schizophrenia, Electric Speech*. Lincoln: University of Nebraska Press.

Ronell, A. (2002) *Stupidity*. Urbana: University of Illinois Press.

Ronell, A. (2004a) *Crack Wars: Literature, Addiction, Mania*. Urbana: University of Illinois Press.

Ronell, A. (2004b) "The Testamentary Whimper." *South Atlantic Quarterly*, 103(2/3), 489–99.

Ronell, A. (2005) *The Test Drive*. Urbana: University of Illinois Press.

Rorty, R. (ed.) (1967) *The Linguistic Turn: Recent Essays in Philosophical Method*. Chicago: University of Chicago Press.

Rose, S-E. (2008) "Auschwitz as Hermeneutic Rupture, Differend, and Image." In *Visualizing the Holocaust: Documents, Aesthetics, Memory*, ed. D. Bathrick, B. Prager and M. Richardson. New York: Camden House, 114–37.

Rudick, N. (2011) *Return of the Repressed: Destroy All Monsters 1972–1977*. Brooklyn, NY: PictureBox.

Saccarelli, E. (2007) "The banality of evil: *No Country for Old Men*." World Socialist Web Site, November 24. Accessible at: http://www.wsws.org/en/articles/2007/11/noco-n24.html.

Said, E. (1978) *Orientalism*. London: Penguin.

Sartre, J-P. (1984) *Being and Nothingness*. New York: Washington Square Press.

Saussure, F. de (1974) *Course in General Linguistics*. Trans. W. Baskin. Ed. C. Bally and A. Sechehaye, with A. Reidlinger. London: Fontana/Collins. US edn (2011). Ed. P. Meisel and H. Saussy. New York: Columbia University Press.

Savage, J. (2001) *England's Dreaming: Anarchy, Sex Pistols, Punk and Beyond*. New York: Saint Martin's Press.

Schapiro, M. (1994) "The Still Life as a Personal Object: A Note on Heidegger and van Gogh." In *Theory and Philosophy of Art: Style, Artist and Society*. New York: George Braziller, 135–42.

Schmidt, C. (2012) *The Swimsuit: Fashion from Poolside to Catwalk*. London: Bloomsbury.

Schroeder, R., S. Everton and R. Shepherd. (2012) "Mining Twitter data from the Arab Spring." *CTX*, 2(4) (November). Accessible at: https://globalecco.org/mining-twitter-data-from-the-arab-spring#All.

Scott, K. (2010) *That Deadman Dance*. Sydney: Picador.

Shannon, C. and W. Weaver (1971) *The Mathematical Theory of Communication*. Bloomington: University of Illinois Press.

Sokal, A. (1996) "Transgressing the Boundaries: Towards a Transformative Hermeneutics of Quantum Gravity." *Social Text*, Spring-Summer. [NB this is the hoax article.]

Sokal, A. and J. Bricmont. (1998) *Fashionable Nonsense: Postmodern Intellectuals' Abuse of Science*. New York: Picador.

Spivak, G. C. (1990) *The Post-Colonial Critic: Interviews, Strategies, Dialogues*. Ed. Sarah Harasym. New York: Routledge.

Stiglitz, J. (2002) *Globalization and Its Discontents*. New York: W. W. Norton.

Sylvester, D. (1990) *The Brutality of Fact: Interviews with Francis Bacon*. Oxford: Thames & Hudson.

Tiqqun (2010) *Introduction to Civil War*. Los Angeles: Semiotext(e).

Tiqqun (2012) *Preliminary Materials for a Theory of the Young Girl*. Los Angeles: Semiotext(e).

Turner, F. (2008) *From Counterculture to Cyberculture*. Chicago: University of Chicago Press.

Ulmer, G. (1985) "Textshop for Post(e)pedagogy." In *Writing and Reading Differently: Deconstruction and the Teaching of Composition and Literature*, ed. G. D. Atkins and M. Johnson. Lawrence: University of Kansas Press, 38–64.

United Nations General Assembly (1948) *The Universal Declaration of Human Rights. Office of the High Commissioner for Human Rights*. Accessible at: http://www.ohchr.org/EN/UDHR/Pages/Introduction.aspx.

Urban, F. (2012) *Tower and Slab: Histories of Global Mass Housing*. London: Routledge.

Vaneigem, R. (2001) *A Cavalier History of Surrealism*. Edinburgh: AK Press; Los Angeles: Semiotext(e).

Viegas, J. (2011) "Innovative Monkeys Stick It to Tasty Termites." *NBC News*, March 9. Accessible at: http://www.msnbc.msn.com/id/41991039/ns/technology_and_science-science/t/innovative-monkeys-stick-it-tasty-termites/#.UCHNBGDAr4M.

Vološinov, V. (1973) *Marxism and the Philosophy of Language*. New York: Seminar Press.

Wallerstein I. (2011) *The Modern World System*, 4 vols. Berkeley: University of California Press.

Wark, McK. (2004) *A Hacker Manifesto*. Cambridge, MA: Harvard University Press.

Wark, McK. (2007) *Gamer Theory*. Cambridge, MA: Harvard University Press.

Wark, McK. (2011) *The Beach Beneath the Street: The Everyday Life and Glorious Times of the Situationist International*. London: Verso

Wartts, A. (n.d.) "Pruitt, Wendell Oliver (1920–1945)." BlackPast.org. Accessible at: http://www.blackpast.org/aah/pruitt-wendell-oliver-1920-1945.

Weddle, R. (n.d.) "Cité de la Muette." *Housing Prototypes*. Accessible at: http://housingprototypes.org/project?File_No=FRA017.

Weedon, C., A. Tolson and F. Mort (1980) "Theories of language and subjectivity." In *Culture, Media, Language*, ed. S. Hall, D. Hobson, A. Lowe and P. Willis. London: Hutchinson, 195–216.

Welsh, J. (2011) "Rare Brazilian Monkeys Know How to Stick It to Termites." *Live Science*, March 9. Accessible at: htpp://www.livescience.com/13138-blond-capuchin-monkey-tools-110308.html.

Werskey, G. (1978) *The Visible College: Scientists and Socialists in the 1930s*. New York: Holt, Reinhart & Winston.

Williamson, J. (1978) *Decoding Advertisements: Ideology and Meaning in Advertising*. London: Marion Boyers.

Wittgenstein, L. (2001) *Philosophical Investigations*. Trans. G. Anscombe. Oxford: Blackwell.

Woolf, V. (1924) "Mr. Bennett and Mrs. Brown." London: Hogarth Press. Accessible at: http://www.columbia.edu/~em36/MrBennettAndMrsBrown.pdf.

Woods, L. (1996) "The Question of Space." In *Technoscience and Cyberculture*, ed. S. Aronowitz *et. al.* London: Routledge, 297–92.

Yeats, W. B. (1919) "The Second Coming." Accessible at: http://www.potw.org/archive/potw351.html.

Žižek, S. (1989) *The Sublime Object of Ideology*. London: Verso.

Žižek, S. (2000) *The Fragile Absolute*. London: Verso.

Žižek, S. (2001) *On Belief*. London: Routledge.

Žižek, S. (2002) *For They Know Not What They Do: Enjoyment as a Political Factor*. London: Verso.

Žižek, S. (2008) *In Defense of Lost Causes*. London: Verso.

Žižek, S. (2012) *Less Than Nothing: Hegel and the Shadow of Dialectical Materialism*. London: Verso.

Index

A Dictionary of Postmodernism, First Edition. Niall Lucy.